Praise for *The Her*

'ing memoir… Giraldi urges us to put aside our
and appreciate bodybuilding as an aesthetic pursuit,
ilder as a kind of "walking poetry": in his narcissistic
n and emphasis on balance, proportion, rhythm and
is not unlike the ballerino.' – **Houman Barekat,**
Times Literary Supplement

's Body, William Giraldi offers a smart, mournful
n what it means to be a man at this point in human
roic size and strength suddenly count for less, leaving
de themselves on such vestigial masculine qualities
both the culture and themselves. Must reading, and
men' – **Richard Russo author of *Nobody's Fool***

t Vesalius, William Giraldi tenders, in *The Hero's Body*,
s contemplation of the epic and catholic incarnations
arts – the heart-wracked, large muscle, high speed,
, sacrificial mysteries of body and of blood. For men
now how they came to be the ones they are, and for
o abide them: a serious, sinewy, humanizing read' –
mas Lynch, author of *The Undertaking*,
inalist for the National Book Award

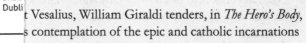

with subtlety about the unsubtle world of clanging
loring with frank tenderness the ways men form
and how those friendships can grow into love. *The
suffused with platonic masculine love, the love of
uddies and motorcycles and the men who ride them,
the author's doomed father… Giraldi has written a
sympathetic accounting of the lengths men will go
emselves through the workings of their fragile and
bodies, and the ways they discover hidden strength'
–*New York Times Book Review*

'*The Hero's Body* provides profound insight into the world of men, their obsessions, their compulsions, their extreme vulnerabilities. This is a beautiful book about bodies that go beyond beauty and into the macabre. Giraldi writes prose that singes as it sings, that never falters in its riveting narrative about strength and speed and grief. I love this book and feel wiser for having read it'
– Lauren Slater, author of *Prozac Diary* and
Lying: A Metaphorical Memoir

'William Giraldi's memoir offers a brilliant anthropological excursion into a world few of us will ever penetrate… To an urban reader used to bookstores and cocktail parties, Giraldi's Manville, NJ, is as exotic as the Kalahari. Perceptive and eloquent'
– *Washington Post*

'*The Hero's Body* offers a wise and thoughtful personal narrative as well as an illuminating portrait of a seductive, if hazardous, American subculture… Grief is a golem that we all have to contend with at some point in our lives, and some of the most arresting passages in this taut but tender memoir involve the author's reflections on the loss of his father… In this gathering of memories, a gifted writer has certainly found the right words'
– *Wall Street Journal*

'Giraldi writes about his life in a way that shows us the depths of masculinity. He makes us see that if masculinity is a mask, it is bonded to the male face. This is one of the best memoirs I've read in years' **– *Financial Times***

'Giraldi has written a powerful memoir that examines the masculine in great detail. Most admirable is Giraldi's love of literature… Throughout this work he continuously astonishes with his highly intelligent verse, apt quotations from literary giants, and creative wording of concepts that are often difficult to convey. This highly recommended book is for anyone who wishes to better understand the male ego, the desire for sheer masculinity, and the need for speed' **– *Library Journal***

'*The Hero's Body* is an epic, the heavyweight champion of this indiscreet genre. Reckless calisthenics, untimely death, saddening masculinity: these might not seem the ingredients for the Great American Memoir. Until you realize: of course they are. This is America, the Land of Violence and Sadness, and this is the perfect book' – **Darin Strauss, author of *Half a Life*, winner of the National Book Critics Circle Award**

'Giraldi's robust and elegant writing delves in a vigorously poetic fashion into the heroic efforts men make to sculpt their bodies – either through bodybuilding or riding motorcycles – and discovers that the truly heroic is being fully and convincingly yourself' – **BookPage**

'In this gripping meditation on men and death… Giraldi's lucid, vibrant prose illuminates the generally unvoiced codes that determine so much male behavior. In the book's flawless first half, he vividly evokes life in a central New Jersey township during the Reagan-Bush era… His narrative provides remarkable insight into the often-stereotyped world of bodybuilding' – ***Publishers Weekly***

'In his compelling memoir, novelist Giraldi uses beautifully nuanced prose to describe growing up in a working-class, hypermasculine New Jersey family' – ***Booklist***

'The best memoirs give you a new perspective, make you see a slice of life you had either dismissed or ignored. William Giraldi's does just that as he lyrically explains bodybuilding and… recounts his father's death. The book is a philosophical journey into the question of masculinity… A very fine memoir… which poetically explains male angst, weightlifting, and a very literate son's deep love for a very fine father' – ***Star-Ledger***

'There isn't a sentence in *The Hero's Body* that lacks vigor or limps onto the page. His prose is sonorously throttled like a twin-barrel exhaust, and as Giraldi feeds "the mandatory obsessiveness of grieving," his attention to language becomes more acute' – ***Los Angeles Review of Books***

'Giraldi provides a respectful homage to his father, who died "attempting to be worthy of an ancient code," but he also pays tribute to the working-class male and the unspoken codes of machismo. A hearty, bittersweet familial chronicle of masculinity drawing on the underappreciated bond between fathers and sons' – *Kirkus Reviews* (starred review)

'The language of *The Hero's Body* captures the adrenaline-drenched world of training and lifting without fetishizing that sphere. What keeps Giraldi grounded is his recognition of the fragility of our bodies, particularly when they are pushed to their limits… *The Hero's Body* is easily the most literary book ever written about bodybuilding… At its soul, it is a New Jersey book about a New Jersey father' – *Literary Hub*

'Obsession and extremity, masculinity, and the heroism of Giraldi's title are the major themes. Christ haunts the pages. So does family, and the strange confederations families inspire, plus the ways they can fall apart and be destroyed… *The Hero's Body* contains beauty, solace, humor, a whole reference library' – *Bookforum*

'Deeply fascinating… A gifted novelist, Giraldi dwells in the world of the dark and complex, and he brings that perspective to this memoir' – *National Book Review*

'Giraldi's own style is graceful and poetic, influenced no doubt by poets like Larkin, Yeats and Auden, whose words enrich this memoir… [A] profoundly moving memoir' – **BookReporter**

'I read *The Hero's Body* with admiration, a deep sense of kinship and joy at the discovery of a new and great champion of working class art' – **Howard Cunnell, author of *Fathers and Sons***

'Magnificent and superbly told… *The Hero's Body* is a living, throbbing, visceral model of what a memoir should be. You simply never want Giraldi's voice to go away' – **André Aciman**

The author's grandfather, on the right, Seaside Heights, New Jersey, circa 1945

Also by William Giraldi

Busy Monsters
Hold the Dark

THE HERO'S BODY

WILLIAM GIRALDI

NO EXIT PRESS

First published in the UK in 2017
by No Exit Press, an imprint of
Oldcastle Books Ltd,
PO Box 394, Harpenden,
Herts, AL5 1XJ, UK

noexit.co.uk
@noexitpress

The Hero's Body is a work of nonfiction, but many of the names have been
changed and certain identifying characteristics of individuals altered.
The gym at which some of the action of this work takes place is
unrelated to existing entities of the same name.

ISBN
978-1-85730-108-6 (Print)
978-1-85730-109-3 (Epub)

2 4 6 8 10 9 7 5 3 1

Typeset by Avocet Typeset, Somerton, Somerset, TA11 6RT
in 12.5pt Garamond MT
Printed in Denmark by Nørhaven, Viborg

To the memory of my father,
William Giraldi (*1952–2000*),
and to my sons, Ethan, Aiden, and Caleb,
so that they may know him.

THE
HERO'S
BODY

PROLOGUE

The four William Giraldis, circa 1978, in Manville, New Jersey

The illness began with a week of all-around lethargy, how you feel when an influenza first gets into you. Soon the headaches commenced – not the forehead pain you have with dehydration, or a behind-the-eyes throb from reading in muted light, but a panging all along the anterior of my skull. Over the span of several days, the panging migrated into the base of my neck. Then the waves came, whole days of dizziness, followed by a stiffening, a gradual inability to turn my head right or left. A body-wide infection now, something toxic thriving in my blood. About twelve days into this, I blacked out in one of my high school's hallways, slumped against someone's locker. I was fifteen years old that autumn, a sophomore. Friends lifted me from the floor and I woke in the nurse's office, my vision tipped and tinting the world into grays.

Then I was on a bed at my grandparents' house, in a darkened room, unsure how I'd got there or how long it had taken, no longer well enough for fear. A minute or an hour later my father was dashing me across town to a doctor who'd recently opened a private practice. We hadn't had a steady family doctor in years; since my mother had left our family when I was ten, my father, a carpenter, couldn't afford medical coverage. He carried me into the office that afternoon, a boneless waif over his shoulder, this doctor knew right away what was killing me.

15

'Meningitis' sounded terminal. The doctor instructed my father to take me *directly* to the hospital, and it was his italicized *directly* that convinced me of my coming doom. He himself would hurry there to perform the spinal tap. I'd once seen a horror movie that had a character infected with meningitis, a wretched young woman, her spine stuck to the outside of her skin – she looked fossilized. So I'd soon be dying of a slow and grisly *living* decomposition, rabid unto death. Supine and panting in the backseat en route to the hospital, I asked my father, 'What's a spinal tap?' He said, 'I think they just tap on your spine with a little rubber mallet,' and I didn't realize that he was trying to be funny. Soon I was unconscious again, yet somehow still aware of being suspended in a capsule of fever and hurt.

A spinal tap: a too-large syringe inserted between lumbar vertebrae and into the spinal cord in order to extract the colorless liquid, called cerebrospinal fluid. Meningitis is an infection of that fluid, which causes an inflammation of the membranes, the meninges, that bodyguard the brain and spine. The most common causes are imperial germs called Coxsackie viruses and echoviruses, although herpes and mumps can also bring on the malady. Some of the germs that lead to meningitis can also stir up such infamous problems as tuberculosis and syphilis. Most meningitis targets are children in their first five years of life, but I was fifteen – I could not comprehend what was happening. If you're among the lucky unlucky, you have the viral sort and it will be caught before it causes too much destruction. But if you're among the unlucky unlucky, like the girl in the horror film I remembered, then you have the bacterial sort that isn't caught soon enough and you end up dead.

Here's how a spinal tap happens when your doctor knows what he's doing: you fetal yourself on the table, knees tight up into your chest. The doctor canvasses your lumbar vertebrae for the best place to harpoon you. He then harpoons you and pulls the plunger to extract the fluid. That's not what happened to me. My doctor-for-a-day pricked and pierced this essential part of me but couldn't extract the fluid. He hadn't told us he was a spinal-tapping virgin, but that's exactly what he was.

I remember looking over at my father, leaned against the heating unit beneath the window, his balding head aslant, his face a mask of stoical consternation, bulky, hirsute arms crossed at his chest in what seemed defiance of this new fact upon me. I imagine he was thinking two things. The second thing was *That looks like it hurts* (and he'd have been right about that), but the first thing was *How am I going to pay for this mess?* It was a good question.

My doctor shot a few more holes into my spine, and that's when my father asked him, 'Why won't it work?'

'I... don't... know,' he said, with those odious pauses between terms.

'You don't know?'

'I just... don't... know.'

And my father said, 'You want me to try it?'

I managed to say no, please, no. He would have handled that needle as if it were a nail, he the hammer, I the lumber. Because he was a master at building things, he sometimes believed he could do anything that took two hands and the right will. His own threshold for suffering was not my own.

He had rare use for doctors, hospitals, aspirin. His stomach did, however, keep Rolaids in business in the years after my mother's abandonment: he'd buy the economy bucket of three hundred wafers and finish it in a month.

My doctor at last surrendered and then talked with some hospital personalities about getting an expert to perform the spinal tap. Benumbed and dim-witted, not fully conscious, I remained on the table with the feeling in my teeth of having just chewed tinfoil. And then – in one hour or two, I couldn't make sense of the clock – in glided the expert. She was a neurologist with the dauntless manner of someone who knows she's an alloy of brilliance and beauty. Dressed in a plaid skirt, white blouse, and heeled shoes, cocoa hair wrapped up in a fist at the rear of her crown, her complexion like typing paper: just seeing her was enough to let me know that I was about to be resurrected.

My father and my failed doctor stood nearby as this neurologist, with the skill of a master who's long been spinal tapping, drew out the fluid everyone needed to see. The feeling that rippled through me when this life juice left my body? An authentic euphoria: my headache fled, my arthritic neck unloosened, my muddy vision cleared. And I thought three short words: *she fixed me*. It felt like love, like an overdue embrace by the maternal revenant.

I sat up then, as out-and-out amazed as I'd ever been in fifteen years, and I inched off the table, feet timidly finding the floor. I grinned at my father because I thought we'd be returning home now, resuming our lives now. I took a solitary step, and, with that dope's grin still stuck to my mouth, I promptly blacked out in a hump at my father's mud-stippled boots. I'd spend the next two weeks in a hospital bed, everyone vexed as to why my vertigo and murderous head pain would not relent.

I had the viral stamp of meningitis instead of the bacterial, and the doctors insisted this was good news – good news that would sentence me to bed as I got more and more waifish, all angles and knots. Each day a retinue of doctors and attendants filed into my room to examine charts and shake their beards and ponytails at me. They took so much of my blood I suspected they were selling it. They wheeled me up and down those antiseptic hallways for PET scans and CAT scans and other scans that showed them nothing, and there was even talk of another spinal tap until I sobbed them out of that plan.

Some pals came to visit, others did not. The news in my high school said that what I had was deadly and contagious both. When I was released two weeks later – uncured, an enigma still – my father left his construction site at lunch time to pick me up. I was 110 pounds. My spinal column still ached in the places I'd been punctured, and my father, specks of sawdust in his forearm hair, said, 'You don't look better even a little.' I wasn't. Another two-week bed sentence awaited me when I got home, and by the time I could stand up without blacking out, it had been more than a month. My grandmother, Parma, was certain that I'd been crippled for life.

After seeing another physician, we were no wiser. Perhaps the persistent vertigo and head pain had been caused by an imbalance of spinal fluid, possibly because my body had been sluggish in producing more after the extraction. Perhaps it was temporary nerve damage from all the freewheeling needlework. Parma felt livid enough to suggest that we sue the doctor, but the suggestion meant little: she knew that my father wasn't the suing kind. When the hospital bills began their monthly assault on our mailbox, they were the new topic of Parma's anxiety. At my grandparents' house, the nightly dinner conversation was usually freighted with dread of one ilk or another. Parma lived in a constant smog of worry that either my siblings or I would be hit with a disease, my father wouldn't be able to pay the bills, the hospital would seize our house, and we'd be living on the corner in a cardboard box with the local hobo. Somewhere in her bustling imagination, Parma believed that there were agents for the hospital who would raid our house and heave us out onto the lawn.

After my meningitis, my father arranged to send the hospital a hundred dollars a month until the hulking sum was paid off – it took seven years. He kept a list of his payments in a black-and-white composition notebook, and, a decade later, after his violent death in a motorcycle crash, I found the notebook in a blue bin and wept with it there on my lap.

BOOK I

The author, on stage, Point Pleasant, New Jersey, 1994

*Youth ends when we perceive that no one wants our
gay abandon. And the end may come in two ways:
the realization that other people dislike it, or that we
ourselves cannot continue with it. Weak men grow older
in the first way, strong men in the second.*

— Cesare Pavese

I

Eight months after meningitis, in the late spring of 1990, recently heart-thrashed by my first girlfriend, scrapped for a football star, weighing barely a buck and a quarter, spattered with acne, both earlobes aglitter with silver studs and my hairdo a mullet like a lemur's tail, and here is what happened to me:

In the deadening heat of a May afternoon, stultified by sadness and boredom, I wandered over to my uncle Tony's house and found him weightlifting in the pro-grade gym he'd installed in one half of his cobwebbed basement, AC/DC yawping from a set of speakers. The song? 'Problem Child.' Tony lived across the street from my grandparents, where my father, siblings, and I ate dinner each weeknight, and so I'd known about his gym – he'd built and welded most of it himself – but never had a reason to care about it. Earnestly unjockish, I'd long considered myself the artistic sort. I kept a notebook full of dismal poems, song lyrics, quotes from writers I wanted to remember. My hero was the reptilian rock god Axl Rose. Filthy and skinny, he looked hepatitic and I thought I should too.

But there in my uncle's basement, my sallow non-physique mocking me from a wall of cracked mirrors, I clutched onto one of the smaller barbells and strained through a round of bicep curls, aping my uncle, who for whatever reason did not laugh or chase me away. And with that barbell in my grip, with blood surging through my slender arms, entire precincts inside me popped to life. Engorged veins pressed against the skin of my tiny biceps, and I rolled up the sleeves of my T-shirt to see them better, to watch their pulsing in the mirror.

Wordlessly I did what my uncle did, trailed him from the barbells to the dumbbells to the pulley machine, trying to keep up, mouthing along to the boisterous lyrics. And in the thirty minutes I spent down there that first day, I had sensations of baptism or birth. Those were thirty minutes during which I'd forgotten to feel even a shard of pity for myself. I didn't know if I was lifting weights the right way, but I knew that I had just been claimed by something holy. I'd return to his basement the following day, and the day after that. I'd return every weekday for two years.

I see it clearly now: I was prompted by more than a need to stave off my melancholy, prompted by forces I couldn't have anticipated or explained. There was the obvious motive, a desperation to alter my twiggy physique, transform it into a monument worthy of my ex-girlfriend's lust, a kind of revenge so important to shafted teenage boys. The footballer for whom she'd ditched me? Just two weeks before I wandered down into my uncle's basement, he'd rammed me against a classroom door, said for me to meet him outside, 'so I can teach you a lesson,' and I was too shaken to ask him what lesson that might be, since *he* was the thieving scoundrel between us. Of course I didn't meet him outside; he'd have ruined me in a fistfight. He and his pals called me exactly what you'd expect them to call me: *pussy, sissy, faggot.*

There was also the chronic memory of that month-long meningitis, the successful shame of my body's failing, the need to fortress myself with muscle in order to spare my father the high cost of my weakness, to preempt whatever disease might choose me next. But the mightiest motive, the one not entirely apparent to me? To obtain the acceptance of my father and uncles and the imperious grandfather we called 'Pop' – to forge a spot for myself in this family of unapologetic, unforgiving masculinity.

Before we return to that basement and those weights, there are certain essential details you need to know about where and how I was raised, details that will help explain how bodybuilding was for me both impossible and inevitable, and how it developed into an obsession that included brutalizing workouts, anabolic steroids, competitions, an absolute revamping of the self.

My hometown's name, Manville, lets you know precisely what you're getting: pure Jersey. A town of plumbers and masons, pickup trucks and motorcycles, bars, liquor stores, and football fields, diners, churches, and auto repair shops, and a notorious, all-nude strip club once called Frank's Chicken House. Go to central Jersey, ask any working-class guy over thirty about Frank's Chicken House, and he'll point the way: the town of Manville, right off Route 206, fifteen minutes from the sylvan spread of Princeton, a town straight from the blue notes of a Springsteen song.

Manville was no Princeton. A meager two and a half square miles of low-lying land, the town is bordered by the Raritan River at the north and east. Roughly once a decade, it gets swallowed by an end-times flood. It was named for the Johns-Manville Corporation, which produced asbestos building materials that ravaged the lungs of its many workers. The manufacturing plant, defunct by the time I was a child, sat on Main Street, blocks-long behind rusted fences, vacant but for the spirits of the dead flitting through those empty spaces in search of better air to breathe.

It was one thing to grow up in this blue-collar zip code, and quite another to be raised by men for whom masculinity was not just a way of being but a sacral creed. I've seen photographs of Pop from 1945, sepia shots made more flaxen by time, thick cloth-like rectangles of paper, curled under at the edges. Pop is sixteen years old in these shots, on a jagged rock wall by the bridge, high above the water. He's with his closest pal, Ed Stowe, both in swimming trunks, both heavy with muscle. They are weightlifters, bodybuilders, backyard boxers, and they've come to this rock wall by the river to peacock the results of their training, to flex their suntanned brawn for posterity. Stowe is Thorish, tall, broad, and blond, while Pop has a powerlifter's density. He resembles the era's ideal of muscular, masculine beauty, Steve Reeves, he of the *Hercules* films, one of the first famed American bodybuilders.

Pop and Stowe do indeed look like men in those photos I remember, not teenage boys. Such confidence and well-honed bulk, square faces shaded with stubble, no magenta sprays of acne. Among his assorted boasts, Pop often recalled shaving in the sixth grade, when the other boys were still tickled by cartoons and waiting for pubic hair. As a teen, Pop had muscle and body hair that let him pass for twice his age, and later they earned him the moniker 'Magilla Gorilla' from one of my crueler boyhood friends.

Pop always spoke of Stowe in a reverential tenor lifted by swells of sorrow. He believed Stowe was part genius, 'ahead of his time' when it came to the particulars of weight training and exercise, nutrition and health. One of Stowe's maverick ideas was that the human body has the ability to cure itself of any illness. It needs neither medicine nor food to recover from whatever malady has attacked it. Sips of water, perhaps a wedge of grapefruit, but otherwise you did not burn the body's energy sources on digestion and you did not further pollute it with laboratory concoctions. You left the wise body alone and waited while it purged the pathogens. Ed Stowe died of starvation in the Arizona desert where he'd gone to consult some turbanned guru of wellness. 'Ahead of his time' is morosely exact: he leapt forty years into the future, straight into the hole of his grave.

When Pop first told me about Stowe, I was twelve years old, with my best pal at the time, and when we biked off into the Manville gloaming, after Pop finished with his stories of Stowe, my pal asked me, 'Did you see your grandfather got tears in his eyes when he was telling us about that guy?'

'Bullshit,' I said. 'No way.'

'There was a tear,' he said. 'I saw it.'

And I said, 'Pop doesn't *have* tears.'

One of my earliest memories of Pop, circa 1978, when

I was three: he cable-tied a one-foot rubber doll of the Incredible Hulk to the grille of his pickup truck. He'd drive around Manville with this green doll scouting the way, and whenever he stopped at our house to visit, he'd exit his truck with the Hulk's dramatic growl and upper-body flexing.

But it was Spider-Man for me. Not Superman and not the Incredible Hulk, those mesomorphic wall-punchers leaving messes of people and property. There was a finesse to Spider-Man, such sleekness and stealth. That liberating mask was the clincher; you could see the faces of Superman and the Hulk, and I thought that a woeful disadvantage. The Spider-Man of the late '70s barely had a bulge anywhere under his fitted suit, even where he couldn't have helped but to have one. Unmuscled, he immobilized foes without harming them, and that seemed to me, at three years old, a noble thing.

Children are natural obsessives. For a month I'd been wearing Spider-Man pajamas throughout the day and making web-shot sounds, my wrists aimed at relatives. To reward this obsession, my family arranged for someone to costume himself as Spider-Man and come to our house. When from our front walkway I saw him approach me in an unwise amble I mistook for menace, I wept and howled and frantically climbed up my father. This must have been disappointing; I was no brave little boy.

Later that year I was in an operating room about to be anesthetized, about to have tubes inserted into my ears. My canals weren't draining; my family had thought I was disobedient but I was just deaf. The doctor asked me this asinine question: 'Would you like a needle, or would you like to blow up a balloon?' and I answered as any child would.

This duplicitous doctor then set a black mask over my face – I remember it descending like night – and four cool hands staked me to the table by my ankles and wrists. Just before the gas unleashed its sleep, I strained to snap free, and my thought was not of Spider-Man web-whirling through the heights of a metropolis, but of Pop, of that great green beast called Hulk.

Pop and my father and two uncles admired weightlifters and footballers, wrestlers and boxers, lumberjacks, hunters, woodsmen. Celebrants of risk, they valued muscles, motorcycles, the dignified endurance of pain. Their Homeric standards of manhood divvied men into the heroic or the cowardly, with scant space for gradation. Heroes were immortalized in song, cowards promptly forgotten. This wouldn't have been an issue growing up except that I wasn't like them. I was made of other molecules, of what felt like lesser stuff. As the firstborn son, as the fourth William Giraldi, the pressures were always there, the sense of masculine expectation always acute. But I was the bearer of patrilineal traditions in name only, insufficiently macho and no doubt under suspicion as a potential pansy.

In his 'Calamus' sequence, Whitman is 'resolv'd to sing no songs to-day but those of manly attachment.' This is a tale of men because my mother left us when I was ten years old, and so our upbringing fell solely to my father and his family. I realized what was happening between my parents about a year earlier. Lying on my bed one night, in the sudden dark of autumn, the deadened limbo of Sunday evening, I listened to my parents quarreling downstairs. Their voices floated up to me as if from a television set in a closed room; I could make out just the occasional word, sometimes a phrase or clause. But the individual words didn't matter; their tone conveyed it all. Disturbances were coming.

When the voices stopped after an hour, and when I heard the door to my parents' bedroom click shut, I slid from bed, crept downstairs to see what clues I could find left over from their quarrel. There, in the dark of our kitchen, lit only by the weak bulb above the stove, my father sagged in a stool at the counter. At first I didn't notice him there, but then he said my name, and I went to him, feeling caught at something, caught *in* something, but I couldn't say what, couldn't identify the new web in which he and I were now stuck.

Unsure of how the separation would play out, this is what he said to me: 'No matter what happens, I'll always be your father.' The following year my mother would be gone, and without balking my father would fill both roles. There is a tale to tell about my mother, too, I know, and perhaps one day I will earn the mercy to tell it, but she is absent from these pages because she was largely absent from our lives, and that absence helped to place me in the hard clamp of the paternal.

Tony brought me to my first bodybuilding show just after my parents' divorce, when I was too young to assimilate the spectacle or understand why it mattered. Sitting in that auditorium, encircled by muscle, by a wall of aftershave, I felt the breath of panic on me, the prelude to a raid of anxiety. I told Tony I needed the bathroom, thinking that he'd let me go alone, that I could take several minutes to shake off whatever was attacking me. A ten-year-old, it seems, can be unmanned among the manly. Instead, I pulled him away from the best part of the show and stood uselessly at the urinal while he leaned against a sink, looking at his watch.

This was when the men of my family still thought it possible that I might evolve into an athletic worthy, maybe a soldier, someone more daringly masculine than what I showed signs of becoming.

There's something else you should know at this point: all through my childhood and adolescence, I had a literary quest under way in hiding, a counterlife carried out quietly on my own, at libraries or at yard sales, whole grocery bags of paperbacks for a dollar. My family didn't have any regard for literature, for the pursuits of language, and was never timid in letting that be known. When Pop once spotted me with a paperback of Poe's poetry, he said, 'I got a poem for ya: Bart Bart laid a fart,' and his chortle sucked all the air out of the kitchen. Physicality mattered; the rest was wasteful. So I cannot fully account for how my draw to literature was possible in a household that was not just unliterary but nonliterary, one in which poems and plays were considered ravingly femme.

A maternal uncle seldom seen – contentedly unmasculine, a committed bachelor, everything about him contrary to the Giraldi male, his apartment an asylum of art books, journalism, Steve Martin records – sometimes brought me to the Manville library when I was a boy of seven or eight. He'd noticed my interest in the Greek god Pan; I'd been detecting it in the trees and weeds, its silhouette at the rear of our property, in the shrubs behind our garage, its flute, horns, and hooves. This uncle led me in researching the agglomerate of Greek gods and goddesses, and it was there at the Manville library, in its squat beige-brick structure at the center of town – I've never forgotten that air-conditioned scent of books, the brew of old leather and new paper – that I found *The Iliad,* a shortened version with ink drawings of those androgen-loaded heroes, their developed muscularity and pronounced thoracic arches.

Later, on Monday and Wednesday nights in winter, the seventh and eighth graders met for basketball practice in our Catholic school's gymnasium. Short and slight for a seventh grader, with no chance at all of succeeding at the sport, I was nevertheless stupefied by the acrobatics of Michael Jordan: he seemed a celestial vision, a beauty made, not born. Pop had erected a hoop above the garage to help me out, and even rigged a floodlight to a pole so my pals and I could practice after the early dark of December, the neighborhood night alive with the crisp thudding of the ball against concrete.

My father never said as much, but he must have considered my basketballing aspirations a bit deranged. Uninterested in the overt masculinity of football or wrestling, trying to conceal an effeminate bookishness, I must have thought that basketball would let me pass as an athlete. I spent most of our team's Saturday morning games where I belonged: on the bench, tying and retying the laces of my unscuffed sneakers.

Once a year for a week, a book fair arrived at our school, wheeled stalls set up in a recessed part of the hallway. The nuns gave us several minutes each day at the stalls, but I never had the money for books, never felt my father could spare the ten bucks, and so I never asked him. From the way Parma fretted over my father's debts, beggary seemed always about to descend on us. On the nights of basketball practice during the week of the book fair, while the taller players echoed and squeaked across the waxed maple of the gymnasium, I snuck down the darkened stairwell to the rolling steel gate that blocked me from the main section of the school. The book stalls were there, lit only by the scarlet glow of the exit signs – my red-light district – and if I yanked up the one damaged side of the gate, I could crawl beneath it and cat-burgle the books I wanted.

Loading my duffel bag with illustrated, abbreviated versions of Poe and Verne, and glossy paperbacks of Greek myths and North American legends, didn't feel at all like thievery to me. It felt like a private and mandatory search for self: private because I couldn't share it with my family (and because the ardent interiority of reading is by definition a private endeavor), and mandatory because I'd somehow, against my social class and family ethos, begun to understand that within the dimensions and dynamism of language lay not just a balm for confusion or curiosity, but some form of deliverance for me. A religion more vibrant and sanative than what I was being sold by the Catholic clergy six days a week.

The convent sat adjacent to our school, and the nuns would sometimes corral seventh- and eighth-grade boys to lug a bureau, or ascend into the attic to retrieve boxes, or brave the damp basement for a ceramic Nativity scene. They once chose me and another boy for such a task, and on the way out I saw, there in the sitting room, sun-dappled by the window, an elderly nun I'd never seen before, her face a road map of creases and clefts, her posture one of European eons, nun shoes like blocks of black wood. A visitor from Sicily, she sat reading the Gospels aloud to herself in a tongue of some other age, Greek or Latin, I didn't know.

I stayed to listen to this startling rhapsodist, to the opulent prosody of whatever she was saying. I could see that she owned the verses by memory because although the Bible was splayed on her lap, her eyes remained shut for minutes at a stretch. She seemed held as if by some welcomed hex. What was that called, that inner billowing I felt just then at the sound of her verses? Why should I have registered such intimations of joy at what I could not comprehend? But I *could* comprehend it: as a braid of wisdom and beauty. A mystery, a religion that meant poetry, a poetry that meant hope. At eleven years old, I had hope for something, *from* something, I could not begin to articulate. But I understood that it had to do with the intricate rhythms of her language and what those rhythms meant, the spaces into which they were trying to reach. At the beginning of *The Power and the Glory*, Graham Greene writes, 'There is always one moment in childhood when the door opens and lets the future in.' This must have been a moment when the future was making itself known to me, the partial realization that language would become my life.

By the time I reached high school, I'd figured out that my family was wrong about literature, that if books weren't exactly happiness, they were – to employ Stendhal's definition of beauty – the *promise* of happiness. Once in high school, I was lucky with my English teachers, discerning women who registered my interest and nudged me in the right direction:

toward Hemingway and Fitzgerald, Flannery O'Connor and Vonnegut, *Hamlet* and *Macbeth* .

In light of all that, my meningitis at fifteen was an embodiment of my role in the family, of the inner fragility they'd long spotted in me. Not that I was forever sickly, but that I was a weakling always with a book in my hand, an unmasculine and romantically vulnerable softie. The meningitis was a month during which I was at my feeblest, literally unable to stand beneath my own weight, but it was a month that in some ways exemplified my entire life to that point. And so when I wandered down into my uncle's basement that May afternoon, I had a stack of troubles quivering within, including the humiliation of having no mother, a humiliation helped by my father's own shame of not being able to hold onto his wife. I was not wholly conscious of those troubles, but this I knew for certain: I needed to make my own creation myth, to renovate my pathetic vessel into a hero's body.

II

In conscious emulation of Pop when he was young, my uncle Tony got serious about weightlifting in his twenties. Like my father, he'd been a wrestler in high school, then earned a black belt in karate. I can recall the poster of Bruce Lee tacked up in his basement, behind the punching bag and speed bag, the bloody scowl of the great martial artist as he's about to punt an enemy. Tony had always seen himself as too unmuscled (he hadn't inherited Pop's effortless bulk), and so, after wrestling and karate, weightlifting seemed the natural next step for him.

In the 1980s, he trained with some hardcore Jersey bodybuilders – animals who squatted six hundred pounds, the barbells bending across their backs as if they were rubber – at elite bastions of brawn that were more dungeon than gym: cracked mirrors, leaky pipes, buckets for puking, heavy-metal music that rattled your bones. No place for the hausfrau or noodle-limbed executive. Realms of self-torture where the 150-pound dumbbells never needed dusting.

When I joined Tony in his basement that first day, he'd

just begun bodybuilding again after a four-year hiatus, one occasioned by the demands of children, but also by the burnout that came from years of harsh training. To train as he did Monday through Friday, and to do it without the accelerant of steroids, after nine-hour days of a carpenter's toil, the hauling of lumber and pounding of nails, up and down a ladder with hundred-pound stacks of shingles at a noontime hot enough to make tar run, all while he was trying to preserve calories so that his muscles could repair, so that he had enough fuel for another racking session at the gym that day – seven years of that will wipe a man out.

Once my uncle understood that I was committed to bodybuilding, once he realized that I wasn't going to go away – it was summer now and I had little else to do – he accepted me as his partner. We trained together every weekday from three thirty to five o'clock, ninety iron-handed minutes, and he taught me the draconian habits he'd learned at those Jersey gyms in the '80s. Uncles provide boys an avenue of freedom that fathers never can, a welcome into the saltier, slightly more pernicious arenas of adulthood.

As the middle brother, Tony was quieter than my father, less antic, and compared to my uncle Nicky, he was not as daring. Nicky once rode his two-stroke Rickman dirt bike down the hallway of Manville High School – I'm told it sounded like the apocalypse. It often works out that way: while the oldest brother gets all the independence and the youngest brother gets all the attention, the middle brother, strained between the two, retreats inward. Not strafed by divorce and debt and three kids to manage alone, he was more available than my father.

Five days a week he and I performed an enactment of that old initiation rite, everywhere in myth and fact, of the grown male escorting the adolescent into manhood by way of challenging tasks. This is what our routine looked like, a three-day cycle:

Monday: Chest and triceps. (Four sets, heavy weight, low reps.)

Tuesday: Back and biceps. (Four sets, heavy weight, low reps.)

Wednesday: Shoulders and legs. (Four sets, heavy weight, low reps.)

Thursday: Chest and triceps. (Three sets, lighter weight, higher reps.)

Friday: Back and biceps. (Three sets, lighter weight, higher reps.)

Monday: Shoulders and legs. (Four sets, heavy weight, low reps.)

It took several weeks for me to learn the myriad exercises for each body part, how to train properly, heavy enough without getting hurt. My uncle was more patient than I'd thought possible. During straight-bar bicep curls: 'You gotta widen your grip on the bar. Too narrow like that and all the pressure's on your forearms. You gotta feel it in your bis: squeeze your bis at the top of the rep. Don't swing the bar, either. Bend your knees half an inch, arch your back.'

During squats: 'Don't go down so far or you won't be able to get back up. You want your hamstrings about parallel with the floor, maybe just an inch deeper. Don't lean forward, either, or you'll fall over. Stay straight up and down. Keep your head up or you'll fall forward. Keep the bar across your shoulders, not on the back of your neck.'

During bench presses: 'That grip is too wide. You see the grooves here in the bar? Line up your grip in those grooves. Too wide like that and you're not working the center of your chest, you're working your armpits. You want muscular armpits?'

During dead lifts: 'You heave the bar from the ground up. Never start with your back or you'll wrench your spine out of place. Start the lift in your feet, your legs, and then unfold with your back, but always an arched back. Head up at the mirror, always head up. A smooth motion, never jerky.'

Near the start of our training together, during a bout of seated dumbbell curls – 'Twist your wrist inward at the top of the rep so the bi *squeezes*' – I performed the first set easily enough with twenty-five-pound weights. When it was time for my second set, I grabbed the twenty-five-pounders again, and Tony said, 'What are you doing?'

We looked at one another in the mirror; he was behind me with a bottle, half water, half orange juice. I said, 'My second set.'

'You just did ten reps no problem with those puny things. You could've done twelve. You wanna grow or not? Get the thirty-pounders.'

And I made the mistake of saying, 'These twenty-five-pounders feel pretty good, though.'

'They feel pretty good, huh? We ain't down here to feel pretty good. We're down here to feel pain. And if you can do ten to twelve reps in any exercise, then the weight ain't high enough. And if the weight ain't high enough, you ain't ever gonna grow. The aim is six to eight reps. So grab the thirty-pound dumbbells, and if you can do ten reps with those, then grab the thirty-five-pounders. Quit pussyfootin' around.'

Each week mirrors reflected the wizardly transformation: the rounding of my deltoids and pectorals, the filling of my biceps, the pronounced horseshoe of my triceps, a thickening and broadening of my back, trapezius muscles bumping up from both sides at the base of my neck, quadriceps sweeping out from my waist in two directions, hamstrings and calf muscles beginning to protrude. Muscle pounds sticking, strength increasing within my very grip, the graduation from thirty-pound dumbbells to forty-pounders to fifty-pounders, sliding more plates ('wheels' was our name for the largest, the forty-five-pounders) onto the bench press, the shoulder press, squats, straight-bar and preacher-bar curls, spitting and moaning, grunting and goading one another with *come on* and *three more* and *push it out*. It was a partnership of inspiriting pain.

Thursdays and Fridays were often slightly less intense because, if we'd trained heavy enough Monday through Wednesday, each body part would be too sore to be blitzed again. That soreness was the goal. It meant we'd been barbarian enough, meant the deep, slowtwitch muscle fibers had been properly damaged during exercise, a kind of controlled demolition by the expansion and contraction that happen while weightlifting. Soreness is a signal that you're growing, because that's how a muscle adds mass: during the reparation process, the amino-acid rebuilding of torn tissue. When I woke each morning and wasn't in pain from the previous day's workout, I berated myself until three thirty when it was time to try again, much more savagely this time, a cussing ninety minutes of severity that erased the backslash between pleasure and pain.

You don't get strong and big while bodybuilding; you get strong and big while resting from bodybuilding. The more you rest and eat, the more you grow. With a gutful of egg protein, I fell instantly asleep each night before eight thirty, and my slumber was so consummate, so weighted, I'd wake in the exact position in which I'd blacked out. No pill, no bottle, no smoke or aerobic intercourse has ever allotted me the immovable slumber that occurred after a session of hellward training. I've been missing that subterranean sleep for twenty years.

What happened to me in the fluorescent corner of that basement was a literal empowering, a structural overhaul. All that summer, those initial results, the evolution I witnessed, manifest in my every step, each time I moved, a solidifying, an engorging I could feel in bed with me as I slept, how the growth was noticed by others, complimented, admired: it all produced an elation I hadn't suspected was available to me. I'd bumbled into being devirginized a year earlier and even that gift, the rapture of sex, could not compete with the fortified sense of self I gained in that basement.

One evening after a workout, I walked two blocks, shirtless, to a convenience store for a quart of milk to drink, and in the tunnel beneath the rails I passed an older girl from our neighborhood, seventeen or eighteen now, someone I'd been looking at half my life. Her name began with a V, and because of her, V still seems to me the most erotic letter in our alphabet. She was forever walking across town trailing smoke and hairspray, walking with purpose, to keg parties and the apartments of leather-jacketed men, I imagined, hoop earrings like bracelets, her purse a satchel of secrets beneath the freckled whiteness of her lovely arm. What wonders that purse must have held: cigarettes and pager, lipstick and birth control pills, gum wrappers with phone numbers inked onto them.

When we passed in the tunnel that day, she stopped and said, 'Billy?' I said yes, and she said: '*Giraldi?*' And when I said yes again, all she said was 'Whoa,' and she stood squinting at me through mascara-laden lashes and the smoke pouring from both nostrils. A week later she'd let me inside her bedroom, that pink and perfumed cave of happiness, Bon Jovi and his chest hair applauding from one wall, a crucifix chastising from another, I trying not to weep from the perfect joy of being invited there. A woman's bedroom and body would always feel that way to me: an invitation inside a chapel for the privileged.

In the 1977 docudrama *Pumping Iron,* Arnold Schwarzenegger, still and forever the doyen of bodybuilding, likened a workout pump to an orgasm. I suppose that's right if he meant an orgasm in reverse: the eruption, the explosion, is inward. Just as an orgasm is an aim of sex, a pump is the aim of the workout. Without it, you feel you've been a radical disappointment to your body. But despite the near ecstasy of those pumps, I cared more for what was permanent, for what I could carry with me through my days, my frame armored against the world's maleficent forces, all those things and people out to crush me. Only those with some sense of coming threat seek refuge in weightlifting.

Buried somewhere in *War and Peace* is an image I've never forgotten: our body as *a machine for living*. What I sought then was a machine much better than the malfunctioning one I had, hoping that it would make life's certain disturbances more endurable, much the way a luxury car makes highway clutter less irksome. And 'machine' is the ideal term, because the grotesque men I studied in magazines and aspired to join looked like a mash-up of the mechanical and the human.

Like my uncle, I was slight with a rapid metabolism, and so had lots of trouble adding that armor. The high-calorie force-feeding was harder than the bench presses and bicep curls. For breakfast: a dozen hard-boiled egg whites in a bowl of oatmeal. For lunch: two cans of tuna fish with four slices of wheat bread and a head of broccoli. For supper: a mound of pasta topped with a grilled chicken breast and flanked by a pile of spinach. Before bed: a quart of weight-gaining protein shake, chocolate or vanilla, chalky or viscous or both, some with the consistency of sawdust. And if I puked it all up, as I often did, I blended another and tried again.

On the weekends: all of the above plus grilled sirloin and potatoes. (Tony once told me, 'When you eat beef, you eat steroids,' and I liked the way that sounded.) And between those meals: muscle-making protein bars as appetizing as sand, added to expensive handfuls of multivitamins and amino acids and tart energy boosters. I was never not eating, never not bothered by *having* to eat. If you think it's difficult to abstain from food, try glutting yourself when you aren't even a little hungry, when you've already consumed more calories in one day than a regular person requires in three. From May to August I'd mushroomed from 125 pounds to 145 pounds, from angularity to rotundity, and because I'd been training so steadily, because I was so lean, my body fat percentage so low, those were pounds with a marbled, fluted density.

My uncle's basement was a ritual space now, our altar of iron at which we offered libations of sweat. From a poster on the wall, we were silently supervised by a deity: the bronzed and golden-locked bodybuilder Tom Platz, his legs so downright brontosaurian – shredded, ripped – he looked engineered by some sinister geneticist. That term, 'ripped,' has infiltrated the common parlance and seems to mean anything from 'muscular' to 'strong,' but we mobilized it to mean only taut skin – skin like parchment, the diaphanous vellum of Bibles – that reveals vascularity and deep-edged muscle separation: no subcutaneous fat, so the muscle tonus shows, the lines and ruts of muscle fibers.

The bodybuilder's regalia helped lend the enterprise its pageantry. We wore T-shirts that looked painted on, sweatpants that bowed through the thighs and tapered at the ankles, wide leather lifting belts to protect the lower back, and weightlifting shoes made by Otomix, well padded and flat-soled. You wanted to be anchored during an exercise, your feet part of the floor so you wouldn't wobble with two hundred pounds in your hands. We used wrist wraps for heavy weights, not just for dead lifts but for chin-ups too, for barbell shrugs, for bent-over barbell rows or T-bar rows, pull-downs and low-pulley rows. The wrist wraps made the metal part of your arms, and then you didn't have to worry about the bar slipping from your damp grip. Your hands will fail before your back does.

My uncle and I didn't gab as we trained, or in those brief rests between sets. This was battle, not frolic. But if we gabbed before and after, we gabbed of professional bodybuilders, those gods and heroes, self-made monuments, aberrations, the *Übermenschen* among us, men superior to the unmuscled rabble of the world. Men with alien ways who puked and bled in search of Mount Olympus. Men who shunned the wimpy Christian ideal that puts a pretty soul above the perfection of physical form. Men who were magnificent Greeks, idolizing male beauty, believing that the bold exterior was an embodiment of the bold interior. Hercules, Achilles, Atlas: just look at them.

Unholy monks of muscle, these men possess the brand of focus that has allowed ascetics to float free of their bodies, except that their focus necessitates a further filling of their bodies. Bodies forged into outrageous artwork, 3-D anatomical charts startling enough to spook Andreas Vesalius, the father of anatomy. Part athlete, part artist, they have the training habits of the hell-bent. Muscle tissue is their clay, their choreography. Triumphant Greco warriors whose no-pain-no-gain credo is Christic to its core: you must rove through hell to reach your heaven. Every professional bodybuilder becomes a nutritionist and chemist, a ritualist and rebel. Masters of nature, they achieve their own apotheosis. To exist in that world of extremity is to leave the rest of us behind almost completely.

Remember how Ovid begins his *Metamorphoses*: 'My purpose is to tell of bodies which have been transformed into shapes of a different kind.' Waiting in the checkout line at the supermarket, you've noticed them on magazine covers,

Muscular Development and *Flex.* You've no doubt picked one from the rack and fanned through it while you waited, to mock, I know, but the curiosity tickles a space in you much deeper than the nothingness of scorn. The unexamined feeling is revulsion; you impulsively dislike the otherworldly aesthetics of them, their suggestion of a hubristic tampering with nature. Their vascularity, earthworms wriggling over striated muscle, and their terracotta complexions, their scant workout garb, penile mounds in spandex, their stern faces orgasmically determined, the imponderable mass of them. Everything looks as if it's about to erupt.

Peer more closely at that curious spot in you, just below the mocking and scorn, and see if there isn't a driblet of respect for the discipline, the religious training and dieting habits required to obtain that eurythmic muscle, the harmony of the whole neck-to-ankle machine. When you're looking at the best pro bodybuilders in the world, you're looking at a balance of form only a handful of human beings will ever achieve. Peek at the world champion, Phil Heath, and see how the linguistics of his body are closer to a poet's than an athlete's. No one, it's true, is born with those aesthetics, and that's why you must think it freakish and wrong. But art isn't born either. Art is built. In his absurdist novel *Body,* the inimitable Harry Crews christens bodybuilders 'the mysterious others,' and 'the mad imaginings of a mad artist.' Start thinking of these men as part artist, part athlete, and not as drug-stuffed showboats, and you might start to feel a subduing of that scorn.

I never possessed the freakish potential to look anything other than athletically normal. I was muscular and round and hard, yes, but not *huge,* the term of choice, the erroneous term, used to describe a commonly muscled man. The pros, the Phil Heaths and Kai Greenes of the world, are both muscular and huge, but *muscular* is otherwise not the equal of *huge.* I was always lean, unmassive, even when I was at my largest and strongest, which was not very large and not very strong, not by bodybuilding standards. In clothes I resembled most other males my age. Still, we trained with only that goal: strong and big. Why else would we have put ourselves through such arduousness as that?

Each week contained at least one round of dead lifts and squats, exacting, injury-prone exercises that also, Tony often said, 'separate the men from the boys.' That was important, as you might imagine: the separation of the men from the boys. He was also fond of saying, 'Squats and deads will show you why you're afraid of the dark' – a bit of machismo that meant *These exercises are monsters most guys can't handle.* Pop once told me: 'If you do dead lifts, you'll never have back pains in your life,' and I never have. While most men strove for convex biceps and domed pectorals because they looked good bouncing down the boardwalk at Seaside Heights, Pop had always focused on his legs and back: 'Your legs and back are what carry you around. You ain't strong if your legs and back ain't strong.'

Squats and dead lifts were to be feared as much as any monster, but tame the monster, make it yours, and then upon you is bestowed great powers. We frequently spoke in those mythical tones. And we called dead lifts 'deads' because, like all underground enterprisers, we relished the argot, but also because after a round of heavy dead lifts, we were virtually dead for the day. Nothing else would get done, and the morning after, our backs and legs would be so sore we'd have to squirm sideways out of bed.

Legs are notoriously obstinate; they don't want to grow. Mine always lagged: calves, hamstrings, quads. You train arms with arms, but you can't train legs with just legs. They demand your gut, your back, and much of your soul. Deads and squats, because they work every major muscle group, prompt overall growth. You might feel the deads and squats primarily in your back and legs, but because back and legs are the largest muscle groups in your body, their stimulation promotes, in a kind of anabolic pollination, the growth of everything else. This is what Pop meant when he'd once told me that the serious weightlifters give most of their love to their backs and legs. They are, in other words, the *Iliad* and the *Aeneid* of body parts. As that summer started to wane, with a new school year just two weeks away and a photo of my ex-girlfriend still in my wallet, I squatted and deadlifted with a maniacal intensity that felt like a trance.

The American high school: that four-year carnival of awkwardness and insecurity, the chancy program of taking human beings at their most psychically vulnerable, those undergoing hormonal monsoons, forced to endure the abounding fissures in their self-esteem, and putting them all on a lighted stage so that the outwardly mighty but inwardly weak can devour those who are weak in both places.

When I returned to school that September, my junior year, people were confused by the twenty-five pounds of muscle I'd made; they poked at my shoulders and arms to see if they were real. No one had seen me since May; my ungodly mullet was gone, my facial acne seared away by sun. John Travolta's iconic opening minutes in *Saturday Night Fever*, the Bee Gees squealing above his goombah strut? My first half hour back in the hallways felt just like that.

Between classes I sat against a locker and force-fed myself tuna fish and wheat bread from plastic containers, making a show of my strangeness and dedication. Teachers and students passed me pinching their noses, and my ex-girlfriend eyed me with a fascination that I hoped flipped her insides. Halfway into the school year, I'd win her back for five romping months. And the footballer for whom she'd ditched me, the one who wanted to maltreat me in the parking lot the previous spring? When we passed in the hallway that first day back, he looked me over with tentative menace, as if he couldn't quite decide how much provocation was called for in a spot such as this. The poor kid was in an unusual predicament: the half-pint he'd tried to pummel four months earlier was now bigger and stronger than he was. I saw his lips move but couldn't discern the words. In an exhibition of bravado I hadn't planned on, I let my bag fall with considerable drama, went across the hallway, and stepped into his face, close enough for him to smell the spearmint of my gum.

'You got something to say to me?' I said.

'If I have something to say, I'll say it.' He was looking, I remember, at my arms, not my eyes.

'You sure?' I said. 'Because we can do this right now.'

Another footballer steered him away then and neither looked back at me as they walked on. If he felt relieved to have avoided a fistfight, he didn't feel nearly as relieved as I did, because the only fighting I'd ever done was with a joystick. Having muscles didn't mean I knew how to use them, and yet they were useful all by themselves.

In less than a year he'd become one of my closest pals when he asked if I'd help him gain strength and size. We'd meet in the weight room after last period and I'd teach him what my uncle had taught me, with the same pitiless attitude: 'You need to use these heavier dumbbells or your arms will always be noodles: like this, watch me.' And: 'If you don't dead-lift once a week – look, like this, from the floor up – then you can forget about ever getting strong.' But he didn't have the requisite ferocity of will, and he didn't have the right genetics, either; he never gained any muscle. The satisfaction of that – of his humbling, of routing him in the weight room, of the closeness we fostered afterward, of the status I bestowed upon myself – was elevating to an almost spiritual degree.

The awe of others that lets you feel worthy of being alive in a carnivorous world you fear is intent to consume you: that reaction is the top reason any kid desires the physical conversion I'd achieved, and never mind what he tells you about the health benefits. Milan Kundera has named youth 'the lyrical age' because, like the lyric poet, the youth is 'focused almost exclusively on himself, is unable to see, to comprehend, to judge clearly the world around him.' Give to that same youth the self-worship that bodybuilding fosters and what you get is a happy Atlas somewhat detached from the normality of others, and one who can begin to see himself as walking poetry.

But I had a cloudless union with my new way in the world,

with the obsessiveness and rigor of it, and could not imagine surrendering that surety of stance or understand how I'd gone so long without that heft in my step, the muscled swagger that, for the first time in my life, allowed me to *feel myself* in my body. Nor could I fathom ever again lapsing into a sadness intent on deleting me, all that inner unrest I perceived as a shameful lack of manliness.

At the end of that first day back to school, as we said hello outside his classroom, my math teacher, the six-foot-three, full-bodied Mr. Roba, former marine and star athlete, blessed me with what remains the most enlarging compliment I've ever been given. He said, simply, 'It looks good on you, kid.'

III

Around the time I was born, one of my father's most cherished friends was a drug-free bodybuilder named Joe Gallo, a hairless and etiolated titan of a man who was, if stories and photographs are to be trusted, not only the gentle giant of fairy tale but an incurable jester to boot. My father talked of Gallo with a pointed esteem, and the key to that esteem had less to do with Gallo's strength and size, both formidable, than it did with the fact that he'd achieved them without drugs. As a child, I couldn't hear mention of that man's name without the words 'all natural' fastened to it like a rivet.

Compact and solid and strong, my father was not what you'd call muscular. He'd lifted weights at various spots in his youth and young adulthood, but never very seriously, and never for the alterations I sought. It never took to him as it had to Pop or Tony or me. My sense now is that although he admired the muscle maker, in a kind of unconscious sedition against Pop, he admired him only so far. Many sons inhabit a contradictory space in relation to their fathers; they emulate in order to earn acceptance while rebelling in order to earn their own identities. I took up bodybuilding in part because I must have sensed that it was something at which I could outshine my father.

One night before dinner, at just about the time those first results began showing, after six or seven weeks of weights, I was swanking through my grandparents' kitchen without a shirt and damp with sweat. We'd just finished one of those blood-gorged workouts that lets you feel half-enraptured. My father said of me, 'Look at him, struttin' around like that, with his arms out like he's Hercules.'

Pop bit into him then: 'You wouldn't know how that feels because you were never good at it.' In the psychological man-games of my family, that retort was a tremendous victory for me. I'd formed an alliance with the top patriarch. The grin I showed my father that night must have said *Take that*. He had never excelled at bodybuilding, and look what happened to him: abandoned and humiliated by a two-timing spouse, dropped into a pit of hardship and debt. Perhaps that's one more reason I'd become so driven with weights, because it seemed to me an assurance against being discarded, forgotten.

It's true that Pop was never more interested in me than when I was weight training. It was he who took the before-and-after photos of me that summer in 1990, a dozen shots at the start of May and another dozen at the close of August. But the impulsive reproach of my father that night did not necessarily mean adulation for me. The men of my family were slow to compliment one another, as if lauding another Giraldi male somehow meant a deficit in their own masculine abilities. There were, however, no objections to praising men outside the family: *that* somehow didn't punch a hole in their conceptions of their own machismo.

Pop, especially, was quick to deflate his sons and grandsons: *jackass, asshole, horse's ass,* always an ass of some ilk. They could rarely do anything well enough, and never anything better than Pop himself could do it. With a hammer or a saw, on a horse or a motorcycle, in a weight room or on a racquetball court, Pop would not concede that any of his brood had the potential to best him. When my uncle Nicky, the youngest brother, earned the New Jersey state record for the largest lake trout ever caught, and when many in Manville and beyond were cheering him for it, Pop's contribution was 'That ain't fishing' – because Nicky had caught it trolling in a boat instead of standing on a bank with a pole, which is how Pop had fished throughout his youth. The ghastly familial myths in the *Theogony* of Hesiod always seem a little like home to me: Uranus jailing his hated children in Tartarus, his son Cronus in turn castrating him, lobbing his testicles into the sea, deposing him. Cronus then eating his own children, of whom only Zeus survives, who later returns to punish his father. Above the desk in my college dorm hung a print of Goya's *Saturn Devouring His Son*.

For the Giraldis of Manville in the late decades of the twentieth century, the psychodynamics are not hard to untie: the vauntingly masculine and competitive are always trying to silence that inner whisper saying *You're not man enough*. It didn't occur to them, as it never occurred to my adolescent self, that a ranting masculinity is often the inverse of what it purports to be.

* * *

Rooting among my father's papers after his death, I discovered a torn-out notebook page, ripped at the bottom. Printed in red pencil, all in caps, was this mantra or epigram, or what he probably thought of as a poem, despite his opinion, common in Manville, that poets were unemployable pansies:

WHEN YOU ARE NOT TRAINING
SOMEONE SOMEWHERE IS
WHEN YOU MEET
HE WILL DEFEAT YOU

That was the kind of bumper-sticker machismo my father went in for. By the logic of that motto, one would never not be training. A champion wrestler in high school, he must have scratched it down in his early forties, just when he'd begun coaching wrestling at Manville High School, at about the time he was beginning to emerge from the cauldron of hurt into which my mother's flight had exiled him.

In a family, there's no distinction as pronounced as the one between those who fit and those who don't. Why did my father not press such machismo upon me? I asked him once, as a teen, before I began weightlifting, why he hadn't tried to mold me into a wrestler, and his reply was simple and perhaps truthful enough: 'Because you never showed any interest.' The full truth no doubt would have been something closer to 'Because I suspect you're one of those unemployable pansies, too faggish for the wrestling mat.' To which I could have replied, 'What's faggier than two half-naked dudes groping one another on a mattress?' He did try to mold my brother into a wrestler, and I was pleased about that; it took the pressure off me if he had one son who was half-interested. They'd even gone together to a wrestling camp at Bucknell University one summer, but as an eighth grader, Mike was already too lanky, too stringy. Wrestlers excel when they have the physiques of fireplugs, low and broad, more *neanderthalensis* than *erectus*. And Mike was already adopting the attitudes of the pot-puffing absentee he'd perfect in high school.

My father might not have pressed machismo upon me, but he certainly nudged, hinted. He reared us on Bruce Lee and Chuck Norris movies: *Fists of Fury* and *Return of the Dragon, The Octagon* and *Lone Wolf McQuade*. He said to me one morning, Chuck Norris's autobiography in hand, 'Bruce Lee was small, but Chuck Norris says he was pound for pound the strongest man he's ever known.' As a child, I too was small, and so I hear that line now as the subtle incitation it must have been, as my father's particular means of encouragement.

Soon I was enthralled by ninjas – lithe but mighty ninjas – after I was somehow allowed to watch those staples of the 1980s ninja-movie craze, *Enter the Ninja* and *Revenge of the Ninja,* cyclones of cinematic violence starring Sho Kosugi. Pop would point and mock when, donned in a ninja suit, I darted from tree to tree in what I thought was stealth mode. Of course the Asian man was too feminine, too hairless, for Pop's standards. When I tried to share with him a VHS tape of a Sho Kosugi film, he mocked him: 'That guy's just a little shit. I'd knock him right over.'

My ninja posture then mutated into a fixation on Sly Stallone's *Rocky* and *Rambo,* the accidental kitsch of

Schwarzenegger in *Conan the Barbarian* and *Commando,* and the ruckus of pro wrestling, all that shirt-ripping and American-hero jingoism of Hulk Hogan. My brother and I, with innumerable brothers across this land in the mid 80s, nearly splintered our spinal columns imitating the maneuvers of pro wrestlers: flying dropkicks, atomic elbows, full nelsons, body slams, pile drivers into pillows.

The original Rambo film, *First Blood,* came to HBO in 1983, and this constituted an event in my family, an excitation beyond reason shared by my uncle Tony and my father. The scene that had stirred them, the scene they wanted me to see, showed Stallone sewing up an astounding gash in his upper arm, a gash sustained after he'd leapt from a cliff and plunged through a ceiling of treetops. In his guttural Stallone voice, my father delivered the most repeatable line in the movie, when John Rambo tells a pursuant policeman via walkie-talkie, 'You want a war, I'll give you a war you won't believe.'

One autumn night after the house had gone to sleep, I watched *First Blood* alone in the dark, all through me that thrill small boys feel when they glimpse someone, some*thing,* they want to become. My father and uncle had insisted that I watch *First Blood* because they must have hoped that it would stir my desire to become someone like John Rambo. And it worked for a while; that night inaugurated a three-year preoccupation with Rambo and Stallone, one that had me dressing, *every day,* in an unsightly patchwork of camouflage, also carrying a survival knife, razored on one side, serrated on the other. The hollow handle contained matchsticks, a compass, a needle and thread in case I had to sew up a gash in my arm.

For a significant stretch of my childhood, still clad in those unsightly camouflage fatigues, I was certain that I'd become a soldier of fortune. I began hoarding canteens, survival manuals, backpacks of nonperishables – the Cold War still had several years of chill left – and magazines that featured firearms, explosives, stories of mercenaries killing enemies of the United States in some Central American boscage.

Our father gave my brother and me a BB gun and compound hunting bow when we were still too short to see over the kitchen counter. With the BB gun I assassinated innocent crows after I'd read Native American stories that told me they were death incarnate, and my brother shot our babysitter, also innocent, square in the face. The BB got lodged in the bone of her chin and had to be surgically excised, and Mike was forced to make the lonesome walk down the street to apologize.

Why this near eye-losing episode did not shame or frighten our father into confiscating the gun from us is one of those mysteries I live with. I can't decide if he thought that violence and injury were the binding aftereffects of manliness – of masculinity realized and asserted – or if he was just too spent to do anything about it, too sapped from single-fathering, from those ten-hour days of contending with two-by-fours.

My father, like Pop, was a fan of Clint Eastwood's renegade cop Dirty Harry, and although I would not have tagged him a handgun enthusiast, I do remember those stickers and letters of thanks from the NRA. At some point, he and Tony bought identical .357 magnums for 'target practice' and 'home protection': nonsense, since he only rarely went to the shooting range and since homes in Manville didn't need protecting. A dark hand-cannon, it slept in an unlocked padded case beneath his bed, and I fooled with it when my father was at work. I'd cock the lever, aim through a window at passing cars, squeeze the trigger, listen to that satisfying *click*. And knowing now that this is how kids mistakenly fire bullets into their own heads or the heads of others, it feels wondrous that we dodged that particular disaster.

A purer mystery is the compound hunting bow; a BB gun can injure and blind, but an arrow through an organ meant the morgue for us or someone else. In the backyard my father had stacked blocks of hay we were supposed to use for target practice, but when friends were over we invariably entered a patch of woods looking to perforate living things. We never did – we had no training and couldn't steady the bow in our shaking arms – but one of us did manage to maim our house, just two inches above the sliding glass door, a permanent hole in the vinyl siding. How we or another child did not end up pierced to death is another of those mysteries I live with.

If all that tempts you into thinking less of my father's parental skills, it tempts me into thinking less of them too. And so does the fact that we neighborhood kids rampaged all over town on BMX bikes, up and down Main Street and residential roads, bunny-hopping and wheelie-popping, soaring from improvised ramps over barrels and one another – plus skateboarding, pogo-sticking, go-karting, anything that involved wheels or contempt for gravity – without once being told to put on a helmet.

Domestic life in the 1980s was an overall less paranoid affair. It shouldn't have been. At eight years old, I spent the night in a hospital bed – bruised, amnesic, concussed – after my front tire got wedged in a sidewalk rut and thrust me over the handlebars, crown-first, into the plate-glass window of a liquor store, knocking me unconscious onto the concrete. When I came to I was blinking up into a silhouetted solar system of strangers' heads revolving around my own hurt skull. Those Manvillians didn't call for an ambulance and even helped me back onto my bike, never mind that I'd been knocked out for half a minute and was bleeding from somewhere beneath my hair.

When I returned home I told my father what had happened, and he said, 'Go play football across the street with your friends, it'll make you feel better.' I slipped on my pads and helmet and crossed the road to where neighborhood kids were clamoring in a backyard pile. The mother took one look at me and called my father to shriek at him, 'He's white as a sheet, his eyes are dilated, he's bleeding, for God's sake, he needs a *hospital*.' Soon I was in the backseat of a car, headed to the emergency room, vomiting into a plastic salad bowl. And after all that, my father still did not think it smart to outfit me in a bike helmet. I suspect now that he considered it a tad girlie for his boy, like tassels on the handlebars, or a basket. Safety was not first. It wasn't even last.

I can't recall any bodybuilding encouragement from my father and I also can't recall ever being bothered by that, not consciously bothered. You'd think he would have taken care not to become a cliché, a trope of masculinity, the reticent dispenser of what's always called 'tough love,' although it never looked tough to me. The Great Santini seems like a spiritually hurt buffoon hiding homosexual impulses. My father was never the Great Santini, not even a little. His tomfoolery was a joy. When Tony was at his largest, my father would make blowing, nickering horse sounds at him, and this was funny without being insulting, since bodybuilders don't mind being compared to robust animals. But my father did subscribe, along with his two brothers and Pop, to a red-meated worldview, the tenderness-is-feminine slant, the encouragement-will-poison-them theory that has left many a son with a cleft at the center of him.

Aside from the BB gun and the hunting bow, there was no planned campaign of masculinization in our household, no overt theater of virility, but I was aware of overtones of proper mannish ways. For one of his birthdays, I bought my father work gloves because he returned home from the job site each afternoon with his hands chafed and scraped, plum-colored blood blisters under his fingernails. A month or so later, when I spotted the gloves untouched in his truck, still bedded down in their packaging, I asked him why he wouldn't wear them.

'I can't have your uncles and Pop see me wearing *gloves* on the job.'

I knew I'd regret it, but I asked: 'Why not?'

I've lost his verbatim reply, but the essence of it was this: *If you can't understand that on your own then you never will.*

Right. What carpenter with testicles would dare protect his hands from unnecessary chafing? But I never forgot that exchange, and when I was old enough to work summers on my family's construction sites – humping planks and blocks, shingles and bricks, wheelbarrowing dirt, hammering nails and smashing my thumb – I made sure not to wear gloves.

Most nights I'd spend half an hour tweezing splinters from my palms, patching holes with Band-Aids, wrapping blisters with bandages.

My father and I warred all through my teenage years: verbally, physically, psychologically. The worst it ever got was a shoving contest in the upstairs hallway when I was sixteen. I lost. He pinned me against my bedroom door, his forearm in my throat, firm up beneath my chin, frothing a millimeter from my face, and it didn't stop until my sister, a Niagara of tears and screams, pounded our shoulders and heads with both her fists. The fault was mine. I was a canker in our home. Disobedient, disrespectful, dismissive. My father, under vigorous financial and emotional strain, still in his mid-thirties, felt unvalued, unloved by me. I wish I could have seen that. All adolescents can't be as swollen-headed as I was. Everyone knew that my mother had left our family because she'd met someone else, a man with money, and yet during one of our verbal shoot-outs, I had the callousness right there at hand: 'You know,' I said, 'it's *your* fault she left us. It was you.' I don't know what I could have meant by that – he drove her away, wasn't man enough to keep her? – but I knew it would wound him, and that's what I wanted then.

'All I ever did was love your mother,' he said, and then he rose from the front porch and walked inside. I won that one, if you can call that winning. I'd give a considerable sum to be able to change my attitude that afternoon, revise those cutting words. Like many father/son relationships, ours improved immensely once I got the hell out of the house.

IV

It can seem inscrutable when an arcane interest such as bodybuilding hops among friends like an infection. Several of my boyhood and high-school pals began bodybuilding when I did, or else I began when they did. We hadn't made a pact, hadn't conspired beforehand, weren't aware of each other's hankering for muscularity. But there must have been something in the water, I thought, because so many of us got sick with it.

Though perhaps it wasn't all that inscrutable. For working-class kids who came of age in the bigness and bluster of the Reagan '80s, who were soused on the action flicks of Schwarzenegger and Stallone, on the bombast of Hulk Hogan, muscled physiques were simply what you pined for. What happened to my pals and me in Manville in the early '90s was part of a grander cultural trend that had jumped to life a decade earlier when the American political mood took a hardright turn. Cartoonish musclemen, typified by Schwarzenegger and Stallone, arrived to supplant the 'girlie-men' of the '70s, to redeem us from the humiliating failures of Vietnam and the emasculating victories of feminism. If we wanted to win wars, actual and cultural and personal, we needed all the muscle we could get. In *Rambo: First Blood Part II,* when Rambo's former colonel springs him from prison so that the great warrior can return to Vietnam in search of POWs, Rambo asks, 'Do we get to win this time?'

I and my pals spent a third of our time talking about weights, a third talking about food, and another third talking about steroids. Of course steroids. We weren't an overly principled lot, even if I had come from a family that was, nor can I pretend that we had a moral skirmish going on: to do or not to do drugs. There was no moral skirmish because we didn't think of steroids any differently from the way we thought of fuel for a motorcycle. Nor were we about to be hoodwinked by the culture-wide hypocrisy that declared cigarettes and alcohol – those convivial slaughterers of the untold – perfectly okay, while declaring steroids – the killer of few – perfectly contemptible.

You can hurl the accusation 'cheater' in the bedroom and you can hurl it in the classroom, but you look silly hurling it among bodybuilders in the gym. For the kind of musculature and might we desired, drugs were as necessary as good genes, and yet were still no guarantee. You can't just inject a torpid stick figure with anabolic steroids and then sit back and watch him transmute into Hercules. All the hard work begins *after* the injection. Contrary to the popular disdain we often heard, drugs are not 'a shortcut,' since the steroidian usually trains longer and harsher, and with more dedication, than his principled and drugless compatriots. This is what we would have said had you confronted us then: *If you have a*

problem with anabolic steroids, good for you, don't do them. But don't
unload your own problem on us.

Nothing except literature was more intrinsic to my adolescent identity, my half-formed conception of selfhood, than muscle strength and the Greco-Roman aesthetics of a champion. A champion of what, exactly, I could not have told you. Of vanity, I suppose, since, unless he's working out at the gym or competing on stage, a bodybuilder doesn't actually do anything with his beauteous bulk. He just ambles around with it, totes heavy objects for Gram, helps Pa with the furniture. Bodybuilding at the highest level, on the Mr. Olympia dais, is more spectacle than sport, an art form as elite as anything you see in the American Ballet Theater. If you think its everyday uselessness is a fault, recall Dr Chekhov's counsel: 'Only what is useless is pleasurable.'

I began aching for steroids after two years of training with Tony, after I turned eighteen and stopped making gains. That aching coincided with his departure from our weekday routine; his work was overdemanding again, his children too needy now, his wife slight with the lymphoma that would eventually erase her. Ever sensitive to abandonment, I did not perceive Tony's leaving as such, and I took that as a hopeful sign that maybe my bolstered exterior was beginning to bolster my interior. Steroid use had to coincide with Tony's hiatus because he never would have consented to it, and it wouldn't have been possible for me to conceal it from him. He knew what a steroidal physique looked like: the gibbous shoulders and biceps, the splashes of acne on the back, the weekly strength gains, the rising poundage, the blessed barbarity of the workouts. He'd passed me the skills and tricks I'd needed to forge on without him, and I had his go-ahead to keep training in his basement.

I recruited my closest friend, Drew; we'd been pals since we were waist-high, living across the road from one another on the North 3rd Avenue in Manville. He had developed biceps, deltoids, pectorals, but his back was flat and lagging and he had spindles for legs. Tony's favorite bit of ridicule for a guy with a weak lower body was 'His legs don't even touch,' meaning the adductor magnus muscles – the inner thighs – weren't developed enough to meet in the middle. Like Pop, I had strong legs and shoulders, and a strong back, and forearms like bowling pins (pals were always feeling my forearms), but my pecs were pathetic (they felt concave to me) and this was a daily fount of embarrassment and anxiety. Drew was one year older and twenty pounds heavier than me, but our numbers in every exercise were equal. We made a compatible duo in my uncle's dungeon, and I felt more than a little pride in being able to teach him the methods my uncle had taught me.

Your body responds immediately when you first begin your bout with the iron, but your muscle tissue is so designed that the longer you train, the tougher it is to add mass. After several months or years, depending on your genes, you plateau. The dreaded plateau, an ogre whose name we dared not utter. It arrives unbidden and unexplained. Your body stalls. You're eating just as much, training just as hard, but your muscle tissue has quit calling you back, is no longer stimulated by the iron. Never mind making gains in strength and mass: now you're battling – eating and training like a loon – just to keep what you've got. It's a spirit-sapping problem.

Or, gratuitously worse than plateauing, you slip, slide back, your numbers start to drop – both your body weight and the weight on the bar – and this is a demoralization that feels epic, an annihilation on your ego.

You could slave for weeks or months, glutting yourself just to gain five pounds of muscle, just to add ten-pound plates to your bench press or squat. And then something happens. The scallywag Phys. Ed. teacher makes you trot laps around the soccer field. (I was usually truant during gym class because I couldn't afford to waste calories on such silliness as that. I needed those calories to grow.) Or you get a cold and miss a workout, and then, God help you, the cold graduates to influenza and you miss a week, ten days, twelve days, you miss scores of meals, scores of them, even the relief of sleep irked by sickness. And then those fought-for pounds, those incredibly precious five or six pounds for which you suffered for several weeks or months, have vanished from you. You could nearly whiff the smoke of their vanishing: *poof.* I was, like an anorexic in reverse, always standing on a scale.

Drew knew an all-purpose drug dealer who ate every night at the pizzeria where he worked, a derelict who'd said that he was about to come into 'a shipment' of steroids from some hardcore gym in New York. Here's how brazen I was: after learning of this derelict's rooftop address – he lived on a roof – I pedaled my twelve-speed bicycle there and knocked on a doorish thing unevenly hung. Imagine being in the paranoid profession of drug dealing and opening your rooftop 'door' one day to find a stranger, some simpering teenage dolt with a handful of cash and the sentence: 'I'd like some steroids, please.'

Who was the derelict here? Disraeli: 'Youth is a blunder.' Yes it is. How does anyone survive the wild tacking through youth? But here's Disraeli again: 'Life is too short to be small.' So there you have it. And so I blundered, trying to explain who I was, and then tried to hand him cash in exchange for the ampoules and needles I wanted. But this newly nervous young man – he must have been twenty-three years old, fit, tanned, tattooed, the frequently barbered sort, that Guido haircut Jersey made famous – said that 'the shipment' hadn't yet arrived but that it 'definitely, definitely' would within a week. 'Definitely, definitely,' he said again, and I remember thinking that a quadruple use of 'definitely' didn't sound very definite at all.

'Hey,' he said, as I was leaving, 'don't show up here again.'

We never heard back from that dealer, but near the end of my senior year of high school, about four months into my training partnership with Drew, a pal of ours was able to get us an oral androgenic steroid named Anadrol. We called it 'Drol.' Made to treat osteoporosis and anemia, and eventually administered to those desperate souls eroded by AIDS, Anadrol was the brand name for the drug oxymetholone. A potent chemical concoction that increases size and strength as nothing else can, it performs its magic by bettering the body's synthesis of protein. That protein synthesis is how all anabolic steroids work, by helping the body produce cells to strengthen the muscle fibers lovingly torn while weight training.

Drol was so attractive to us not only because of its efficacy, but because it wasn't an injectable. A lot of my pals had hang-ups about addiction and disease. They dreaded needles – in the early 1990s, 'the war on drugs' was still used as a fearsome equivocation, HIV still a nightly news flash – and so weren't capable of harpooning one into the white foam of their buttocks. The irony is that injectable steroids are much less harmful to your health; unlike pills, they get immediately assimilated by the body without having to pass through the liver and other important parts. Drol, on the other hand: it unleashed hellfire upon the liver. I frequently thought I could feel mine sizzling.

But in only two weeks I inflated from 155 pounds to 165 pounds, and this for someone who could go many tormenting months without gaining a solitary pound. The new stony roundness of my deltoids and biceps, my lagging pectorals at last catching up, the added body mass I felt in each step, the sway of my quads under sweatpants, the spread of my lats (*latissimus dorsi,* those back muscles behind the armpits) – I can recall the inebriation of it still. It was as if I'd finally managed to get myself fully born. Never mind the high blood pressure that caused enfeebling headaches: I'd eat twelve ibuprofens per day, which tore up my stomach, which in turn caused me to eat twelve antacids per day. Never mind my puffed-up face: certain steroids cause water retention, so I had chipmunkish cheeks that were not cute. Never mind, too, the back acne and irritability: back acne was new to me, but irritability – I'd been thinking of it as a sensitive person's anomie – had been a near-constant for years.

Ever stolid, my father did not watch me as I sauntered through my days, did not notice the added mass on me, my complaints of headaches. Or if he did, he never said anything to me about it, and I have trouble explaining that. Wouldn't a committed father have confronted his teenage boy about a body full of steroids? Tony noticed. At a picnic, a family member asked me: 'How are you doing?' and my uncle countered with '*What* are you doing?' He meant 'What *drugs* are you doing?' But he never mentioned it to me again. Perhaps he thought it was my father's task to fix the trouble I'd given myself, or perhaps he thought it wasn't trouble at all. Like most families, mine often chose to cover its eyes and ears in an attempt to maintain peace. They pretended that problems weren't problems because meddling caused *other* problems.

A teenager is already a squall of hormones; that mortifying passage from boy to man shouldn't be further disrupted by synthetic testosterone or something called oxymetholone. But don't believe the after-school specials and alarmist brochures: steroids don't make marauding goons, don't turn placid males into Visigoths. On anabolic steroids, you are only more of what you were. The patient stay patient; the impetuous get impetuous and are glad for the excuse. Here's what I know for sure: I raised the physical stakes for myself. I required this next step. To ignore the all-natural code of my family, to become the only Giraldi to flood myself with steroids, I must have been pantingly desperate for some semblance of power, for my place among men.

I had no intention of shipping off for college, no spurring from my father to do so; my grades were painfully average, and despite my private life as a reader, I didn't think that the university world was open to me. I wanted to linger in town because I was in love with a girl who was lingering too, and because I wanted to weightlift. By the time I was paroled from high school in '92, a coven of boyhood friends had begun training at a gym in the next town called the Physical Edge. I'd known for several months that the dungeoned isolation of my uncle's basement would no longer suffice. Every bodybuilder eventually requires an atmosphere of incitement and arousal, a dynamizing gym republic, full membership in the cult.

I'd been all along too sapling, too uncertain of myself, not muscled enough to join the Edge or any of the less fervid gyms in the area. I remember fearing ridicule, the possibility of not belonging, of being jeered back through the door by freaky-looking beasts. But I was stronger and more muscular, more steroidal, than many of the pals who were already training there. It was the combination of Anadrol and graduating high school – the wideness of adulthood before me like the prelude to embrace – that gave me the necessary poise to walk into the Edge that first day.

Set back in a spottily wooded industrial park, behind leaning plots of corn, the Edge was a crimson-and-silver sprawl of modern equipment and Olympic free weights, five thousand square feet of mirror and metal. An aerobics room of chants (*and one and two and three*), an alcove of stationary bikes, treadmills, and StairMasters. Manifold machines of transformation, pulley machines and Smith machines, squat racks, flat and incline and decline benches, a battalion of gray dumbbells, black barbells, red faces pinched and grunting under them. Framed photos of pro bodybuilders in muscular tableau. Everywhere the iron-to-iron slap of plates beneath speakers pealing Soundgarden, Nirvana, Metallica, such distortion-fueled bruit. Everywhere the scent of rubber, oil, and sweat.

On my first day there, I tried to carry myself as if I were accustomed to such onsets of stimuli, but I'm not sure I succeeded. You've seen a six-year-old at a summer carnival, his eyes and limbs manic to take in, to test, all things, all at once? It was like that for me. When I tell you that the Edge was electrified by eroticism, I don't mean covertly. I mean the eroticism was flagrant, women and men tending to their vanity and fending off their deaths, quarter-dressed and sweating, spandex shorts with priapic knolls or else split crotches blotted with damp, nipples in salute, the aromas of bodies in extremis, arms and legs aglint with their exertions, the unsubtle flirting between sets of lunges, sets of squats, workout moans and faces remarkably coital, part brunt, part bliss.

For two years I'd been reading in muscle magazines about gyms such as this, but those articles must have been too puritanical because they forgot to tell me about the humming sexuality, the pre-orgasmic splendor of the place, those about-to-give-birth attitudes. Nurse Whitman said it: *Urge and urge and urge, / Always the procreant urge of the world*. For an eighteen-year-old kid who'd misplaced God and didn't much mind, it was a festival of carnality and better than any heaven you could have conjured for me.

It's true that the Edge was the district primarily of the weightlifter and dogged bodybuilder – it was like being in a wilderness of erections: large, hard, vascular men planted everywhere around you – but for the sake of its survival, the gym also humored normal people, the loafered and the desk-glued who clicked keyboards at various firms in the vicinity, some of whom were hand-held through timid exercises by trainers who looked like surfers. The presence of these normal ones was welcome, as planets welcome their moons. It was they who gawked, who provided the stunned audience for our daily Mardi Gras of muscle. A gym such as the Edge was a gym only in the most literal, practical meaning. For those of us who would make it our home, who would come of age there, and become the ambassadors of its kingdom, its physical utility was only one part of its value.

I've heard certain tweeds describe a gym as a microcosm of society, complete with its own lexicon (*pumped, shredded, juiced*), its own cruel hierarchies (the largest men and fittest women, those Santas among elves, rule the upper stratum, while the pencil necks and chubbers are the unfortunate helots), and its own regulated behavior (don't you dare touch a machine or weight when a world-beater is using it). That might be accurate, gyms might have their own flesh-and-iron ecosystem, but for me and the circle that would adopt me, the Edge was theater and church before it was anything else, the ancient triumvirate of ritual and drama and play. We relished the stage-like atmosphere of it all, this theater in the round, relished its most performative aspects, the music and the pageantry, the costumes and the exhibitionism. You should have seen the multicolored outfits I stretched over my frame. An elastane one-piece, striped in turquoise and white, was not the worst of it. A night at the gym often felt like a night of kabuki in a strip club.

Or else our body mass as Mass, because for the many failed Catholics among us, bodybuilding was both a form of homage to and revolt from the flesh-centered mythos of Catholicism. We said to the Church, in effect, *You want a fixation on the flesh of our battered Messiah? We'll make ourselves into messiahs, self-saviors. With this iron we'll torture ourselves into godliness.* The Satan of *Paradise Lost*, that unrivaled insurgent, describes himself and his legion of the fallen as *self-begot, self-rais'd / By our own quick'ning power*, and that's the kind of sublime, steroidal ego to which bodybuilders aspire.

We wanted to be totems, objects of veneration and warning, of the extraordinary and the occult. A tired psychologist will tell you that we wanted these things because we were internally minuscule people with the psyches of hurt birds, and I don't deny the trace of accuracy in that claim. But the more exciting assessment might be this: we wanted sexiness and seduction and exhilaration, some communion with the sacred in a culture that no longer acclaimed the sacred, and, above all, we wanted brotherhood. We wanted to belong.

I began by training with those boyhood pals who'd joined the Edge before me. The way we trained, we couldn't train alone. We required partners, spotters to supervise the high poundage we lifted.

During a bench press the spotter helped raise the barbell from the rack, and then he was there either to prevent you from dropping the thing onto your esophagus, or to prod you through a round of forced reps. We used forced reps at the end of a set when the muscle was mostly spent. The spotter gripped the bar to help us complete two more, three more, four more, shouting us through the burn – it was like a delivery room: *push, push, push, push* – and that's partly how big guys get big, by shocking the deepest muscle tissue into expansion. Your muscles don't *want* to grow. They're perfectly content to remain as they are, which is why you need a shock campaign if your goal is size and strength.

My boyhood pals were frequently helpful but our schedules were never quite in sync. More important: they were muscular and strong but without the necessary violence of mind, the savagery of will I'd learned from my uncle. I don't mean they didn't care about training; I mean they were too well-mannered, their attitude toward the weights much too polite. I needed to pick fights with those barbells and dumbbells and plates, to kick and spit at them, grab them as if I had to throttle their heft in order to keep that heft from throttling me. After a hellacious, hollering set of straight-bar curls, I'd slam, clang the bar back into the rack, as if to tell it: *You lose.* My pals wanted a workout; I wanted warfare – against the weakling I'd been. They didn't mind eighty per cent engagement; I considered that a waste and a shame when it wasn't a sin. What was the point of this enterprise if you weren't going to bring every particle of yourself to its execution?

Here was the Giraldi family machismo at last making itself known in me, the machismo I'd internalized now seeking vent. Maybe with that uncompromising attitude I stopped feeling, for a time, as if I was not really Pop's grandson, not really my father's son. I didn't carry that awareness with me through my days, wasn't unduly conscious of needing to impress either Pop or my father. They weren't privy to my training methods at the Edge; they never went to see what my life was like there. Pop had once or twice visited Tony and me in the dungeon – he stood aside to comment and correct – but my father, entangled on multiple fronts, never did. That's not an accusation. What happens in the gym between a man and his partner and their muscles is not unlike what happens in the bedroom between a man and his partner and their genitalia, between the confessing and the confessor, and so uninitiated spectators can be a concentration-kill.

There's something to that. At the Edge, you made sure your awe stayed furtive. You didn't openly goggle those Atlasian others, but rather tried for glimpses in that funhouse – everywhere the mirrors gave the impression of rooms within rooms – because there was a contradictory sense that a workout was private. A public and publicized privacy, but privacy just the same. And yet in most cases the furtiveness wasn't necessary at all. Those who were rubberneck-worthy *wanted* your awe and ogling, wanted to see the lust and wonder on your face. That's part of why we'd made the Edge our home – it was what we lived for.

V

The Greek athletes at the gymnasium shaved their pubic patches. Hairlessness as a symbol of youth's vitality. Porn stars barber their genitalia in a suggestion of pre-pubescence. Look how *smooth*, how godly, is that magnificent sculpture, the Farnese Hercules.

Our upstairs bathtub half-filled with tepid, milkish water, tinged with pink, my body afroth, throat to toes, with shaving foam. I was seated on the rim of the tub with a razor, rivulets of blood like raspberry sauce in whipped cream, wincing through the nicks. How was this done? The two blades of the razor kept getting crammed with hair. I'd slide it three inches and it was crammed.

So I had to knock it against the tub to loosen hair from the blades, but when I did that, the cartridge detached from the handle and disappeared into turbid water, and then I had to grope around for it, which is why my fingertip was bleeding now too. Plus the razor I used was meant for a tender male's face, and so the blades were dulling rapidly against my body's wool. I'd gone through three cartridges already.

I'm saying this took forever. Women did this *every week*? Perhaps it got simpler, more efficient, but I wasn't sure how, because, contorted though I was, I couldn't see where I was shaving. In addition to the body's collection of knobs, the ankles and elbows and wrists, those unseen corners and nooks were what was bleeding most earnestly. Behind my knees, the under-pockets of my groin, beneath the ridges of my buttocks, also those raised moles, one in my left armpit a tragedy of crimson teardrops. It didn't at all seem imperative or comfortable, or *safe,* to shave my pubis and scrotum, too, but having gone that far, why not just deforest my genitalia of its personality? Everybody was doing it.

We shaved ourselves because you couldn't see the suffered-for striations and vascularity, the rutted divisions between muscles, if we were coated in hair. Your thigh, for example, is not a single lump of flesh; it's four elegant bands, hence its name, quadriceps. So hairlessness was required of both the competitive bodybuilder and the serious aspirant, and now that I was serious, too, now that I was training at the Edge, down the drain swirled my hair. Although it wasn't really swirling down the drain, I saw when I finished; it was stuck, splotched on the sides of the tub and clumped there at the grate, a whole inch of it.

My naked skin, dry now save for the runnels of blood, still felt wet, felt newly bloomed into a missing breeze, felt as if I could have used another bathtub full of aftershave lotion. There were eddies, shaving foam, sanguinary footprints on the floor, plus used Gillette cartridges like shell casings at a massacre. I was trying to mop this impressive mess when I heard it behind me: 'Good God in the morning.'

I'd left the bathroom door ajar, and there stood my father, blistered and filthy from work. 'Good God in the morning' was, for some reason, his way of saying, *What in God's name have you done?* He had much-used variants of that exacerbated expression, such as 'Oh my aching back,' which meant *What trouble have you caused for me now?* Several years hence, when I'm 'helping' him paint his friend's living room, I'll drop a newly opened gallon of china white onto the carpet, and we'll both just stand there looking in astonishment at this bungle, and he'll say it over and over: 'Oh my aching back.'

I pressed the towel to my lap and we had this familiar two-line exchange: 'Oh hey, Dad, what're you doing?'

'No, Bill – what are *you* doing?'

(My friends delighted in this exchange – they thought my father buddy-like, trenchantly comedic – and in the hallways of our high school they said to me, 'No, Bill – what are *you* doing?')

The paradox of bodybuilding, its mixed signifiers, the collision of the masculine and feminine. Tough guys *shave*? I said, 'I'm shaving, Dad.'

And then he said it again with a wagging head, before shambling down the hall to his own bathroom: 'Good God in the morning.'

It took a month for me to be adopted by the prelates and priestesses of the Edge, to be welcomed into the sanctum of the gargantuan. Two things happened at once: a colossus named Victor approached me about training together, and the gym's manager asked me to work the morning shift from five to ten. The job put an Edge T-shirt on my back and its keys in my pocket: a vicar now, a cleric. I can recall that surging of honor in me, of pride at having trained harshly enough to be noticed, chosen. It's what all of us are working and waiting for in this world, to be chosen ones. I'd open the Edge at five, man the front counter, peddle memberships and merchandise, blend fruit shakes spiked with protein powder, offer training tips to newbies, stroll about the place feeling clued-in and authoritative, keys clanking at my side, then go home to nap and eat and read, and then return to the Edge at 5 p.m. to meet Victor.

Short and broad, a foot and a half thick from front to back, Victor waddled around on diamonded quads and calves, with whopping arms and rashes of acne from anabolic drugs. His training partner had just been hit with a hernia during a set of bent barbell rows, and so Victor was in pursuit of a dedicated replacement. His choosing me was an uplift, confirmation of my rigor, of muscularity that earns praise. It was like being asked to the prom just when you feared you might be too homely to go. We trained with the drive of vanquishers, with profanity and spittle, a return to the partnered intensity I'd had with my uncle.

The camaraderie at the Edge happened the way rewarding camaraderie normally does, with ease and unspoken understanding. We dubbed one pal 'Sid,' after the pro wrestler Sid Vicious – six and a half feet and 250 pounds of blond beef – and we dubbed another 'Rude,' after the mustachioed and curly-locked wrestler Rick Rude, ripped through the midsection, world-class abs and obliques. Pedro was wee, only five feet two inches, a trainer with an office at the gym, with beautifully rounded muscle bellies and a gargoyle inked into his bicep; he lay naked in the tanning beds and once came out saying, 'I think I burned my rooster.' (The shorter you are, by the way, the easier it is to stick muscle to your skeleton, especially the legs. Tall guys are forever in lament over their lagging quads, hams, and calves.)

Bob the Cop was always 'Bob the Cop' to distinguish him from the other Bob who wasn't a cop, but both had height and bulk and pectorals like halved volleyballs. It was useful to know Bob the Cop because if ever another cop pulled you over in town, all you had to do was mention him, present his business card – 'Bob's a friend of mine; we train together at the Edge' – and the cop who'd just interrupted your day would instantly know what that meant. The bodybuilding compatriots of Bob the Cop don't get tickets in this town.

The other Bob – thirty-five years old, owner of a car dealership – sometimes trained in the morning or afternoon. He was constantly having to stagger his schedule, circumvent his fiancée, train when she'd least suspect it, because she'd outright forbidden him from bodybuilding, from every aspect of gym life, its drugs and its fanatical kinship, such nuptial-wrecking zeal. She was smart, in other words: an emergency room nurse, privy to how some men cannot weight-train casually, with the calmness of only fifty per cent investment – privy to how they get squeezed by the obsessiveness of the sport, and to the health trouble that can be sparked by the drugs we used .

If Bob wanted to do some bicep curls at home with her tiny purple dumbbells, if he wanted to go for a bit of a jog, or jump some rope, do some sit-ups, all that was okay. But God have mercy on his soul if ever he stepped foot in a gym

81

again. Bob gave us, his pals and coconspirators, wallet-size photos of his fiancée – all lips, cleavage, yellow locks from Rite Aid – with instructions to warn him should we ever see her coming, warn him so he could escape out the back door. He parked his Trans Am in the rear of the building. If ever I answered the phone to find a woman asking for him, I was to reply, 'Who? Nope. No one here by that name.'

The nighttime priestesses of the Edge were Pedro's girlfriend, Rude's fiancée, Sid's wife, and a Titaness called Christine, her outfit usually a prototype for the porn version of *Barbarella*, a woman so unjustly beautiful she seemed to have stepped from the pages of Petrarch. She rearranged all your body's chemicals as you looked at her; you could feel your endocrine glands going haywire, the stuttering of your pituitary. And she was so mighty with weights you dared not cross her. Victor and I were often just getting our asses out of her way.

A beautiful woman in the room will make some men try harder at whatever they do, whether deadlifting or dentistry. The callousness of sexual selection at work: your double helix needs to impress her even when your backward self has no hope of ever smelling her sheets. The women in our sect were like mists of cocaine in the ventilation system; they could wake you right up, turn a middling workout into a memorable one.

We had a hard time remembering how ordinary women and men traversed this world without muscle, without our shields to fortify themselves against all the missiles aimed at them. And for me, in certain exalted moments, that was especially true. I *tried* not to remember it, because those memories were appended to feelings of sickness and vulnerability, fourteen years old in a hospital bed with meningitis, then dumped by my first love for a footballer.

If you want to know about the essence of eroticism in the bodybuilding underground, I suppose you'll have to tack a *homo* onto that term. Imagine us there in the locker room of the Edge, a tribe of hairless, naked men bayoneting one another's buttocks with needles, massaging the cramps from one another's deltoids and quads, positioning one another into poses before adoring mirrors, bestowing compliments on muscle shape and density, in post-workout exhaustion sprawled on benches like the Barberini Faun, in unknowing imitation of the fifth-century Athenian gymnasium at which beauteous, post-pubescent boys exercised fully nude (*gymnos* is Greek for *stripped, naked*). And the original Olympic games, in legend founded by Hercules himself, were spectacles of masculine nudity.

In the West, our entire mode of thinking about the male body and male beauty has been handed to us by those fifth-century Greeks. The prominent social place they allowed for sculptures of that beauty is unmatched in antiquity; just look at how they conceived of the human being, what godliness they glimpsed in us. For those Greeks, one's carapace of muscle was not only a signal of athletic dexterity or a warrior's prowess, but also indicative of inner, non-physical energies. It meant fortitude and fearlessness.

You see it everywhere in Greek myth and drama, the importance of self-mastery, the glorification of the individual through physical battle, through a struggle not with your own spiritual state, but with a corporeal world always attempting to clobber you. This is why the Greeks believed that the individual, the self and its selfhood, was inextricable from the condition of the body: the cultivation of one compelled, required, the cultivation of the other.

It's no surprise to know that the Academy and the Lyceum (those two vital gymnasiums, arenas of physical aptitude and beauty) lent their names to Plato's and Aristotle's programs of philosophical inquiry. The great thinkers did their cognitive exercises within sight, scent, and sound of young, naked, athletically perfect men, as if the mere proximity to their muscle and might would stroke the brain cells. It seems to have worked. In a conversation with a fatso named Epigenes, Socrates declares that the youth has both a civic and ethical obligation to develop his body to its peak potential or else he'll live a wasted and ridiculed existence.

So the inner and outer were indistinguishable, and they mostly stayed that way until St. Paul debuted his new hero, the Nazarene. Flip through the medieval Christian thinkers, peek inside Augustine and Aquinas, and you'll spot the *odium generis humani,* the anti-idealizing of the physical form, the severing of flesh from soul, a belief in the inherent imperfection of the flesh, and a marked preference for the health of the spirit. In his hymn 'Pange Lingua Gloriosi,' when Aquinas writes: *Now, my tongue, the mystery telling / Of the glorious Body sing,* you know whose body he's talking about.

Christianity cares about the fallen, filthy body only insofar as it will be resurrected after Christ's second coming. Even the Renaissance resurgence of Greek ideals in art, so effective at wedding the Hellenic with the Christian, didn't put a damper on Christianity's disdain for flesh. That makes sense, doesn't it, if you consider Nietzsche's contention that Christianity is for literal losers, for the many weaklings of the world. When you're a limping asthenic being bashed by imperial muscle, of course you'll say that muscle doesn't matter. Of course you'll elevate the incorporeal, the soul, to the highest ranking. The secretly envious usually pretend that what they envy isn't all that enviable. It's impossible to imagine Atlas offering his aggressor the other cheek to slap, or Hesiod or Homer uttering Christ's third Beatitude in the Sermon on the Mount: 'Blessed are the meek: for they shall inherit the earth.'

But Christianity is meant for, *designed* for, the meek. It's the perfect fit for the gimped and depressed, for those who feel beneath one boot heel or another. Don't worry about your physical, worldly deficiencies and flaws because glory will be yours in life after death. Bodybuilders would rather not wait that long for glory, and they aren't about to be despotized by anybody, or concede that there's something hallowed about meekness. They are exceptionally plugged in to the palpable, the carnal, the world as it is and not the world to come.

You're probably wondering: didn't bodybuilding strike any of us as extremely *gay*? It did not. If a mocking sexologist had shown up to point out how gay we were, we would have said that he didn't get it. The manly code, the manly discipline, the manly sport and art: '*You* try it,' we would have told him, right before smacking his glasses off. We would have insisted that our arcane passion resulted from wanting to astonish women. We were all of us suspiciously vocal about wanting lots of women.

But let's be honest: despite the skirt-chasing, the real aim of our arcane passion, entirely hidden from us then, was to astonish *one another*, to gain the attention and affection of other elite men, the grandees of the Edge. And we, the ultra-masculine, had transformed into stereotypical females in order to do it. We repined for the approval of dominant males, shaved and tanned ourselves, wore tiny clothes, were food-obsessed, weight-obsessed, always standing on scales, secretly worried about our brittle images and self-worth, our always tremulous control. With one another at the Edge we made a show of whoops and high-fives, not unlike those syndicates of teenage girls who embrace one another at the mall with shrieking brio.

Except for me the show wasn't merely theatrical. I'd found my tribe among them, a substitute family, the Edge a home more meaningful than what my father provided.

Many of us also had gynecomastia, what we called 'bitch tits' – I still have mine in the left pectoral – nodes of fatty tissue beneath the nipples caused by an excess of synthetic testosterone. Your body is looking for the right testosterone-estrogen ratio, so when you deluge your blood with synthetic testosterone, the body cooks up more estrogen in its quest for homeostasis, and more estrogen means, among other things, the physical traits of a female. It means breasts. They could be moderately painful, to boot, but it wasn't the pain that bugged us. Pain we did not mind. Tits we did. Some among our number went under the scalpel to undo the humiliation.

The acne harvested by steroids, the high blood pressure, the bitch tits and frequent headaches: tolerable consequences of trying to meet the Western standard of male beauty, much the way anorexic women become famished, hirsute, hideous in their quest to be loved. The male bodybuilder and the female anorexic are equal though opposite manifestations of steady social arm-twisting. Women will be thin, men will be muscular, or both will be nobody. The equivalence of genders is nowhere more apparent than in a gym.

I was twelve, twelve and a half years old, pumping gas at a station in the next town. The owner, we'd heard, was a notorious 'fruitcake,' his wife an elaborate blind. But this confused me, because with a sashay like that, I was certain there was no blind big enough. Certain *queer*-scorning pals warned me not to pump gas there because the owner would trick me into the bathroom and try to wedge himself into my jeans. But I didn't believe he'd do this – he'd never been anything but kind to me – and I was proven right. He didn't.

But I did this to him: it was one of those August middays when the asphalt was about to melt, the heat coming as much from below as above. I was working a shift with one of my best pals, who was also not made nervous by the owner's sashay, although this pal was a part-time gay-hater who amputated *fruitcake* to *fruit,* and rather enjoyed saying it, enjoyed saying it so much he greeted *me* with it: 'Hey, fruit' and 'What's up, fruit?' and sometimes just plain 'Fruit,' in the lilt you use when you say someone's name upon seeing him after a longish spell.

(This aside is not quite poetic justice but it falls within a nearby taxonomy. The same pal with *fruitcake* always on his lips was one of three brothers, two of them extroverted, all sons of a brash fireman. The first son was a heavy-metal head and car mechanic; the second, my pal, a titanic football fiend; and the third, the youngest, was – always had been – inward, awkward, skulkingly cautious, too effete in the macho oxygen of his household. Over the next decade he centimetered himself from the closet, to the no doubt thunderous disquiet of his family. Before I left Manville for good at nineteen, I placed a copy of Housman's *A Shropshire Lad* discreetly on the youngest brother's desk: a token of fraternity from one misfit to another. So my pal who called everyone *fruitcake* when we were twelve years old would be, before long, confronting that slur in a fashion he couldn't then fathom.)

In this tsunami of August heat a quivering Ford pickup, rusted through the quarter panels and missing its tailgate, dinged the bell for gas. My pal and I were mawing pizza slices and gumballs in the office, and I walked out into a ninety-eight degrees that felt more liquid than gas. The guy in the pickup, a laborer with a granite paunch, week-old beard, engine grease to his elbows, said what you'd expect him to say: 'Fill 'er up.'

And so that's what I did, filled 'er up. When she was full, he handed me the cash and the Ford grumbled away. And not ten minutes later, as I was feeding another thirsty tank, I saw this man sweating back into the gas station, from the direction in which he'd just departed. His thumb was jabbing over his shoulder. 'What did you put in my truck?' he said.

'Your truck?'

'What did you just put in my truck?'

'Gas?' I said.

'Did you just put diesel in my truck?'

I looked at the diesel pump, and there it was, looking back at me. Yes, I'd just put diesel fuel into his apparently gasoline-engine Ford. But he'd pulled up to that pump and told me to fill it. Of course the pumps were close enough to kiss. But I should have known what got diesel fuel and what did not. And of course now I was prodigiously frightened, the fear of imminent bodily harm.

'Get X on the phone right now,' he said. X was the owner. I hurried back into the office to call him, but before I did, I called my father. 'Dad, come to the gas station,' I said. 'I've got a problem here.'

My pal, a fresh gumball in his face, said, 'You really did it now, fruit.'

Soon my father was there, and the owner, too, and my father said: 'We'll have to siphon it out.' The owner was embarrassed by this, I saw, but he was missing the rage I'd expected. The guy I'd just dieseled had an icy attitude toward my father – he wouldn't shake hands – as if he was to blame for my gas-station stupidity.

From the garage the owner and the dieseled guy gathered tools, tubes, red cans, and didn't include my father in whatever remedial plan they had. In the shade of the building – it was four o'clock now – my father leaned with one foot up against the white brick, no doubt wondering what he should do about this, waiting to be of some assistance. His look said to me both *Good God in the morning* and *Oh my aching back*.

And it was then that I noticed, in his navy blue, hole-strewn sweatpants, the flaccid bulge in his lap. He must have scrambled from the house to come here. Perhaps he'd just stepped from the shower when the phone rang, and he must not have had time to hunt for underwear, and now he had this flaccid bulge at the center of his sweatpants. I was mortified by this; feeding diesel fuel into a gasoline engine seemed charming in comparison.

The owner and dieseled guy left to undo what I'd done, and my father left too, although I'm not sure if he went with them. Later I would learn that he'd paid to fix the guy's truck, handed over cash he did not have to reverse my mistake. I finished my shift at the station that day; I wasn't fired. In fact, the owner was compassionate toward this blunder: the heat, my youth, my father's willingness to pay, etc.

No, I had to wait a few more weeks to get fired. It was another shift with my *fruitcake*-saying pal and we were knocking around in the mechanics' bays, making the car lifts rise and fall, handling hydraulic tools, objects we should not have been touching. A grease gun hung from the steel beams so the mechanics could simply reach up for it when they were beneath the opened hoods of cars, and I leapt to grab this gun, dangled from it, the trigger engaged, salvos of grease unloading upon everything.

I never thought to mop this mess – I hoped it wouldn't be noticed? – and so I left these ejaculations of engine grease all over the garage bays. On the day I was fired, I pedaled home and spoke those words to my father: 'I'm fired, Dad.'

'Yeah,' he said, 'that sounds about right.'

VI

A gym has several seasons a day, and the early season, during my shift from five to ten, was far less severe than the evening season. It was the mellower, coffee-scented spring of morning you'd expect. Most of the a.m. crowd consisted of those civilians who wouldn't have meshed well with the evening behemoths. They were fit without being muscled, healthful without zealotry, professionals who entered in spandex and sports bras, sweatpants and sneakers, and exited in pantsuits and heels, dress shirts and ties.

There were the silver-haired ones, as well, those who were up at five not because they'd pried their slumped frames from bed, but because sleep had betrayed them, deprived them of its gifts. When you have fewer days ahead than behind, dawn rushes upon you, mugs you awake, as if in reminder of your truncated time. I was very fond of them all and their normality; they talked to me about their jobs and their retirements, their kids and grandkids, and they seemed steady, easeful in their lives, in the lives I imagined they had when they finished at the Edge each morning.

Normality has a soundtrack. Instead of the amygdala-arousal of Metallica or AC/DC required by the working-class night crowd – power chords that shook your spine – I'd play Pink Floyd or the Eagles, the tuck-in-your-shirt solace preferred by bourgeois white people everywhere. Sometimes I could get away with a smattering of Guns N' Roses, with Axl Rose's irreligious screech. (In '88, not long after *Appetite for Destruction* came out, I bought my father the cassette so he could play it on his Kenwood stereo – the only costly item he ever gave himself during those gaunt years – and perhaps know what was seething inside my newly teenaged self. Whenever I heard Axl wailing 'Welcome to the Jungle' from his bedroom, it sounded to me like hope, like I might have a chance in our household.)

Sometimes the morning crowd let me get away with the lipsticked baying of the glam bands that in '92 still held a cobweb of relevance: Cinderella and Ratt, Warrant and Faster Pussycat. In their dervishing falsettos you could almost smell the illogical mix of male pheromones and hairspray. Those glam rockers and their leotarded, yelping masculinity – men who'd morphed into women to croon about how much they loved women – had an uncomfortable amount in common with bodybuilders.

The abusive cheese of '90s Aerosmith was always welcome, and because we were in New Jersey, so was anything by Bon Jovi, and perhaps, on occasion, the Boss of *Born to Run,* though the Boss of *Nebraska* I could forget: too contemplative, too downtrodden for the spandexed. You have to understand how important, how primary, music is at a gym: riots erupt, coups are caused over the wrong kind.

Let it not be too distortive or eardrum-slamming among the average ones, nor too sedate, too Paul Simon among the monsters. A revolution is always one song away.

One duo never gave me any lip over the music I played: Hudson and Father Antonio, the about-to-be-married Catholic and his weightlifting priest. I'm not certain how they'd begun training together, and I remember thinking it incoherent that a priest should pump iron. (But in the Book of Job, Yahweh asks the stricken man, 'Hast thou an arm like God?' Admit it: if you have a god, he's no stick-figure wonk.) Thirty years old, humble, always hidden in a sweatshirt and sweatpants, sienna curls past his ears, Hudson was a man of great rarity, so magnanimous he accidentally made you feel bad that you weren't a gentler person.

On melancholy mornings I'd vent to him about a girlfriend at Rutgers who was in the process of jilting me; bodybuilding, it turned out, was no security against being jilted. Hudson would listen in a kind of nodding serenity, and then respond with the most non-New Jersey, quasi-Buddhist acceptance and sensitivity I'd ever heard from another male. *Forget that bitch* was the level of relationship wisdom I was accustomed to at the Edge, but Hudson was all nuance and subtlety and, without putting too bathetic a point on it, love. His strategy, wholly new to me, was to remind me of my value without demonizing the girlfriend. If he felt he didn't offer enough comfort during a particular dialogue, he'd call me at the gym when he returned home to give me another twenty minutes of his time.

The girlfriend at Rutgers – let's call her Val – had been my girlfriend in high school, a senior-year miming of commitment and love. That relationship, like most high-school relationships that attempt survival after graduation, was dying from loss of blood, from an impact of expectations. No suturing could have saved it, but I was in ironclad denial of this. She had a blond beauty that rewired my hypothalamus – oglers said she could have passed for Uma Thurman – and I was under the desperate misimpression that if only *I* could be beautiful enough, muscular enough, wise enough (I penned one of her college English papers, on Hemingway), then I could make her return the affection I felt. That strategy, as you know, never works.

At Hudson's wedding, officiated by Father Antonio, I read a verse from Corinthians – 'If I speak in the tongues of men or of angels, but do not have love, I am only a resounding gong or a clanging cymbal' – and years later, long after my life at the Edge had ended, long after Val had gone, I heard, I don't know how, that his marriage hadn't lasted. I spent several hours feeling unstrung by that news, and several more trying to find him after years of lost contact, but I could not.

Father Antonio gave me my first invitation to speak to a classroom, to Catholic-school kids, but not about bodybuilding – about reading. He'd seen me one morning behind the front counter with a copy of Flannery O'Connor. Among the morning crowd I read openly, without dread of the question *What the hell is that?* In the evenings, doing cardio on the exercise bikes, I resorted to that well known ruse, a reversal of the classic *Playboy* mag inside a textbook: into an issue of *Flex* or *Muscle & Fitness,* I slipped yanked-free pages from a battered Goethe or Keats paperback, or else I didn't risk it at all and left literature home.

One gets adept at keeping two sets of books, at managing a bisected life. Father Antonio's curiosity about my holding a copy of Ms. O'Connor's stories was unsullied by latent accusation, that small but suspicious rising in the voice that meant *A muscle-head doesn't read; who are you fooling?* And never mind that I'd been wed to reading for a decade already before I picked up my first barbell.

The only weightlifting priest I'd ever met or heard tell of, Father Antonio was rare in beholding no contradiction between a Homeric shell and a Christic soul. He was at home in modern paradox – which is probably why he beheld no contradiction in me either, why it was not jarring for him to see someone with my physique, someone so ensconced in the bodybuilding headspace, holding a copy of Flannery O'Connor. When I went to speak to the classroom of Catholic grade-school kids that autumn, I tried to promote the magnifying satisfactions of literature – I read from O'Connor's story 'Parker's Back' – and they gave gracious nods, the courteous impression of agreement.

But before I left, a boy asked about my biceps, about weightlifting: 'How much do you bench?' and 'How big are your arms?' Others asked if I would flex for them, if they could feel my arms. It might have been a mistake to wear an Edge T-shirt. Later, I'd interpret this as my failure to convince them of the personal relevance of O'Connor; they weren't really listening to the sentences I'd read aloud, to my analysis of how the images and rhythms worked on the page, the codependence of style and matter. But maybe I was wrong about that. Why couldn't they have both, the biceps and the books, just as I had both?

I stretched my shirt sleeve up past the shoulder and stood at the blackboard flexing my right arm, and a gaggle of twelve-year-olds, all males, rushed to me there – those poor darlings who for the next several years would be stranded in a purgatory of inelegance, limboed between boys and men, with all the worst traits of both and none of the charms of either – and they took turns feeling my bicep and forearm, as if testing the firmness of fruit, the firmness of their futures.

'Why do you *want* those muscles?' a girl asked from her desk, her hair a storm of black curls, her mouth a grid of metal. It was the most reasonable question I'd been asked all day, but I didn't have a chance to answer because a crew-cut boy with buckteeth beat me to it. 'For chicks,' he said.

Let's call her Daisy. Every morning she arrived with the sun, came to the Edge half-nude, half-clad in lavender – mere eight inch strips of elastic across her chest and lap – came for sit-ups and the Stairmaster, for the aerobics classes and pulley-machines. Ten years older than me, silken yellow hair choked back into a ponytail, Daisy sat at the front counter after her workouts, sucking at a straw in the whey-protein shake I'd blended for her, sometimes interested in a fitness slick, sometimes in a novel, rarely in anything at all I had to offer. After ordering her shake, she seemed gravely committed to resisting all conversation, as if each dawn she'd made a pact with her temptation counselor not to chat up the eighteen-year-old at the Edge.

That went on for more mornings than my ego cared to count. Even when it was only the two of us there, her face stayed locked on a magazine, a notepad, a book. Until that morning when the book was Fitzgerald's *The Beautiful and Damned*. Our exchange sounded like this:

'They're pretty miserable, those two.'

'Who?' she said.

'Anthony and Gloria Patch,' I told her.

'You read this?'

'Yup.' Like every American high-schooler, I'd been given *Gatsby* in tenth grade, and when our class finished with it, I went in search of more Fitzgerald. *The Beautiful and Damned* seemed to me an unimprovable title.

'You read books?' she asked.

'Yup.'

'*These* kinds of books?' and she showed me the cover, showed me the kind she meant, the serious kind, the kind serious, unmuscled readers read.

'*Those* kind,' I said, and if I'd been more calculating, I'd have feigned a wounded bafflement.

Mornings at the counter were different after that: her gradual glowing, an uncoiling. Since college she'd been nursing a medium-grade Fitzgerald fetish, and so, trying to catch up, intimidated by her knowledge and the many sentences she'd memorized, I abruptly had a whole drift of Scribners paperbacks on my bedside stand.

At some point phone numbers were exchanged, midnight talks shared, ostensibly about F. Scott but the subtext was all about our own antsy fluids. Val had not been returning my calls – she was just then in the process of banishing me to the marchlands of her heart, enthralled by college life at Rutgers, one of sororities and frats, a drunken rollick that could not include me – and so I didn't for a minute consider this cheating.

Soon I was at Daisy's condo, an after-dark, unplanned stepping-out, in a town much swankier than Manville, BMWs and Benzes dreaming in driveways, lit shrubbery that looked imported from the Orient. She had a city of white boxes in her garage, boxes filled with baby oil, each with a picture of an overjoyed, over-soft infant on the side. A couple of times a week she'd empty several bottles into her bath water, marinate in it for an hour or more, and her skin, as I would experience that night, was like the satiny backside of the baby itself.

When you're the sprig I was then, and the woman grinding herself into your lap is not only a decade older than you but a decade ahead of you – degreed, salaried, mortgaged – what you first feel are inklings of the paradisal, an adrenalized confidence and joy, but then it's something else. Then it's much more substantive, a confirmation of your selfhood, a validating of your spirit; it's a welcome to the altar of your contentment.

It's not quite accurate to say that Daisy seduced me that night; what happened in her bedroom was closer to consumption. I remember a robust gibbous moon cutting through blinds, the mirror atop her bureau alive with it, illuminating the underthings, the T-shirts, shorts, and socks that had been tossed hastily onto her carpet, her bookshelf boasting two feet of Fitzgerald. And I remember the scent too, always the perfumed, lotioned, laundered scent of a woman's sheets.

Her grip on my deltoids and biceps wasn't merely bracing as she ground into me, nor was it merely a caress. Rather, it was part massage, part claw, talons attached to my arms as if she could keep them. She said my name and I did what you do: I said hers back. And that's when she demanded, 'Call me Daisy.' And I called her that until the moon showed me her bun of lemon hair shaking free and she began to tremble toward release. Soon she'd switch jobs, switch gyms, and I wouldn't see her again, although I'd remain intensely grateful for that single night she gave me, and for her leading me deeper into Fitzgerald than I might have otherwise gone.

Parma had convinced my father that he needed what's routinely called personal time, that his life couldn't be a conveyor belt of kids, work, chores. I can hear her say it still: 'How's he ever gonna *meet* someone if he never goes out?' I was ten years old when she bought him a membership at a Jack LaLanne gym two towns away. For roughly four decades, from the early 1950s to the late 1980s, LaLanne was the preferred fitness czar for everyday Americans; his television program, *The Jack LaLanne Show*, which ran from 1953 to 1985, had a lot to do with that. But his gyms were of the sort that I and my set would, eight years later, regularly tease for their unembarrassed lack of masculine asperity and grit, their neutering sounds of Duran Duran and Phil Collins.

But a lack of asperity and grit was exactly what my father needed then. He was only in his early thirties, although, said Parma, 'he looks forty,' and so she paid for his gym membership with a mother's gung-ho hope that it would both dilute his unhappiness and introduce him to a female. 'He needs a *woman* in that house. It's not *natural* for a man to cook and clean, and I can't help forever.' My family was big on declarations about what was and was not natural.

I'd recently overheard Parma and my father talking – adults often have an ignoramus's inability to detect the antennae of children, when and how often those children can hear them, and how incredibly much those children care to comprehend – and my father said he was worried about bringing a woman into our house, worried about destabilizing us kids (my sister was eight, my brother six), worried about how threatened a new female might make us. If I felt guilty about this, I cannot now recall. It seems as if I should have felt at least a little guilty about the lonesome bachelorhood my psycho-emotional needs had helped to force upon our father.

Parma was capable of periodic gestures of hope, I know, but overall her disposition was unsinkably grim. That mood of hers, her dire sense of drama, set the tone in our family, and so there was habitual talk of how bad we three kids had it: 'Those poor kids, without a mother, it's so hard.' That's the reason my father hadn't brought a woman home; he believed, with Parma, that we kids were contents under pressure, canisters of ineffable internal suffering.

My father worked out at Jack LaLanne on weeknights while my siblings and I were at my grandparents' eating supper and scratching through homework. Not long after his gym life began, there was indeed a swelling of chatter about a woman. This appeared supernatural, if for no other reason than Parma, consistently wrong about human living, was right about Jack LaLanne.

Whatever reservations my father had about bringing a woman into our house had been dashed, because this woman, Kim, was about to spend the night – on the sofa, but still, she was spending the night, because she lived an hour away. Our father and Kim had a date, my siblings and I had a babysitter, and because our father was sawing lumber until noon the following day, we were given warning and we were given injunction: 'When you wake up, Kim will be here' and 'Please, for the love of God, do not terrorize Kim.' Somehow the earnestness and gravity of that injunction did not reach me.

I went to sleep that night positively giddy with the prospect of a woman being in the house upon my waking. My father was gone by six, I rose at eight, ahead of my siblings, and the first thing I did, before I even shook myself fully awake, was dress in my ninja regalia, mask and all – this was the apex of my Sho Kosugi period – including tabi boots and a utility belt into which I tucked my weapons, the nunchucks and shurikens I was too young and knuckleheaded to have, and yet I had them. I also owned a black grappling hook with a knotted rope I'd ordered from a catalog, and this was good news, because we had an open upstairs hallway, loftlike beneath a cathedral ceiling, a balcony that overlooked our living room. Lately I'd been practicing my crafty descent from the balcony onto the cushioned armchair below.

I'd later be told that what I did next was unequivocally wacky behavior, even for a ten-year-old – 'borderline mental illness,' my father said. But here it is: in my ninja suit I crept across the carpet to the spindles of the balcony, and I saw, down there asnooze on our sofa, the woman called Kim. Her hair – what was that color called? sangria? currant? – was cropped close, spiky like a man's, and this sent tides of delight through me because all night I'd been expecting a commonplace do, a number or mousy mane, permed just past her shoulders.

I secured the grappling hook's talon to the banister and rappelled, knot by knot, to the armchair, then ducked behind one of the two sofas, on my knees at the corner of it, spying on her erotic snores. Then, step by glacial, silent step, I approached those snores, my own breath clinched. I was close enough to smell her now, a fruity odor, part shampoo, part disinfectant. I'd punched nose-holes in my mask for ventilation, un-ninja of me, I know, but I couldn't breathe in the thing otherwise.

Her face was warmed by skylights: a creamy complexion, the dimmed galaxy of freckles across pronounced cheekbones, lips like azaleas. I was standing over her, bent at the waist, only two feet between us, my heart bobbing in my breast. And when her eyes flashed open – the sleeping mind sometimes knows when a delinquent is watching it – the sound she made was not so much a scream from the mouth as a moan from the throat, a clipped moan stuck somewhere between surprise and injury. Of course I rushed away, retreated back up to my bedroom, bolted the door, left Kim there on the sofa wondering if she'd been poked or probed. Even a visual trespass can feel filthy. I have no memory now of what followed, of what we five did that day after my father returned from work, but I know that evening she left and never came back.

My decade-old self, the child as traitor: the unconscious saboteur of my father's romantic hopes. Such maliciousness, such bristling, can hide in the heart of a child. He gets even for perceived wrongs, for whatever marring he feels has been unjustly done to him, and he gets even against those who deserve it least. Of what was my father guilty? Of driving away my mother? What hazard did Kim present to me? The splitting of my father's affections? Of course my creepy ninja act was not to blame for her going away and never coming back, but neither was it darling boyishness: a ten-year-old is not a five-year-old. The latter can get away with all orders of mischief; the former is just two years shy of pubic hair.

During those childhood years, there would be only one more appearance by a woman in our house, a fellow divorcee with two children of her own, a Manville girl, someone who'd known my mother before she'd disappeared, someone who could have been Carly Simon's stunt double. Her relationship with my father, if you could call it that, was ill-fated from the word go. It couldn't have lasted a month. He kept up his membership at the Jack LaLanne gym for a while longer, but he never met another woman there. He'd be single for seven more years, his only female love from the woman who bore him.

VII

Victor and I, along with some other pals from the Edge, had been traipsing around central Jersey some Saturdays to attend different amateur bodybuilding competitions. And at one of these shows, as we watched the teenage division, my pals became convinced that I could beat every guy up there, that I had the desirable aesthetics to excel on stage: 'You could take those dudes, bro,' and 'Dudes all got toothpick arms, bro,' and 'Those dudes ain't stacked like you, bro' (most of our sentences contained a *dude* and a *bro*). And it was true, mostly; one kid carried about as much muscle as a high-school swimmer.

That Saturday morning, reclined in an auditorium somewhere in the intestines of our state, after what was really the most piddling instigation of friends, we decided: in two months, I'd represent the Edge in the teenage division at the Muscle Beach bodybuilding competition in Point Pleasant, New Jersey. This decision, it seems to me now, should have been paired with a feeling of momentousness. I'd never before done anything like it, was not a performer, naked or otherwise, at ease on stages. But I remember no momentousness. What I remember is the sense of inevitability, and a desperation not to disappoint the guys at the Edge who wanted me to do this.

At only 175 pounds, I was in no way large, nothing close to what you see in magazines. If you put normal clothes on me I looked like any athletic kid, a lacrosse or football player perhaps. But my arms and shoulders were well built and round; those were always my kindest body parts. Unlike my lagging chest and calves that always needed extra doses of loving anguish, my arms and shoulders grew without too much coercion from me. And my waist was only twenty-eight inches, which allowed me that coveted V-shape. Bodybuilders can't be fireplugs.

Also, because I was naturally light and lean, with an over-rapid metabolism that made it an Augean effort for me to gain weight, I had the body-fat percentage of an Olympic runner, five to six per cent, and for the bodybuilding stage, that's a blessing you cannot inject. What's more, in addition to having full muscle bellies, I had narrow joints, the joints of a fifth-grader. All of which meant that I appeared much more rotundly muscular, much more the bodybuilder, than I actually was. That appearance, or call it an illusion, is indispensable for the competitive bodybuilder. When he's onstage, nobody cares about how much he can bench press. It's not a strength contest; it's an art contest.

A weightlifter wants mass; a bodybuilder wants that too, but at a certain point, in preparation for a competition, he's focused on conditioning, on diaphanous skin and vascularity, a symphony of form, the symmetry of his physique, how it all gels and melds: trapeziuses curving into deltoids curving into pectorals, biceps flowing into forearms, hamstrings into calves, quadriceps into kneecaps, lats into a tiny waist. And so the bodybuilder is a renegade aesthete, an underground artist whose medium is muscle tissue, whose implements of creation are food and iron.

That stereotype with which bodybuilders are saddled – self-aggrandizers and simps, inauthentic athletes, all show and no go – has always been an injustice put forth by those with no eye for harmony on the human body, or those too fearful to admit the animality in man, too fearful to catch our own reflection in fellow hominoids, in the mighty chimp from whom we've sprung. Tell some people they're a primate and watch their faces become uncomprehending.

Balance and proportion, rhythm and harmony: these are the terms of representational art. Indeed, bodybuilding can be viewed as a continuation of both the heroic and aesthetic traditions in Western art. If you believe that this heightened focus on the body is vain or narcissistic – Ovid: *It is myself I love, myself I see; / The gay delusion is a part of me* – ask yourself this: how different is it from a writer's world-be-damned focus on his book, a painter's on her canvas, or an actor's obesity or emaciation for a role? Is bodybuilding really more egoistic than a ballet dancer's brutal pursuit of perfection?

Its proportions, mastery, vitalities, its self-containment and control, its suggestions of the ideal, reaching after Platonic form – don't be so eager to dismiss the developed body as art. The person is not an object, I understand, but whether you like it or not, the body *is* an object, albeit one in a constant reciprocal waltz with the self. That doesn't make bodybuilders self-demeaning objectifiers; it makes them sublime celebrants, Whitmanian crooners, singing the body electric.

Much needed to happen in only two months. I had to make the technical transitions from weightlifter to bodybuilder, which began with weaning myself from the drug I was injecting each week, a miracle called Sustanon 250, a blend of four different synthetic testosterones (we called it 'Suzie'). A mass-building, oil-based anabolic steroid, Suzie causes water retention, which blurs vascularity and muscle striation. She makes you strong as hell, yes, but also puffy, and puffy is not the aesthetic you're after onstage. Puffy will be japed straight out of the auditorium. So no more Suzie for me.

Instead, my set at the Edge scored me a steroid called Winstrol-V (drug name: stanozolol) from a crooked veterinarian who was also a weightlifter. We lovingly named it 'Winny,' our true-blue mistress, a water-based injectable used during dieting because it helps promote the hard, dry aesthetic you want onstage, while letting you keep a bulbous muscle density, since dieting can flatten you right out. Whatever you do, don't flatten out. You'll find this drug not only in every hardcore gym across the land, but also at any given horse race. Winny makes the horses whinny. It also burned when I injected it. An oil-based steroid such as Sustanon felt not bad as it went in; a water-based one such as Winstrol felt like a lit match inside the muscle.

I looked forward to the injected singeing caused by Winstrol, as if that burn was a signal, a promise, of its efficacy. If you pressed the plunger slowly you could mitigate the burn, but punch it down quickly with your thumb and the burn was twice as hot as it needed to be. I always punched it down hard, then sat to imagine it dispersing through my blood, bolstering amino acids, bonding cell to cell.

What I'm speaking of here goes beyond the NO PAIN NO GAIN bumper stickers you would have seen on trucks and Jeeps in the parking lot of the Edge. I mean to suggest something about in-the-world asceticism – from the Greek *askēsis,* which rather fittingly means 'exercise' – about the degree to which this pursuit provided a brace for the soul, how the workouts and lifestyle were a quasi-spiritual undertaking, whether we realized it or not. What else did we have to believe in with equal intensity, what else worthy of our worship?

It's true that we didn't subscribe to any ilk of mystical babble, and it's true that I've always found emotional pain an unenlightening waste – Nabokov: 'Human despair seldom leads to great truths' – but the bodily pain we fashioned for ourselves at the Edge was something else altogether: the exalting in, the election of, this particular anguish. We were contented self-crucifiers. You'd want to say that we ignored all delight for this anguish if it weren't true that the delight *was* the anguish. It's what Sadeans have been trying to show us all along, those sexual deviants and their assorted utensils of orgasmic torture.

What I did not look forward to, not ever, was the contest diet. The nutritional demands are the most unforgiving element of this life. Only half of a bodybuilder's physique is forged in the gym; the other half is forged in the kitchen. For the previous two and a half years I'd been eating cleanly: not a Big Mac, not a french fry or cupcake. But with those scant exceptions, I ate what I wanted because I had such a difficult time gaining mass, a metabolism in a hurry: lean burgers and occasional pizza, all-beef hot dogs and Parma's ambrosial meatloaf, hummocks of pasta and mashed potatoes (no butter), sandwiches of all sorts, buckets of fruits and nuts, even the occasional Snickers, plus the vanilla MET-Rx protein shakes we blended with orange juice (they tasted like creamsicles).

That diet, however, won't mold a body into contest shape. The aim is to fine-tune the body, to get it sensitive to every gram of carbohydrate and protein, expectant of a uniform meal every two and a half hours – imagine that: eating a full meal every two and a half hours for eight weeks – so that it knows precisely when you switch from, say, chicken to steak, from red potato to white potato to sweet potato, from brown rice to white rice. When you're already lean, already on the way to contest shape, carbs can actually alter your aesthetics. Muscles remain fuller, rounder on potatoes and pasta, leaner and less round on rice. Carbs are like coal into a steam engine: when they hit the system, they stir the metabolic rate, and you want to keep the metabolic rate high so your body doesn't hold on to anything it doesn't need. That's exactly how we get to be jolly fatsoes, when our metabolism isn't trained to burn what our bodies consume but instead holds onto it for future use. But since we're jolly fatsoes, that future use never comes.

The guys from the gym – Rude, Sid, Victor – sat me down at a large desk in an unused office at the Edge and debated the best possible diet for me, Victor scratching it all down on a pad as I stayed silent, scratching down my own notes. If someone unchurched in our ways had been among us that evening, here's the onrush of obsessiveness and mystery he would have heard:

'At his body weight, he needs forty grams of chicken protein per meal, and then I'd switch to turkey protein about four weeks out. He's lean enough now for chicken.'

'He's too lean, and we need to keep the mass he's got. I'd give him fifty, sixty grams of beef protein for at least three of his seven meals, maybe even four or five. Screw that turkey shit.'

'He'll put on too much fat with steak, dude, even a lean cut. I'd stick to chicken. And depending on how lean he gets close to contest time, we might have to switch him to fish, I'd say tilapia or halibut, seventy grams a piece, no more than eighty. We won't know that till four, five weeks out.'

'He ain't gonna put on any fat, dude, look at him. He's got veins everywhere and he ain't even dieting yet. Diet him down too much and he's gonna flatten the fuck out. He's 175 now and he needs to be at least 165 onstage. So we're talking ten pounds here.'

'He ain't got ten pounds of fat on him. Maybe five, you ask me. The rest is water. I'm recommending at least a gallon of water a day to flush the water he's holding.'

'A gallon? Try two gallons.'

'He'll be pissing every ten minutes, dude.'

'That's the point, dude. He'll piss out whatever water he's holding. Most guys lose a show, it's because they're holding water, not fat.'

'That water will vanish a week after he stops the shit he's on now, the Suzie, and starts up with the Winny. He'll peel pretty easily on the Winny.'

'What Winny we'd get him? Oral or injectable?'

'Injectable.'

'Winny ain't no guarantee of losing water. I'm saying if he wants to get peeled, he drinks two gallons a day, end of discussion.'

'What about his carbs? I'm thinking six-ounce baked potatoes all the way through. Why even screw around with rice, right?'

'Depends on how full he stays. If he's full enough come contest time, we can switch to brown rice, sure. Or else drop the six-ounce potato to five, maybe five and a half. No less than five.'

'That's fine if he's sick of potatoes, sure. If he's sick of white potato, let him switch to red potato or sweet potato. I don't like messin' around with rice, white or brown. He can lose his roundness. It's either pasta or potato, in my book. He's lean enough.'

'As long as he stays in the per-meal, fifty-to-seventy-gram range with the complex carbs, he'll be fine whatever carb he wants. Let him switch between potatoes, sure, though sixty grams of pasta is good in the evenings to hold him through till morning. He'll need that.'

'He can't be on rice for those last two or three meals or else he'll wake up starving at 2 a.m. Let him have sixty grams of pasta and seventy grams of sirloin for those last two meals, and the rest of the day he can stick to forty-gram chicken breast and five-ounce potato.'

'What's he putting on the pasta for flavor, anything? Shot of hot sauce or something?'

'No, nothing, nada, zilch. Plain pasta.'

'What vegetable are we talking here?'

'String beans will work. Never cauliflower, though. Let's keep it green, whatever it is.'

'If he's feeling hungry at all, not full enough, he can switch to Brussels sprouts too. Those'll keep him feeling fuller.'

'That slimy shit at the bottom of the poultry package? Those are his nutrients right there. He's gotta drink that shit if he wants nutrients.'

'Any fruit at all? He can get away with an apple or orange if he wants the taste.'

'No goddamn fruit at all. No *sugars* at all. Those simple carbs are too quick. Show me any dude who's ever built or maintained muscle with fruit.'

'I'm just saying, he can afford an apple for the taste. I'm talking one a day, if he needs it.'

'Fine, if he's desperate, but it's gotta be in the morning when his metabolic rate is highest, but otherwise, screw the fruit. Complex carbs will stay steady for him. The sugar is in and out. It's a waste.'

'It ain't a waste on the tongue, that's for damn sure. After seven meals of boiled potatoes, grilled chicken breast, and steamed broccoli, the dude's gonna be hurting for a taste of sugar.'

'Let him drink a Diet Coke then. He should be drinking six of those things a day anyway. Caffeine's a diuretic.'

'He can nuke the potatoes, easy enough, but the chicken and broccoli should both be lightly steamed. Heat's too high on a grill, you can burn the protein right out of the chicken if you're not careful.'

'Don't boil the shit, whatever you do. I see dudes boiling their chicken. Turns it to rubber.'

'Make sure there's no salt, not even a pinch, on the veggies and chicken. Maybe a dash of paprika, a dash of pepper. Throw the salt into the garbage when you get home.'

'My advice: throw out *everything* in your kitchen you can't eat. Just get a big-ass trash bag and load it right up.'

'Empty your fridge when you get home, Billy Boy.'

'Empty that thing right out, dude. Keep the chicken and beef and veggies, but ditch everything else.'

The dialogue went on like that for another maddening half hour until everybody was in some form of agreement about what I was going to eat and when I was going to eat it. I'd have to drop eighty bucks for Tupperware and prepare each day's seven meals the night before.

Then it was time for them to inspect my physique, to scrutinize my body's lingua franca, to assess which annotations awaited it. Victor twisted shut the blinds and I stripped down to my briefs and stood at the far wall, rotating when they told me to, while they leaned back in office chairs, their sneakers propped up on a vacant desk fit for an imaginary CEO.

'His abs need work. His midsection is flat enough, but those abs need to pop more.'

'The diet will make them pop.'

'His calves need help.'

'He's gotta go easy on his delts and bis, they're already jacked, and if he gets them even more jacked, he'll be all out of proportion.'

'Damn, his chest is weak.'

'He's got that little-ass waist, though. The round shoulders and little waist give him that sweet *V*. Plus his quads got a pretty nice sweep to them. It's a good overall shape.'

'Width-wise, he's weak in the back, but he's thick enough through the middle and lower back, I'd say. And what he lacks in back width he makes up for with those delts.'

'All that crazy-ass deadlifting and bent-over rows, he better be.'

'I'll tell you what: deadlifting is done for him. No deads going into a contest unless you're begging for an injury.'

'Yeah, Victor, make sure. Stick to one-arm dumbbell rows, low pulley rows, maybe some dumbbell rows on the incline bench.'

'T-bar rows are okay, I'd say. Pull-downs are okay too, wide and narrow both. I'd rotate wide and narrow.'

'What about squats? He nixing squats?'

'Depends. Light squats are okay, I think, nothing too crazy. Ten to twelve reps, three good sets.'

'His weight can't go too light or else he'll lose mass.'

'He'll be fine with leg presses. He can go heavy with them and not get hurt. Squats are a goddamn gamble pre-contest, unless you're doing 'em on the Smith machine.'

'Stick to the Smith for squats, yeah, and stick to leg extensions and ham curls. Don't screw around with too many barbells now or else you're asking for injury.'

'We can barbell curl, though.'

'I ain't talking about bis. His bis are golden.'

'I'd say stick to as many machines as possible. Not now, but at about four weeks out, stick to machines. You'll be depleted as hell four weeks out, and about eight pounds lighter, I'd guess, so you won't wanna mess around with barbells then anyway.'

'And remember, he's getting *smaller,* not bigger, as he goes into the contest. That ain't good news for his chest, I'll tell you that.'

'But those delts and arms and quads – he'll be golden. He's golden from the front.'

'Not so much from the back, though.'

'It's the *teenage* division, for fuck's sake. He ain't going against Lee Haney. It's his first show.'

'These next eight weeks, all his focus needs to be on chest and legs and back or else we can forget about any symmetry.'

'Yeah, Victor, you dudes really gotta go light on his arms and delts, dude. Forget about those behind-the-neck presses you like.'

'I'm saying he can forget about barbells *entirely.* Anyone listening to me here?'

'What about cardio? What are we recommending?'

'Bike. Keep him on the bike.'

'You feel like a gerbil on a stationary bike. Let him do the StairMaster.'

'So he can feel like a mountaineer? Screw that. Stick to the bike. He'll be too beat for the StairMaster. Plus he can read those weirdo books of his on the bike, those little poems or whatever the hell they are.'

'Nothing wrong with the treadmill, either. He should switch between the bike and treadmill. See how he feels. He can read his little poems on the treadmill too.'

'Forty minutes for him? Fifty? Seven times a week? Less? More? What?'

'Forty at least, maybe a full hour. Seven days for sure. Depends how much water he's holding. Depends on if those abs are popping or not, what his striations look like. Let's see what his fat percentage is about two weeks from now.'

'Yeah, give the diet two weeks. He won't need more than two weeks to see results. He's lean already. He's always lean.'

'Shit, I was too at eighteen.'

'Good to be eighteen.'

'Fuckin' *great* to be eighteen.'

VIII

There's a fetishizing pleasure involved in the accumulation of steroids: the smooth, tiny ampules, no taller than a pinky, both clear and brownishly opaque; the white pill bottles, both square and cylindrical; the syringes of various gauges, packaged like toothbrushes; the bottles of injectable B12 for enhanced appetite, a scarlet liquid that caused a five-minute high, a giggling full-body warmth, as if a tonic lava loose in the blood. I lined them all up, tucked them into a velvet-padded, polished oak box with a flip top. I'd open the box, behold and hold them, scan the alien-lingo medical scripts printed on their labels, shake the vials, watch the oil or water breathe minor bubbles. Pot smokers, coke snorters, junk shooters share a similar hobbyist's delight in ritualized minutiae: rolling the joints, cutting the lines, heating the spoons.

I began accumulating caches of steroids, whatever I could buy, whenever a new shipment arrived. Better to have them and not need them than need them and not have them. Our connections weren't the most dedicated lifters; you got the feeling they enjoyed the drug dealing better than the bodybuilding. Some of the drugs came from Mexico, where they are easily had without a prescription, and others came from hardcore gyms in New York State. I bought not only the drugs I'd already taken – the Drol and the Winny and the Suzie – but the drugs I wanted to take in the future: the Deca (Deca Durabolin), the D-bol (Dianabol), the Test (Testosterone Suspension). We uttered their sobriquets much the way I imagined top brass uttered launch codes for ballistic weaponry: with a sinister affection.

Several boyhood pals from Manville were cycling with Suzie but were too skittish to inject themselves, so I'd do it for them in the locker room at the Edge, or else at my house at night after my father was asleep. They'd often have to pace themselves into courage, wiping wet hands on the legs of sweatpants, gassy with nervousness, until finally they'd say, 'Okay, hit me,' and I'd say, 'Okay, on three,' but I always plunged on two, plunged into the upper-outer quadrant of the buttocks. Unless the needle was blunted from repeated use, it was never as painful as they'd been planning for.

Word of one's drug stash passed like bacillus through the raw oxygen of the Edge, as it does through any incestuous gym. I often had the best drugs because, between working and working out, I was at the Edge eight hours a day during the week, four hours a day on weekends. I knew who had what to sell and when. Pals began approaching me with 'Billy Boy…' If they began that way, with the 'Boy' and the ellipses towing the 'Billy,' I knew what they needed, and I happily sold it to them for the same price I paid. Injecting drugs was okay; making money off your friends was not.

Bob the Cop was a compatriot in the drugs-and-muscle milieu we'd built at the Edge, but he was understandably queasy about being perceived as such. One night in the locker room, he said, 'Billy Boy…' and put a mammoth arm around me – I was eye-level with his jugular notch – and I said, 'Sure, Bob, no sweat.' But he didn't want the exchange to happen at the Edge, so he offered to come by my house, and this he did on a Saturday morning, in his uniform and police cruiser – he was on duty. He bought five hundred bucks' worth of Dianabol and needles in my kitchen, and I was rendered giggly by the combination of his size, his officer's uniform, and the discrepancy of what we were doing, a cop car humming out in the driveway.

I blended us both MET-Rx shakes then – Crystal Light for me, orange juice for him – and at the kitchen counter we discussed the D-bol, how many milligrams he should inject and how often, what results he should expect and how soon. We discussed the Edge too, the training habits and dietary demands of our set. My father, I thought, was not due home until noon or later, but when we heard the front door creak open, I knew it was him. And before he turned the corner into the kitchen, as his bootsteps were coming our way, I knew what his face would say after seeing a cop car in our driveway: *Oh my aching back.*

Bob the Cop usually had the immovable massiveness of a blond Kilimanjaro – he would not startle, would not stun – but as my father's bootsteps came nearer, he got a slight squeak in his voice as he tried to appear normal, to continue talking about training and diet. (I'd wrapped his ampules and needles in paper towels and tinfoil so that the

119

package resembled any workingman's hoagie.) And then my father was there in a patch of sun, tanned gingerbread from summer middays, caulk in his wrist hair, mouth slightly ajar, eyebrows forcing his forehead up into a paragraph of wrinkles.

After those initial seconds, after Bob the Cop introduced himself – 'Mr. Giraldi, a pleasure to meet you, your Billy's a good boy, just stopping by to talk bodybuilding, he knows his stuff' – and my father understood that this cop in our kitchen was not there to incarcerate me, it was difficult to decipher what he was most taken by: the police uniform or the mountain inside it. But he got that look I sometimes saw on him when in the presence of such masculine superiority, such sheer physical excellence: a look two parts awe, two parts longing, one part love – a look that said, *Let's be friends.*

Whatever exchange we had after Bob the Cop drove away has been lost to the many deletions of decades, to time's bizarrely indiscriminate backspacing. What I do know is this: my father continued not to show excessive interest in, never mind enthusiasm for, my bodybuilding, and he didn't even pretend to care about my obvious steroid use. And yet – how can I explain this? – I felt *loved* all the same.

I understand if this will sound like rationalization to you, like a son's bodyguarding of his hero-father's memory, but here's my step into hypothesis: he was allotting me the father-free territory in which I could measure the depths and angles of my selfhood. Perhaps he recalled his own emotions, his own coordinates of mind, at eighteen, his need to be liberated from Pop's influence, interests, endorsement.

I mean to suggest that my father left my bodybuilding alone not because he was resentful that I'd been shepherded into this portion of my life by his own younger brother – because he was hurt that he'd played no direct role in my most masculine endeavor – but because he somehow feared that his meddling, his overexpressed approval, would sully what I'd cultivated independent of him. Some teenagers will abandon a quest the second they suspect their parent shares it or appreciates it. Remember how dispirited you felt, how quickly you bailed, when the obscure band you worshipped was suddenly popular with the rabble.

I can't say now for certain if my father would have been right about that – I doubt it – but what matters is that he must have apprehended me as the seditious son who didn't want his father's interference, who somehow needed to evolve in its absence, and he'd have been right about *that*. Consciously, at least, I never pawed after my father's attention during my bodybuilding years, and the pursuit was all the more crucial to me when I sensed that he really didn't get it. When I knew that the pursuit was mine alone. At home at day's end, we four in our house, I was content to be asked no questions, to offer no explanations, to prepare my meals and mix my shakes without being interviewed, without needing back pats and pep talks.

Still – there's no getting around this – my strength-and-size obsession makes emotional sense only when seen as an attempt to impress my father, to conform to the manful standards he'd inherited from Pop. That's the thing about the developed body, and how it differs from the developed mind, from the life of ideas: there's no explication necessary. Through its acquired aesthetics, the body is its own advertisement. What it means is how it looks. In that way, it also has its own semantics: the body as sentence, its demonstrable syntax and vocabulary, muscle as diction, the punctuation marks between muscles, the commas and semicolons of tendons, the style of striation. It is both the symbol of the things it communicates – grace, power, beauty, vitality – and the things themselves. In the classical conception of Western art, form soared over content, but for the bodybuilder, as for literature, form is wed to content. The style *is* the substance.

Writing about Muhammad Ali, Norman Mailer offered this: 'There are languages of the body.' I didn't need to speak with my father about bodybuilding because my body spoke for itself. All I needed was to *show* him, and he knew. He didn't have to respond, only look. The look *was* the response. This is the route many men take to express and assert themselves to one another. Deeds, not words. Recourse, not discourse. The physical over the emotional, or the emotional embodied in the physical – embodied in the body. Reticent in tongue, we men are garrulous in act.

And he knew. Knew what, though? That I was at long last manful, worthy of our name? Or was my father not beguiled by my muscle-making because he suspected, as so many suspect, that the enterprise is femmy, faggy? Our shaved smoothness, nude brotherhood, walking erections, the spandex and banana sacks, the tanning booths and food fixation. At the gym, the spotter spooned in behind the lifter, his quads to the man's hamstrings, pelvis to rear, his arms hooked under the lifter's armpits, cupping the chest in an effort to keep the man squatting, keep him from yawing forward with such weight: an outsider looks at that and is perhaps helpless not to think of buggery. Of course he'd be committing a category error, a debauching of context; such a workout is actually the neutralizing of sexuality, just as one soldier carrying another across a minefield has no conceivable eroticism. No different from a brother's embrace of brother, or when that cone-breasted great aunt excitedly stabs you in welcome. The erotic resides always in the crotch of the beholder.

Be certain to experience the gamut of emotions when you're young, said Gogol, because when you're older, that gamut will not avail itself to you. Once you emerge from the trenches of adolescence, the one emotion you can frequently rely on will be regret. I can only grasp now in the dark for what my father really thought about my bodybuilding, and regret that I never asked him, that I was too cocksure to care. By the time these questions became important to me, he was already gone.

I must have been in the first or second grade, perspiring out in a baseball field at the edge of town, close enough to the river to smell its muddy wend, the summer now enormously ablaze, the sun all places, all at once. This was Little League practice, the coach the father of two boys who lived on our block. One son was the pitcher, a year older than me; the other son was my classmate, the star hitter.

We didn't have a baseball household, not even close. Baseball isn't a motor or muscle sport, and so it wasn't considered masculine enough. We didn't give a damn about the Yankees, the team everybody else in Manville rooted for. And yet somehow there I was, squinting in that unbelievable barrage of sun, a shortstop in a white-and-marigold Manville Pizza uniform. Local businesses sponsored this Little League, provided the outfits, and the teams were called by their names: the pub or the pharmacy, the insurance company or the confectioner.

On this day, my father came to practice to participate, humored by the coach, who knew he had no baseballing ability. He came directly from a sun-charred day of roofing or framing. The coach, in contrast, was a foreman of some kind; he wandered around a plant with a clipboard and hardhat, made leisurely phone calls in a swivel chair, ate elongated lunches in an air-conditioned office. There they were, two snapshots of fatherhood, side by side at home plate: the rested and the ragged, one broad and tall with a greedy erectness, one much shorter, stouter, as if in perpetual duck of a right hand. One in pressed khakis, a laundered shirt, and smudgeless sneakers, ashen from the indoors, and the other in clothes that looked meatground, boots that were battle-worn and too heavy to walk in, his hands and limbs a pastiche of blood-sketched nicks and scratches.

My father's task was to stand at home plate, next to a basket of baseballs, and hit flies and grounders to us so that we might scamper after them. You know the trick: you've got to lob the ball in front of yourself with your left hand, then quickly regain your bothhanded grip on the bat, then swing to send the ball soaring out among the waiting ones. Except my father couldn't do this; he just couldn't regain his grip on the bat quickly enough, and so the ball belly-flopped in the packed sand at his feet, or else he missed when he swung and so the ball again belly-flopped in the sand.

This happened for an excruciating three or four minutes, his sunburn dialed up a notch by embarrassment. With my mitt at my forehead to block the mugging rays, I said aloud, but not loudly, 'Come *on*, Dad,' and I said it again, wriggling, each time he missed, each time I heard the sandy belly flop of the ball. When finally he made the bat connect, it connected with insufficient slap and the ball barely made the pitcher's mound. The pitcher, the coach's son, was glancing about and rolling his eyes – he made damn sure I saw him rolling his eyes – but if the other kids were impatient and disappointed too, they didn't readily show it. The truth is, I was trying not to look. I was trying to keep my focus on the bat in my father's hands, as if telepathy could send it the will it needed to succeed.

He began hitting them after that, although not every one. I think he tried to send a ball my way, between second and third bases, but his aim was off. The ball would not obey the bat's commands, whatever orders my father attempted to transmit from his body to the birch, and I didn't have the chance to scoop a grounder, never mind snag a fly. The coach, clearly piqued by this – or was he secretly pleased by the physical failure of another man? – ended my father's participation. And for the rest of the practice he stood exiled behind the fence, his fingers gripping the chain-link with the mild hope of a prisoner, too proud to go home though he looked hacked-at with fatigue.

I've no other memory of that Little League season: not a practice, not a game, not a pizza party afterward. Nor, I am certain, did I ever join Little League again. Here's the memory I do have: not long after this mortifying afternoon, we neighborhood kids were typhooning through someone's front yard, a melee that was half football game, half wrestling match. At one point I saw the coach's son – the brash pitcher, a soda can taller than me – kneeling there on the grass, smiling to the left of our pile. And here's what I did: I rushed at him, and with the full momentum of my body weight, I thrust a knee into his ribcage. What came from him had no sound, a fish-mouthed fight for air, and he toppled to his side, his neck and face a palette of indigos. He couldn't speak or breathe, but I knew he could hear, and so I stood above him as he struggled.

'Let me see you roll your eyes now,' I said.

He hobbled home then. Some parent from an adjacent home instructed me to go apologize. I had to cut through yards to get to the coach's house, and when I arrived, the coach and his wife were with their two sons on their front porch, their brash pitcher no longer so brash, sobbing there in his mother's lap.

'Sorry,' I said, but I could feel myself smiling as I said it.

'You get *the hell* outta here,' said the coach.

So I did. I walked back home, down their driveway and through their yard. The pot of ferns they had sunning there on the bottom step of their rear porch? I kicked it over.

IX

Excommunicate all the sugar from your diet and watch your dreams go syrupy with visions of Willy Wonka, sticky collages of chocolate pudding and candy bars. Each week – each *hour*, it often seemed – I got leaner, harder, more striated, more vascular, skin more diaphanous. And weaker with weights, looser in clothes, a sucked-in face, more ravenous for cake. As my family scarfed down raviolis and stuffed shells, Parma's buttered bread and lasagne, I sat secluded in the hallway with my Tupperware containers, trying to swallow a chicken breast drier than cardboard.

It was a desolating assault on my psyche to be getting smaller and weaker when the sole mission of my training for the last two and a half years had been to get larger and stronger. Several times I attempted to tell Rude and Sid that I was not cut out for this, not muscular enough to perform onstage, that losing strength and size was my misery, but I could never get to the end of a sentence without hearing one of their stomping rejoinders: 'Go change your tampon' or 'Untwist your panties.' So you see what I was up against.

Each evening after our workout, Victor and I pedaled nowhere on the exercise bikes for fifty minutes. He was doing cardio with me in a gesture of fellowship. I tried not to let anyone notice that I was holding Goethe's novel of passion and self-destruction, *The Sorrows of Young Werther*: one self-involved romantic reading about another (although Auden saw Werther as an 'egoist,' and perhaps that tag, too, applied to me, to all bodybuilders). Published in 1774, *Young Werther* sent a blast of suicides across Deutschland, and in its youthful assertions of self-consumptive doom, it helped define the European Romantic movement. Every dreamy stripling in the eighteenth century craved the book – 'They should be ashamed of themselves, all these sober people!' – and there I was, trying to read it covertly on an exercise bike at the gym. Although, all the oomph slurped out of me by the vampiric demands of the diet, I cared much less about what my brethren thought of the books I read. The abolishing of sugar and fat, the curtailing of carbs: it saps your fighting spirit, demotes you to slow motion. In the tanning bed, I'd often fall asleep within the first minute.

Near the end of the night, the guys opened the aerobics room and we practiced my poses and contest routine beneath a constellation of lights. The image in the glass sometimes startled me. That bronze sculpture had my eyes, though unnaturally lit against darkened skin, distended in a face angling toward the skeletal. There are eight mandatory poses on the bodybuilding stage: Front Lat Spread, Front Double Biceps, Side Chest, Back Lat Spread, Back Double Biceps, Side Triceps, Abdominal and Thigh, and Most Muscular. Each pose is designed to highlight not only the muscle group in its name, but also that muscle group's relation to other muscle groups.

Take the Front Lat Spread: the chief aim is to show the width of the back, the *latissimus dorsi,* by placing both pinched hands on the waist, sucking in to pronounce the thoracic arch, and swinging out the elbows to reveal the breadth of the lats beneath the arms. But the pose also reveals the density of the chest by packing together the pectorals. It reveals, too, the deltoid development, the roundness of the overall shoulders, but specifically the condition of the middle delts.

What's more, you can't forget about your legs just because you're flexing your back. You pose from the floor up, which means that a pose such as the Front Lat Spread begins with the flexing of the calves, then the quads, then the back, shoulders, and chest. That's how you're being scored: on the fluidity of the body as a whole, on how each muscle group merges with its neighbor.

But one doesn't only pose. A bodybuilding contest has two segments: prejudging in the morning – this is when the judges score you – and the night show, the spectacle for the crowd during which a pro athlete will often guest-pose, and during which each competitor performs a choreographed routine to music. We were given a minute and forty seconds to be ballerinos, to present our physiques in time to melody and rhythm and tempo. The bodybuilder competes against other bodies the same way a motorcycle racer competes against other racers, but the competition is also against the self: the rider's against his own body on the bike, the bodybuilder's against his own body on the stage. How fast you can push the bike or body without crashing.

The competitive poses are normally performed with the other guys in your weight class, each man shoulder to shoulder so the judges can compare physiques. This was a problem for me because the teenage division was not divided by weight; rather, it was an open division for anyone nineteen and under, which meant I was going to be competing against guys who were much larger than me. So in order to do well, I needed superior conditioning: harder, leaner, more symmetrical. I had the V-shape, plus the tiny waist and joints that helped with the consummate illusion, but symmetry was going to be an issue because my chest and hamstrings were still delinquent, my calves still minuscule.

An hour of posing, an hour of Sid, Rude, and Victor contorting me into the proper configurations, and then one more hour of practicing my routine to the song I chose – 'Plush' by Stone Temple Pilots, because I thought it had the right drumbeats for posing – were themselves a workout. Those ludicrous two hours would sound something like this:

'Dude, you gotta bring down your left shoulder about two inches during that Side Chest pose. Look in the mirror: it's too high, see? Make it even with your right shoulder.'

'And you're forgetting about your right ham, bro. Smash your legs together so the ham comes out. *Push out* your right ham with your left quad.'

'Don't forget that right calf too. Bend your left leg just a bit.'

'His right bi is killer in that shot, though.'

'And his chest looks not bad there actually.'

'That's about the only place it comes out. And thank God that shot doesn't show abs, because there's no abs to see.'

'Not yet, but they're coming out.'

'Victor, seriously, dude, you guys gotta be killin' abs more.'

'Good quad separation in that Most Muscular pose. That's his best shot, I'd say.'

'The right quad isn't as separated as the left. Dude, make your quads even. Flex them *equally*. Be sure to hit that pose from the floor up, bro. You want to *unfold* the flexing from the floor up, like this, watch me.'

'Don't just focus on the bis and quads in that shot, because the abs are part of it too. Think total body, forget about the name of the pose.'

'In that Abs and Thighs shot you gotta blow it out more, blow it out so the abs pop, and then tilt just an inch to either side, pivot to show the obliques. You *pivot* at the waist.'

'You can't have that straining look on your mug, either. Can't you relax your face more than that? You can't faint onstage, dude.'

'His glutes are gettin' ripped. His Back Double Bi is not bad. See, his glutes are squaring there? That's key to the Back Double Bi.'

'Pull in your trunks, Billy Boy, we can't see all of your glutes. You don't want a goddamn G-string up there, but your glutes are gettin' lined, dude, and the judges need to see that shit.'

'Yeah, you sure as shit ain't gonna win with size, so show what you got to win with.'

'He's gettin' to be nails.'

'His bis got a good peak in that Back Double Bi. I wish his lats were wider in that shot. He's losing thickness in his lower back too.'

'Straighten up in that Back Lat Spread, bro, you're pitched

too far forward. After you expand, come back up from the waist. Don't let off the expanse of the back as you do it. Remember: pivot back up from the waist.'

'The upper back is killer. Sweet tie-ins with the bis and delts and traps. They pop in that shot. The fluidity is there.'

'Hams and calves, dude. Hams and calves, come on. Not just bis. Fuckin' focus here.'

'I'd do the right side for Side Triceps, not the left. Bring the left shoulder down half an inch. Look, see? You want the line from one shoulder to the other to be even. You wanna be level. Think about the *lines* your body is making.'

'You gotta get it into your head that just because this is a Side Triceps pose, you don't forget about the lines your body is making. Your *whole* damn body. So keep your right fist even with your right heel in that shot. Bring in your leg an inch. Think *symmetry*.'

'And the left pec in that shot too, bro. Squeeze the left pec by bringing the left shoulder around just a bit, half an inch.'

Then we'd break, I'd breathe for five minutes, mop my sweat, guzzle from the fountain before Sid or Rude would tell Victor to start the posing song on the boom box.

'Dude, when the song starts, right there at the guitar, you come alive immediately. You see dudes waiting too long to begin after the song starts. Don't do stupid shit like that.'

'Your solo time up there is yours, so let's focus on your arms and delts and quads, I'd say. Your routine, your motion has to favor your strong parts.'

'When the drums hit right here, *boom,* you hit a Front Double Bi, then, watch, you swing out of it right here and into the next drum hit, and then *boom,* right here, hit a Side

Chest. See? Be steady as you do it. Be *fluid*. Not all jerky.'

'Yeah, you want fluidity of motion here. Don't be so damn stiff. Loosen just a bit between poses. Be loose until the drum lets you hit a shot, bro. Follow the drum, not the guitar and not the lyrics.'

'Should he mouth some of the lyrics? I see dudes mouthing lyrics all the time, you know, like they're really into it.'

'That's gay, mouthing lyrics. Plus, listen to this singer: he sounds like a dope addict. You can't even tell what the hell he's saying.'

'Follow the rhythm of the tune here. See, look: when the tempo of the song drops, right here, you drop, like this. Drop to one knee and hit a Double Bi, then *boom,* swing into a Side Triceps, like this.'

'Be sure to use the stage. Play to all sides of the audience. Do a Most Muscular pose to the left when the guitar picks up here – listen, right here – and then move to the right and hit another Most Muscular, *boom,* like that, but always on the drum hit. Don't flex fully into the pose *until the drum hits.*'

'And Billy Boy? No one wants to see a sourpuss up there on stage. Fuckin' smile – it ain't that hard.'

In a corner of the aerobics room rested a five-foot stack of blue floor mats, and on a few of those nights, after two hours of training and two more hours of posing, the gym about to close, I'd climb on top, my duffel bag for a pillow, a towel for a blanket, damp still through my clothes, and fall quickly asleep, somehow partially aware of the gym shutting down around me, lights clicking off, doors locking, leaving me to my womb of exhaustion.

* * *

Mid-August, the contest was just twenty-eight hours away, and I was water-depleted. The goal at this crucial juncture was to keep my body as full and round as possible on the right carbs and protein while drying the remaining fluid from in between my skin and muscle tissue. Carbs require water to be assimilated, and because I wasn't drinking any, that required water was being pulled from beneath my skin, creating the dry, see-through aesthetic needed for the stage. The problem is that dehydration can feel like influenza, your bones somehow boards and jelly both. Also: try getting down your gullet an unseasoned, not-moist chicken breast and baked potato every two hours when your mouth's interior is a caul of Elmer's glue.

The guys at the Edge had instructed me to ban any stress from my week because stress creates a spike in cortisol, a steroidal hormone, and cortisol creates havoc with the body's processing of protein and glucose, which could cause a diminished muscle fullness, or the retention of water, which meant the blurring of muscle separation, a minimizing of the alps and ridges of my physique. The stress they meant was my girlfriend at Rutgers, Val; they sometimes overheard me quarreling with her on the phone at the Edge. Once, Victor caught me wet-eyed and defeated in the locker room, though he pretended not to notice.

But how was that supposed to happen, I wondered, the at-will banning of stress from one's week? What button did I press for that? Did they not understand that the triumph of stress stems from its unwillingness to be banned? I'd seen it with my father in the years after my mother left us. And wasn't being nearly naked on stage in front of thousands of discerning citizens *inherently* stressful? I'd been so zeroed-in on the training, the diet, and the posing that I'd altogether forgotten to consider the coming anxiety: I'd never been on a stage before.

Our set at the Edge rented out half a motel in Point Pleasant – several others were competing in the upper divisions – and the day before the contest we caravanned down in vehicles stocked with coolers of chicken breasts, potatoes, and protein shakes, with duffel bags of bronzer and posing oil, drugs and needles. And if we'd been nabbed and searched by the police? We had Bob the Cop's business card. Everywhere on the boardwalks and beaches of Point Pleasant, on the sidewalks and in parking lots, waddled the women and men who'd arrived to attend and compete in the show: artificial tans, chiseled faces, chromatic muscle clothes, Oakley sunglasses.

In my and Victor's motel room, Rude and Sid ransacked a bed for a sheet, then flattened it on the clay-like carpet near the opened door. I peeled down to skin, cupped a handful in my lap – steroids are said to shrink testicles, but mine stayed stubbornly normal – raised the other arm, and the guys, having donned respirator masks, sprayed on a carob-hued coating, a mandatory glaze to darken my tan by about four shades, otherwise the stage lights would delete me. It fumed of chemical cinnamon, but sweeter, and went on cool. Victor held a clattering box fan to blow the toxicity out into the afternoon. What looked like blunt carob under the motel lamps and the day's remaining light would be a sheath of copper shine on stage. We'd settled on this carob-hued bronzer after Rude and Sid bickered for half an hour among the metropolis of bottles they'd erected on the bureau, each a different shade of brown.

'He needs this coffee-colored one, this one here.'

'Screw that, no way, that's gay. Let's use this mocha one.'

'Dude, that's too *dull*. The lights won't pick up that shit. Let's use this hickory. See, it's got this nice reddish tint.'

'What's he, an Injun? This pecan one looks sweet. This is the one.'

'Pecan is weak, dude. How about this caramel? This caramel will do the trick.'

'We don't need a trick, we need the right color. Let's use this umber. I used this umber once and it was sweet. The lights fuckin' *love* this umber.'

Dehydrated and craving cake, much too twiggy in the mirror, I saw every color as identical. I could not comprehend what they were carrying on about. When they began quibbling over what color trunks I should don, the red or the blue, Victor and I stepped into the bathroom so he could hit me with a needleful of Winny. I normally had no trouble injecting myself, but my grip was slick and shaky now, and since I'd sheared all the cushion from my body – my glutes were square slabs of stone – the needle felt twice as thick going in. That Winstrol burn I'd always savored? Not anymore.

Then we went outside and sat on the curb, dark gray cumulus hinting of thunder. And I remember wondering what time my family was going to show up the following day, my father, Pop, and Tony, if they'd arrive in time, leave Manville early enough to dodge the certain snarl of Jersey shore traffic. A black kid and his father pulled up to an adjacent room in their Oldsmobile – a kid my age, I thought, who was clearly there for the contest. They were dressed as we were dressed, lugging what we had lugged, the coolers and duffel bags. I could see the rounded mass beneath the clothes, the swaying quads in his step, and I said to Victor, 'I hope that dude's not a teenager.'

He hesitated before his reply, waited for the kid and his father to disappear inside their room. 'You could knock him out,' he said. The tender lies we friends tell one another: are they told to preserve the other's delusion, or to preserve our own? I'd never knocked out anybody in my life.

My senior year of high school and English class was under way, a lecture on Vonnegut's *The Sirens of Titan*. Then Alisyn, my sister, two grades behind me, appeared in the rectangular glass of the door, waving me out into the hallway, tears inking trails with her makeup. An ex-friend of mine, a weightlifter jacked on drugs, larger and stronger than me, had just accosted her, perhaps pushed her, threatened her, it wasn't clear – she was sobbing and I couldn't make out her sentences. Whatever had just happened had to do with me, I knew; my friendship with him had recently detonated from rivalry and rancor, a collection of jealousies, envies, perceived betrayals. The pettiness of seventeen-year-old boys. I calmed my sister, escorted her to her classroom, and then, on what felt like adrenal autopilot, stalked both floors of the high school searching for this kid.

I spotted him in his classroom, in the center of the front row. I banged open the door, rattling the glass in its frame, and in a swift stride, picked up the short wooden stool sitting empty there at the blackboard and stood before him at his desk with the stool cocked at my side. The teacher shrieked, fifteen kids gaped. The ex-friend didn't try to rise, just smirked up at me, his face a pufferfish, flushed and swollen from steroids. All I had to do was swing and his skull would break, his cheekbones crack, his teeth scatter onto the floor. He'd earned that.

The cliché is 'heat of the moment,' but I didn't feel any heat now that I was there before him. What I felt was the cool awareness that I didn't want to hurt him that badly. I didn't want the consequences of that hurt. I lowered the stool with one hand and jabbed a finger at his face with the other: 'You go near her again and I will end you.' And he did an unexpected thing then; he didn't protest or offer denials or reciprocal promises of destruction. Instead, he folded his arms at his chest and pouted – a first grader's disappointed pout, but disappointed in what I couldn't say.

By this time the teacher was tugging at my sleeve, yanking me toward the door. I let the stool drop and I left, returned to class in time to learn something about Kurt Vonnegut, the clutch of his moral imagination. But I wasn't there long; the vice-principal was at the door now, saying, 'Let's go, get your stuff, Giraldi,' and he led me from the building, suspended me for the rest of that week. And the conversation that night at the dinner table sounded just like this:

'You didn't knock him out?' Pop said.

'He attacked your sister and you didn't knock him out?' my father said.

'He didn't *attack* her,' I said. 'He scared her, is all.'

Pop said: 'He scares your sister and you don't knock him out?'

138

'I let him know what he needed to know,' I said. 'He won't go near her again.'

'He goes near her again, you knock him out,' my father said. 'What are those muscles for if you're not gonna knock him out?'

So that, then, was the chief value they saw in the physique I'd begun to build: how well it let me knock out another male. And if I had tried to tell them that I didn't comprehend my body in that way, as a hammer to inflict damage on other males? What good would that have done? I said nothing.

X

The morning of the show, the prejudging portion, a muster of attendees mistaking gaudiness for godliness, not an overweight ice-cream lover among them, skin enough for a porn convention, outfits with an emphasis on both the 'out' and the 'fit.' The air inside the auditorium was charged and hard to breathe, crammed with bovine strut, men grazing from containers, ripping protein bars with their teeth. Female bodybuilders hulling through hallways like the genetic joke of some insane god, women who'd made themselves complete strangers to ovulation, their faces mannishly square from steroids, breasts abolished, voices baritone – Atlases in drag.

Victor stood with me in a queue near the face of the stage so I could sign in, receive my number badge, and hand over the CD with my posing song for later that night. We tried to spot the other teens, to gauge my competition, but they all looked the same to me: sandals, thigh-flared workout pants, hoodies zipped to the throat, duffel bags like pocketbooks beneath their arms.

Backstage, Victor sprayed another sheath of bronzer on me, then added an enamel of posing oil, its odor like the flavored lubricant in your bedroom. The noxious fumes of the body paint were a smog in that tight air, every man backstage laminated with the stuff, his face scrunched, trying not to inhale it. We stood or sat in our posing trunks before mirrors, eighty mostly-nudes from all weight divisions, pumping up with dumbbells and barbells, some lying on the floor with their legs up on benches to reduce water retention in their legs, eyeballs spookily aglow against newly coppered hides, nobody speaking, each sizing up the other, everybody emotionally withered from the diet. A paramedic stood sentry in a starched white button-up in case someone passed out, his stethoscope round his neck and ready to sound our unhinged hearts.

I nudged Victor in unease, nodded to the teens who dwarfed me, the full lobes of their pectorals. Two teens in particular were blessed with size and superior scaffolding, both humped with muscle; their *ears* looked muscled. One of them was the kid we'd spotted at our hotel the day before, his skin a dazzling obsidian; he needed no bronzer. I'm sure I'd never duped myself into believing that I had those same genetic gifts, and yet there I was, having been talked into this, an impostor backstage with these teen freaks who would trounce me.

Victor whispered, 'You're shredded, bro. That dude's not peeled like you,' and 'You're nails, man, got veins everywhere,' and 'Don't sweat them dudes. You're *nails*.' But it was impossible not to sweat because I was wearing nine layers of epidermis in a Sahara of body heat. There were eight guys in the teenage division and I was sure – it was a stomach-pit surety – that I was better than only two of them. So: sixth place for me, it seemed. You don't get a trophy for sixth place, and you make no one proud.

Soon the teens were summoned to center stage, lined up by number, elbow to elbow, our backs flared, legs and abs tensed, behind us a silver-spangled curtain on loan from a strip show. The announcer called the first move, four quarter-turns to the right, and then he called out the mandatory poses, one by one, beginning with Front Double Biceps. We held each pose for twelve, thirteen seconds, and although that's not long to clench your breath, the body feels it as much longer because the flexing forces an onrush of blood, the dilation of veins, each muscle group leaping distinct and hard. What's more, you've got to be aware of the other guys because the wily ones will try to inch forward on the stage in an attempt to stand out.

I was pinned there between the two largest teens, crushingly aware of how little I must look, merely planar by contrast. I could hear Rude and Sid shouting at me, though not Victor (Victor didn't shout). I heard 'Abs!' and 'Calves!' – reminders to flex them, to pose from the floor up: calves first, then legs, then abs, then the upper body. During the rear poses, Rude shouted, 'Hams!' because apparently, I was forgetting about my hamstrings, which were rather easy to forget about because I didn't have any. Sid yelled, 'Glutes!' and I squeezed my buttocks into striated squares.

We'd practiced each pose for several weeks and yet, when you're a first-timer, an unfortunate thing can happen up there. In the heat of it, all the posing prep falls aside and you begin simply trying to keep pace with those beside you, aping whatever they do, because surely, they have more experience than your sorry self. Pose by pose – Side Chest, Back Lat Spread, Back Double Biceps, and the rest – I simply tried to keep up with the leviathans who flanked me, looking side to side to see their poses, their stances, whatever in the world their faces were doing.

The head judge then scattered the lineup, microphoned where he wanted us to stand: 'Number 22, next to number 19. Number 20 in between Numbers 21 and 18.' This meant they were comparing the best physiques more scrupulously. I knew it was an ominous sign to be on either end of the line because that meant they didn't care to compare you, and not, alas, because you were incomparable. You wanted to be at the center of the lineup; that's usually where the top placers appear at this point. Although I wasn't at the center, I also hadn't been exiled to either end. So, the slightest fattening of hope, then, among such pounding doubt. And once again the judges bullwhipped us through the eight compulsory poses.

Those who contend that bodybuilding isn't a sport because it lacks utility, a specific function of physicality, have never attempted rounds of competitive poses in lanes of scorching spotlight. The skill lies first in the difficult mastering of muscle development and nutrition, in the wedding of power with grace – grace is the body thinking clearly – and then in this racking exposition of the outcome. Hitting and holding those poses in such heat, with a body that dehydrated, with the elbows, shoulders, and thighs of others nudging greasily into me, was as difficult, as technical, as building the muscles in the first place.

I can half understand the cynic's charges of homophilia: those male bodies, ninety-eight per cent nude, grunting and sweating, slick together. But it doesn't come remotely close to feeling that way. It feels like combat, not prelude to coitus. The bodybuilding stage, with its strictness of rules, its rigidity of judgment and ferocity of competition, its stress and its heat, destroys any possibility of eroticism. The art/sport display, the objectifying of the body into pure aesthetics, into lines and form and flow, empties it of all sexuality. You actually forget you're naked. That's why no bodybuilder ever worries about sprouting an erection on stage; there's simply no space up there for an erogenous zone.

After that second round of compulsory poses, the judges dismissed us, thanked us, and I walked off stage cramping in my quads. Victor was there in the wings with a towel and he patted the sweat from me. The head of a Poland Spring bottle peeked from the side pocket of his shorts like a periscope, and when I grabbed for it, he swatted my hand away. Then he unscrewed the cap and carefully filled it with barely two milliliters of water, which evaporated on my tongue before I could swallow. He and the others from the Edge would remain to watch the prejudging of the other weight classes, but they instructed me to return to the hotel.

'Go lay down, stay off your feet.'

'Put your legs up on pillows to keep the water out of 'em.'

'For the love of God, whatever you do, don't *drink* any water.'

'Find a hamburger and eat it. You looked a little flat up there. You need to fill out. A hamburger will fill you out.'

'Sips maybe to get the burger down.'

'*Sips,* fucker, no more than sips.'

'But overall, great, man. You held your own up there.'

'You looked killer, dude.'

'You looked great.'

'You looked *good*. It ain't over. Tonight still matters. At this point, the judges are eighty per cent sure of the placements, I'd say, so tonight still matters. You can't screw up anything between now and then.'

'Yeah, you looked a little flat, as I'm saying. So go get a hamburger. Get two. No water.'

That might sound counterintuitive, a mooing hamburger and bun, but my body fat percentage was so low, my metabolism so high, and my anabolic rate so efficient after those many weeks of training and diet, that the burger's density of fat and carbs would get stuffed directly into the muscle bellies, keeping them round and causing my veins to surge. A hamburger for the average American is a cardiac catastrophe in the making; a hamburger for the bodybuilder on contest day is a necessary nectar.

I found a plaque-friendly grill on the way from the auditorium – you could smell the cholesterol a block away – and bought the hamburgers. Trying to eat them in my motel room without any water took an hour. After jerking shut the blinds I dialed my house and then my grandparents', but no one answered at either place. Without traffic, Point Pleasant was an hour south of Manville, and I wanted to remind my family to leave early enough; the show began at seven. On the bed, on a sheet already dyed with streaks of bronzer, needing to sleep and feeling myself fill from the burgers, I

145

lay half in dream, half in fearful remembrance, and what I dream-remembered was this:

Six months earlier, Victor and I and some others from the Edge attended the prejudging portion of a minor bodybuilding contest held at a high school auditorium in north Jersey. One of the competitors was mentally disabled, maybe twenty years old; you could see the slight warp, the frozen twitch, in his face. He wasn't just unmuscled – he looked shriveled from malnutrition, earnestly straining and oblivious. He'd applied a layer of oil and shaved his body, but nobody had told him about self-tanner, and so he glowed ghoulishly on stage next to dark copper hides, all of them many times more massive. The universal nightmare in which you're naked in front of a crowd of people mocking you? This blanched stick figure was that nightmare incarnate, except he didn't know it.

Somehow this had been allowed to happen, but no one seemed to know what to do about it now. The judges and other competitors were paused in perplexity and embarrassment, and then determined to move forward, and then paused again. The head judge's voice in the microphone quavered with *umm*s and *err*s. He looked left and right for help from the other judges, but no help came. The fifty or so spectators reddened, quaked with quiet laughter, and I could hear the whispers around me: *Who let a retard onstage?*

The guys from the Edge slid low in their seats, their baseball caps yanked down over their brows, literally crying from the unexpected comedy of this. I was afraid my own tears would come then, and that they wouldn't be from laughter – that release of emotion would have been the end of me at the

Edge. Because I could see, there in the front row, a blocky silver-haired man in mismatched garb, his eyeglasses built for star-gazing, something warped in his face too, pitched eagerly forward in his seat, ignoring the ridicule, beaming encouragement and faith up to the ghoulish kid who'd been wrongly placed on that stage – beaming at his son.

Backstage at the night show, after Victor varnished me with a final layer of posing oil, I could hear the auditorium filling, the balanced pre-performance din. I asked Victor to check if he could spot my family in their seats, but he couldn't make out anyone. Hundreds of spectating faces somehow coalesce into a single face. I'd heard someone say that the traffic on the Garden State Parkway was clogged for miles into Point Pleasant – early August was the crest of beach season, carloads in swarm for a Saturday night's play – and I guessed that my family was idling in that clog. The teens would be first to compete, and so I was certain that my father, Pop, and Tony would miss me onstage.

It all unfolded quickly then, in the way events do after so much buildup. The teen division was instructed to form a queue at the curtain, and each guy would perform his solo routine before we were called onstage for another posing competition. When it was my turn, the announcer sang my number and name in the drawn-out, faux-dramatic manner of every boxing announcer you've ever heard. I walked in to the clapping, the orchestra of whistles and hoots from the Edge crowd. The way the lights were angled, I couldn't see farther than the judges' table and the first two rows. The rest was a bleary canvas of beiges and blacks. But my body could *feel* the noise of them all, their mass humming along my bones. Flashbulbs were going off to my right like a squadron of fireflies who knew my name.

When the song began, I performed my routine – a banana-sack ballet, as I'd come to think of it – just as we'd rehearsed it for the last several weeks. Or at least I *tried* to. It felt hectic up there, and I was conscious of missing certain beats, of being either a second too quick or too slow to hit a pose. I thought I could hear Sid or Rude shouting, 'Time!' over my song, by which he meant *Keep in time with the music.* The guys who'd gone before me looked somewhat clumsy in their choreography, and so I strained for agility, for elegance, aware that elegance can't be had by straining. And just as I was starting to relax, to feel semi-assured in the routine, to remember all my beats, the volume descended and the song disappeared. I'd seen guys bow at this point, or else kiss their hands toward the audience in appreciation, but I swiped my wet brow and waved goodbye, squinting into the lights as I tried to spot my family.

I stood by in the wing, stage left, while the others performed, baby-sipping from a water bottle, hopped-up now, feeling a muscle tautness just shy of cramping, Victor behind me with a towel, blending my sweat into the oil, saying, 'Killer job, you nailed it,' but I didn't believe that. Gawking at the obsidian beauty who was just then performing to a hip-hop blend of Naughty by Nature and the Wu Tang Clan, I couldn't believe that. After the last guy's routine, we were all summoned to center stage to go through the mandatory poses. I was near the heart of the lineup again, dwarfed again, and if the guys from the Edge were yelling reminders at me, I couldn't hear them over the crowd.

Then came the posedown, an unscripted minute of free-for-all posing to whatever guitars burst through the speakers, all eight guys elbowing for a spot at the lip of center stage, the sweat and oil stink of us, trying to smile, some of us virtually hugging, trying to get around one another. The music stopped at sixty seconds, but guys were still hitting shots for the judges, and everybody had to be ordered back into line. This posedown was for the audience; it didn't matter for winning or losing because the judges had already finalized their decisions during the posing competition.

Now we statues stood at the line, waiting to hear the top five numbers. When your number was yelled, you stepped forward. If your number wasn't yelled, you didn't place, and you remained lonesomely at the line. The top five would stand on the dais, but only the top three would be handed trophies – two-foot, two-tiered oak and silver-sprayed sculptures of a muscled demigod in mid-pose, forty pounds apiece, expertly crafted. My number was among the five. And so, I'd be fifth place, I thought: fifth among eight. But when the announcer yelled the number for fifth place, it was not mine. Nor was fourth.

At this point, something begins to happen to the enlivened competitor, the formerly insecure one who an hour earlier thought he'd take sixth place. He begins to think not about the possibility of third place or second place, but about the possibility of *first* place. It's an optimistic delusion based upon the suddenly fortuitous, a reversal of fortune (*peripeteia* was its name on the Greek stage, although the reversals there were almost always in a direful direction). My brief rationale was this: I thought I'd be in sixth place, but now I'm in the top three, and if I can be third, then I can be first, because the distance between third and first is much narrower than the distance between sixth and first. Well, of course it is, but that didn't mean that there was *no* distance between third and first, and to remind myself of this, to dispel the delusion, all I had to do was glance at the other two guys who remained in the lineup with me.

Third place was announced and it wasn't my number, and I began to suspect that major errors were being committed. I twisted the badge on my trunks to check it, to make sure I was seeing and hearing numbers correctly, because the kid to whom they'd just given third place outmuscled me by about twenty-five pounds. Only I and the obsidian beauty now, the toothpick and the sirloin, and when they gave me second place it felt like relief to me. Not relief that this madness was finally finished and I could down a canter of water and a chocolate bar, although that too, but relief that rightness had prevailed. The world now and then peddles justice.

It didn't feel anything like justice to the third placer. I wasn't aware of this at the time, but in photographs from that night, we three perched and posing on the dais with our trophies, I can see his indignant smirk, his awareness that he'd just been robbed of second place. And robbed he surely was, although why, I don't know; perhaps because the judges didn't like his attitude (he'd been pushy, arrogant during posing), perhaps because his skin was denser than mine, his routine less graceful.

I walked behind the curtain with forty pounds of trophy, through the backstage flurry to dress myself, to receive high-fives from Victor, congrats and shoulder pats from giants all around. In the silent, fluorescent hallway that led to my seat in the auditorium, I bent into the water fountain to gulp for an uninterrupted two minutes. But what flooded me then was a mix of pride and bliss, a mix I'd never felt before, and one I'd have to wait sixteen years to feel again, when my first son was born.

My father, Pop, and Tony were there in seats at the rear of the auditorium, and when I entered they rose to greet me, each grinning, nodding, and I hoisted the trophy to chest level as if to say, 'Ta *da*.'

'That's one hell of a trophy,' Pop said. 'I didn't think you'd make better than fifth place.'

'You did good,' my father said. 'I had you at third place.'

'I had you at second,' Tony said. 'You were better than that third place kid. He was big but he had no shape.'

Before we took our seats, my father, with a calculated slyness, handed me a small paper bag, as if he didn't want anyone else in the auditorium to see it: an assortment of Snickers and Reese's Peanut Butter Cups. He said, 'I thought you might be craving one of those.'

I said, 'How'd you know?'

He said, 'I know things,' and together we finished off that bag of chocolate.

XI

It happened on a Saturday afternoon that autumn, October or November, all the oaks aflame. The road to the Physical Edge cut through farmland and plots of forest, and I remember clicking off the radio as if quiet would pronounce the color. I turned into the parking lot of the Edge and spotted a huddle near the glass doors, others leaned against cars, some sitting on curbs, heads framed in hands as if with something to ponder, or else grief-hit. On Saturdays, the only business open in this industrial complex was our gym, and so from a distance I knew these were my people and not others from adjacent buildings. There was Victor's red Camaro, Sid's black Ford pickup, Rude's Harley, Pedro's silver Corvette, Bob the Cop's cruiser, and a dozen other vehicles I'd learned to associate with the faces of their drivers. A fire alarm, I thought. A mistaken fire alarm must have chased everyone out into the parking lot.

When I approached the huddle at the doors, these were the sentences my friends spoke to me:

'We're shut down, dude.'

'Out of commission, man.'

'Shit out of luck, bro.'

Chains snaked around both sets of door handles, the entrance and the exit. Taped to the inside of the glass was this notice on gym letterhead: THE PHYSICAL EDGE WILL NO LONGER BE OPEN. THANK YOU FOR YOUR PATRONAGE. Sixteen hours earlier, when we'd all been here training, we'd detected no portent of this. There'd been no whispers, nothing aslant. So, imagine: one morning you leave your house of several years to report for another normal day at work, and after that normal day, you return home in the evening to discover your locks have been swapped and a note that reads, *This is no longer your home.* I heard someone in the huddle say, 'We're gymless,' but what that really meant for me was *We're homeless.*

Because I was an employee, the others looked at me as if I might have some corrective wisdom, but I had nothing of the sort. I'd never met or spoken to the owners. Bob the Cop was making furious calls from his car phone, others complaining that they still had clothes in their lockers. I pressed my face against the glass, hands ovaled to my eyes, peering into the new dark of our beloved space, everything right there and familiar but abruptly severed from us. When I joined the huddle to see what we were going to do about this, I could tell how deflated they felt. These normally verbose, resourceful individuals had been jarred into a kind of paralysis. Men of immensity and machismo, women who'd always seemed to me unflappable, were drooped now, looking at their sneakers as if about to sob. Refugees now, orphaned by the owners of the Edge.

The scene quickly turned into a makeshift funeral as more

of our set arrived, and it wouldn't have seemed out of place for someone to break into 'We Shall Overcome,' except that it didn't seem as if we would. Emboldened by my second-place finish in the bodybuilding competition two months earlier, I planned to compete in another, more prestigious show that April, but that didn't seem doable now. This was the end of something. In the coming days, we'd hear rumors of bankruptcy, but we wouldn't learn for certain how we'd come to be orphaned. They owed me a paycheck I'd never see, although that didn't even register on my scale of sorrow, because I knew what the closing of the Edge would do. It would scatter us all to other gyms in central Jersey. It meant our affection for one another would have no place to thrive.

I remained there on the curb that day long after everyone else had gone, waiting for someone to arrive and rectify this misdeed, but no one came. And every day for a week I showed up there to see if anything had changed, in the hope of catching someone inside, someone who might tell me what had happened, who might let me walk through a final time, touch the equipment, offer a proper farewell, kneel once more in our house of worship.

Things continued to unravel after that. My father sold our home, took my siblings, and moved in with his new girlfriend, a woman he'd been dating for a year, the mother of one of my sister's friends. There was no room for me in her condo; I wouldn't have elected to go if there had been. I took an apartment in town, a place I could neither afford nor fill, a two-bedroom with pine floors, early-'80s appliances, a sliding glass door that looked upon real homes across an expanse of grass dotted with spruce. It was forever empty, echoic, and I bled my bank account to be there, borrowed money from my father and Pop, although 'borrow' was a joke and everybody knew it.

Dinnertime with my grandparents was a nightly inquisition: 'When are you getting a job? Can't lift weights for a living. You think about college? What about being a cop? That kid from your class, what's-his-name, over on Bosel Avenue, he's becoming a cop. Good benefits, cops. Or else you better start thinking about construction with your father and uncles. You're not exactly cut out for that work, we know, but it's a living, and better than nothing.' Before returning to the emphatic silence of my apartment, I'd drive slowly past my boyhood home, nearly stop in front of it, and look at the windows burning amber in the winter night, see if I could spot foreign shapes through the sheerness of drawn curtains, shapes living a family's life in rooms that had made me.

Victor and I drove overlong distances each afternoon to try out other gyms, but none ever welcomed us as the Edge had; none ever fit. We'd see Pedro at one gym, Sid at another, Rude at another, and we'd embrace and reminisce and try to revive our enthusiasm, but our workouts were shit, the weights not right, the music all wrong (REO Speedwagon, for Christ's sake). The clientele at those gyms was mostly piddlers, and the managers scolded us for training as we did, for smashing the barbells back into the racks, for our spitting, cussing intensity, an intensity impossible to maintain in those climates. Our set from the Edge muttered to one another those absurd senior-class-yearbook vows of not losing touch, made wispy attempts to remain in contact, but that never works, the forcing of unions that had once developed organically and without effort. Take away the nucleus and the electrons spin off and away. There were phone calls, a stray Friday-night revel at a restaurant, a bachelor party with New York strippers, and then nothing.

Val and I had been providing occasional CPR to a relationship that was desperate to die; but she stayed with me during the winter break from Rutgers, and for that month of pretending, the serpentine home of her body helped absorb the echoes of my empty rooms. Her voice, even when she lied, *especially* when she lied, had the throaty allure of a chanteuse. When she at last killed the relationship in January, those echoes returned, but louder. Always the dumpee and never the dumper, I was unstrung each time it happened. Textbook shrinks would later tell me that I was experiencing the original wound of my mother's abandonment: as a child I didn't have the equipment to process such abandonment, didn't have the emotional utensils even to acknowledge it, and so as a teen I lived out the grief of that large wound through fleeing girlfriends. A better question might have been why girlfriends were always fleeing.

And then came the ice storms, entire zip codes crippled beneath inches of frigid glass. The snow and ice lasted weeks, appeared never to tire of their own terrible beauty. For whole days at a time the ice entombed me within my first-floor apartment. The wind gusted ceaselessly through the night like angry souls unleashed, sealing the windows and doors, rounding the brick steps in a promise of deadly descent. I'd lie on the sofa at night in the dark – after Val left

I could no longer sleep in the bedroom, could not scrub it free of her scent – and listen to the ice pelt the sliding glass door. Out back were domes of lacquered snow, sheds and patio grills thickly packaged in white, icicles like great fangs jabbing down from street lamps glowing dull lime.

TV weathermen seemed pleased to be of such use; their increased airtime lent them a mien of scholarly importance. In the mornings I'd wield a blow dryer against an opaque window to melt a porthole for me to peer through, but there was nothing to see except the silent heft of winter, all that curvaceous cold. If I made it outside and down the steps, I could barely reach the sidewalk without injury, and couldn't shovel: the metal one would bend, the plastic one break. On walkways beads of salt lay uselessly atop ice like seeds strewn for pigeons suddenly extinct. No one could drive anywhere, and that didn't matter: cars sat in surrender to their interment.

Good boots helped. Snowplows had carved slick conduits through the centers of most streets, and that's how I hiked to the grocery store. Except the grocery store wasn't open when I arrived. And so I hoofed and slid over drifts and waffled paths for another mile to a convenience store whose shelves looked ransacked by marauders. If I passed a fellow hiker, he watched me through goggles and a ski mask as if deciding whether or not to kill and cook me. An orange snowplow would scrape past trailing a mess of sand or salt, its single yellow light twirling in impotence. I felt further stranded when it didn't stop to pick me up. Somehow I'd make it back to my apartment, and that night the icy gusts would come again, sealing me inside again.

The monotony of doldrums, their stalling, sputtering of

time. Hours would pass, but when I looked at the clock its arms hadn't budged since the last time I checked. My appetite obliterated, a clenched stomach from the instant I woke until the gray bowl above began to darken. Fetal on the sofa with a pillow clutched to my gut. It took me an hour or more to talk myself into standing up. At dusk I forced down protein shakes because I couldn't muster the will to chew a meal. Pacing from one room to another, then hallucinating Val on a kitchen stool, on the toilet, in the bathtub. One afternoon I discovered her unwashed panties wedged between the sofa cushions – pink cotton gossamer that once held worlds – and I slipped them over my head, reclined there to inhale her. Winter continued as if it enjoyed astonishment.

When streets became passable I exhumed my car with a pickaxe and potfuls of boiling water. It took six hours, such were the crusted mounds that had shored against it, flotsam from snowplows. A route to a gym that usually took an hour took twice that, and I was worthless once I got there: my body weight down, strength gone, incentive sacked. Victor clapped me with back pats, offered buckups, but his voice came as if from underwater. Another tempest of ice and snow would make misery of roads and we'd go another week without training.

Once, asleep on the sofa at noon, I woke to a doorbell. It seemed this tolling had come from the dreamland I'd been sucked down into, but then I heard it again: it was mine. I'd never heard my own doorbell before. My father stood on the top step, dressed like an Inuit: fur-lined hood, padded Carhartt overalls, chunky Sorel snow boots, his cheeks lashed red from wind, his lips chapped, veined with cracks of blood. He was holding something up in a dramatically displayed pincer grip.

'You lose something?' he said.

'What's that?'

'Your wallet,' he said.

'Where'd you get my wallet?'

'Arty the electrician gave it to me.'

'How did Arty the electrician get my wallet?' I said.

'He found it in the WaWa parking lot, half-buried in a snow bank.'

'Oh,' I said.

'Oh?'

'I haven't been to WaWa in three days,' I said.

'You lost your wallet three days ago and you didn't notice?'

'I've been...'

'You've been *what*?' he said. 'Were you sleeping?'

'No, no. I was... looking in the want ads.'

The previous tenant had tied a thermometer to the porch lamp. Its mercury, a bulb of blood starting at minus forty, could rise no higher than nineteen degrees. The cold came like pins through my T-shirt and sweatpants.

'Did you have cash in your wallet?' my father asked. 'Arty said he found it with no cash.'

'Yes. Forty, I think. Or thirty maybe.' I looked into the lonely folds of the wallet. 'But there's money in here,' I said.

'Naturally, Bill. I couldn't give you back an empty wallet.' *Naturally* was one of my father's pet terms. Should I get Pop a birthday present? *Naturally*. Was Yamaha better than Ducati? *Naturally*. He squinted over my shoulder into the curtained dark of the apartment as if looking for whatever had turned me this way.

'Are you feeling all right?' he said. 'You look like hell.'

'I'm fine,' I said.

'Come for dinner tonight. I've been asking for weeks.'

'I will,' I said. 'I'll come tonight.'

Back on the sofa, I crawled into a placenta of blankets, and when I emerged it was 8 p.m. and long past dinnertime.

That winter I began walling myself in with books, stacking them around the sofa as if to repel the cold, abutments of new hardbacks and paperbacks, columns of slipcased fiction I found secondhand. If I came across an essay by Dorothy Parker or a story by Raymond Carver in an anthology, I was soon at the bookshop unloading all the Parker and Carver titles from its shelves. The hordes of books were manifestations of the selfhood I was reaching for, a sensibility externalized, a worldview I could see and hold. They were rather like muscles in that way, embodiments of the strengthened self I wanted, at a time when I seemed always just minutes from collapse.

Raymond Carver's fiction discovered me with the same restorative jolt as bodybuilding had three years earlier. He'd been dead for nearly a decade, but his stories were new to me, and just then offered a much-needed brotherhood of working-class melancholy. On the coffee table in front of the sofa I'd stacked a tower of his paperbacks, those unmistakable white Vintage Contemporaries, his name a thing of hope in a colored band at the head of the spine. Immediately upon waking, the light of morning like steel, spruce still oppressed by snow, in me a living void, I'd reach for Carver's stories with the guarded faith of a pilgrim.

'Fever,' from the collection *Cathedral*, was my father's story almost exactly: Carlyle is abandoned by his perfidious wife, Eileen, and must care for two small children without her; he struggles for competent babysitting, for an eclipsing of his sorrow, and along the way earns triumphs too tiny to make much difference. The Carverian world is a spiritual tundra, an alcoholic wasteland in which the American Dream means disappointment and malaise: not because it has died, but because it never was born. Communion, if it comes at all, comes from minor human interaction. Forget about grace; grace means a feeble paycheck. If you're lucky, the electricity won't be turned off.

Carver was my first convincing intimation that something might be made from grief, that I myself might fashion artistic assertions from my own failings. There was some rescue in that: my sadness could be *useful*. Until this time, literature had been a font of pleasure and of wisdom: the satisfaction of beholding a well-carpentered sonnet, the beauty of a novel's sturdy plinths and joists. But why did reading 'Ode to a Nightingale' at fifteen – *Now more than ever seems it rich to die, / To cease upon the midnight with no pain* – relieve my own trendy death wishes? What spell was at work there? To be personally addressed by Keats in that way seemed a wizardry I'd never explain. Later I would understand. Reverse the ineffable and be found. The elemental vitality of the right words in the right order. Name the thing to gain dominion over it. The comfort, the good fortune of finding sentences and stanzas which

161

equipped me with descriptions of my own half-explicable anguishes.

But how would *I* be capable of such wizardry, of reversing the ineffable, of naming? Until Carver, I'd been only a dabbler in written words: a sheaf of stray lines, impulsive poems, what might have made a song lyric for an especially inept rock vocalist – what Proust once dismissed as 'merely phrase-making.' Instinctive volleys of self-expression. But there was no *assertion,* no armature, no order, no strivings into the accuracy and surprise of language. In Carver's expertly built stories, in their sneaky simplicity and demotic prose, I glimpsed possibilities of the architecture I might use. Faulkner, Bellow, Proust: they divested me of whatever motivation I might have had to conceive my own fiction. I could never do *that,* what they did, how they did it. Bellow's *Augie March* seemed not of this world, seemed crafted of a linguistic magic and intelligence I'd need different DNA to perform.

But Carver's 'Fever,' and 'Vitamins,' and 'A Small, Good Thing': those I might attempt. And not just because they were about people I'd known my whole life (the handyman, the salesman, the janitor), or because their sadness let me feel less solitary (literature must be about more than the merely identifiable), but because their sentences and structures contained a crucial quality of the spoken, the conversational. Their narrative ease extended a hand in invitation, and that's part of why Carver was so beloved by so many, how he influenced so many, because his stories said, *I welcome you. Come in.*

And so, seated at a desk in the bedroom of that silent

apartment, at a secondhand computer the size of the Liberty Bell, the winter in extended wrath, I began. The telling of stories. The circumstances of which were mine, yes, but, what? *Altered* somehow. *Imagined into order.* How should those circumstances proceed? Take an instance from a life – my own, say, or my father's – and give it shape, augment it into meaning. Let it find its form. Beginning, middle, end. Get characters talking. Have them want something – no, *need* something. The meaning, the structure of the meaning, would come from the characters' needs, from finding words that equaled their troubles. Because in life, I was certain, all the meaning had gone missing. Life had none of the symmetries, none of the parallel significances, of literature.

Is that where those periodic spasms of delight came from, spasms that for a few seconds at a time alleviated my despair? Not because I was expressing my bewilderment through characters who were me but different, my father but different – self-expression is simple: go punch a hole in the wall – but because I was attempting to fashion harmony from disorder, to go in search of what was within me? Attempting to manifest meaning in chaos? Because I was making, because I was naming, and from that making and naming emanated a sense of control, the satisfaction of control? Yes, here was what people inevitably refer to as 'a calling.' And the calling felt religious in its specifics, in its choosing of me and not a neighbor, not a friend. And the calling was relief, because I knew then, during those icy maelstroms, and then as the kicking cold relented into the kiss of spring, I knew what my life would be.

* * *

When the time came to step onstage again in April, in Hackensack, New Jersey, I wasn't prepared. In several ways, my physique was improbably better than it had been at the first contest in August: fifteen pounds heavier, rounder and more symmetrical (I'd got the drug cocktail right). But all that unkind winter I'd despised each workout at inadequate gyms, suffered through each force-fed meal, and without the camaraderie of the Edge, I couldn't find importance in this anymore. I'd skip workouts to begin another story or to reread Carver. During the days leading up to the show, I'd polluted my diet in a manner I could not clean: striations disappeared, one muscle bled into another. I drained a liter of water and fell asleep in my car in the parking lot before prejudging. Victor told me he couldn't discern a single abdominal muscle from his seat in the audience. It didn't matter. I took fourth place out of ten and walked offstage. Nowhere among the unreliable acoustics of memory can I locate the song I used, or much of anything else. Not my posing routine, not a single other competitor.

Friends planned to meet at a nearby diner to glut upon all they'd been forbidden for many weeks, but I drove back to my apartment and inhaled a pound of peanut M&Ms while revising yet another Carver-influenced story, another domestic drama, this one about an intruder who might or might not have broken into the home of a struggling couple. The judges had handed me an embarrassing plastic trophy in Hackensack, and when I moved out of that apartment in May, I placed both of my bodybuilding trophies into the dumpster. *Placed* them, not *dropped* them, because although I didn't want to see them anymore, I also didn't want to see them broken.

'One needs a town,' wrote Cesare Pavese, 'if only for the pleasure of leaving it.' I left Manville first for a year in Myrtle Beach, South Carolina, and then for another year in Boston, Massachusetts. And I left for a reason people have always left small towns: not because I didn't value it, but because I believed that my development waited elsewhere. And because some young writers, after they reach the final page of Hemingway's or Conrad's biography, get hit with the fantastic inkling that unless they light out of town, unless they make motion of their lives, they won't have the raw materials from which to invent compelling literature.

It's not true, of course. Dickinson proves that. A garden, a library, and an imagination were her only requirements. O'Connor said that any fiction writer who survived childhood had ample material for her lifetime. But I needed to leave Manville. During my more than two years away, when I wasn't eyeing the clock at vapid places of employment – a restaurant, a newspaper, a telemarketing firm – I taught myself to write fiction by doing it very badly across six hundred pages, two novels and dozens of stories I would later shred from sheer embarrassment. It would take several more years of practice, and several hundred more pages, for fiction to stop being easy for me, to stop coming in spates, and only when it stopped being easy, only when each sentence became a labor, did I begin producing work that might make it out into the world.

I'd been to Myrtle Beach with a friend just before my second bodybuilding competition and, while training at a tiny World Gym there, had been offered a job for the summer, what turned out to be glorified janitorial duties. And so I had one more summer among the radiantly hale, though mostly as an observer this time. My bodybuilding and steroid use were finished, but it would take several months of not training for my physique to revert to the string bean it had been before I started with weights in my uncle's basement. The furnished studio apartment I found was part of a complex against a golf course, the rent an unlikely $350 per month, first-floor views of a peripheral and little-visited nook of the course, beyond it undulating green and beige. On the day I arrived, the keg-bellied landlord met me to deliver the keys and, looking into my Buick, said, 'Rob you a library?' I'd choked the backseat with eight milk crates of books, several hundred titles I couldn't do without. When the golf course was vacant, I'd carry Chekhov or Gogol beneath a copse of pines and lie on a mat of needles, trying to work out how they'd achieved such resplendent effects.

If ever someone asked why I'd quit bodybuilding, I said the truth: I didn't have the genes to make anything of it. But why quit training entirely? Because some of us, if we can't do a thing full bore, won't do it at all. We sense something wasteful, something shameful, in halves. Most of the men in my family are infected with that urge to dichotomy: it's extremity or nothing. I stayed at bodybuilding for those three years because it had once kept me from the craters of depression, but I must have begun to suspect, in some weakly lit sector of myself, and especially during those final six months, that it couldn't last, that my future was something else. Did I not miss it? I did. But what I missed was impossible to resurrect. For someone who once could not envisage life without muscle, without the shrine and shelter of a gym, I fled that world with a regretless ease.

My father visited me in Carolina that summer. I have photos of us on the beach, at my apartment, making golf balls soar at a driving range. He wasn't a reader but he accepted the manuscript I handed to him, a story I'd recently finished. I can vividly recall him on the sofa with it, reading about a man not unlike him, an about-to-be deserted husband who's making a last effort to change his wife's mind. I can see him turning pages with a face that oscillated from puzzlement to surprise, and I can remember precisely what he said when he put it down: 'That was a strange one.' In the spring of the following year, when I asked him for a few thousand dollars to spend two months at Harvard Summer School, in a literature class, he wrote the check and I left Carolina for Boston.

Out from underneath the mortgage of our home, from the debris of his marriage to my mother, he had money again for the first time in more than a decade. He bought a Honda CBR900 that summer, his first motorcycle in twenty-three years. It must have seemed a rebirth to him. He'd said he wanted to ride up to visit me at Harvard Summer School, but that plan, vague from the start, never materialized. He worked all week, Saturday was for resting, Sunday for motorcycle racing.

The instructor of the literature class laded me with titles for which I've always been grateful: *Under the Volcano, On the Road, Rock Springs* among them. The classroom and campus life, I saw, were considerably better than a collection of part-time drudgeries. My dorm that summer turned into a sexual UN that was as fulfilling, as loving, as anything I'd experienced at the Edge: Japanese and Koreans, Germans and Danes, Brazilians and Turks, most of them dazzling talkers and virtuoso smokers who sated my lungs with Lucky Strikes, all of them gloriously unlike anyone I'd known in Jersey or Carolina. When late August came and they returned to their worlds, I sobbed from the sting of losing them.

I'd spend another year in Boston, at a soul-smashing job as a telephone enroller of senior citizens who sought frolic on educational trips. In a derelict East Boston walk-up, in an iffy district friends wouldn't visit, my weekends passed in a galloping solitude, in manias of sentences, none of which would be salvageable. The apartment canted toward the back, buckled in the middle. I'd sit on the lopsided porch meshed in with broken screens, half expecting it to crumble under me, exhaling smoke at the gloomy view of redbrick walls and the detritus of lives. That whole winter was a cocoon, winter as only New England knows winter.

In the closing weeks of the following summer, I returned to New Jersey to attend Drew University. My father helped me sardine my stuff into his work van, the same van my brother and I would clean out the week of his death. He then drove me the forty minutes north to the town of Madison and we toted crates of books and clothes into my dorm room, a garden-level double I'd have to myself. I could see from his face that he was delighted for me. 'Not bad,' he said, inspecting the closet, the bathroom, the desk drawers. 'Not too bad.' Out in the cul-de-sac where we'd parked, he passed me a hundred-dollar bill, and we embraced there, stiffly and manfully, in the August afternoon.

The last photos I'd ever take of him would be in that same cul-de-sac, two years later, on a Sunday in mid-spring, just a month before his fatal motorcycle crash. He stopped to visit me on his new bike, a Yamaha R1, wearing full racing regalia, and the photos show him as he was about to leave: pulling on his gloves, strapping on his helmet, tightening his boots. In one shot, taken before he zipped the suit to his throat, there's something I only recently noticed, something I'd forgotten: tucked against his chest is my first story publication, a glossy magazine that has long since been shuttered. He'd spotted copies on my desk and asked to have one. There's only a sliver of the magazine visible, and in all the hours I'd spent looking at these photos since his death, I'd mistaken it for his T-shirt. Whether or not he'd read the story in the month he had left to live, I cannot say. But he'd made that gesture for me, that show of interest I imagine must have been genuine.

I watched him pull away that afternoon, glide slowly from the cul-de-sac and through the wooded lanes, the bike's chrome-throated growl fearsome and majestic in the Sunday calm of campus. When I could no longer see him, I could still hear the engine as it approached the front gate. I waited there, my breath quickened, and when he made it to the main road, he hit the throttle, and I listened to the air-slicing wail, the aluminum song of his rising through first gear, through second, through third, his sublime screaming toward the highway that would take him home.

BOOK II

The author, on Pop's lap, his father standing, Manville,
New Jersey, circa 1975

We die with the dying:
See, they depart, and we go with them.
We are born with the dead:
See, they return, and bring us with them.

— T. S. Eliot

I

One of Pop's many motorcycle crashes, the specifics of which have not faded in the thirty years since he first told me this story:

A summer Sunday in 1981, in Flemington, New Jersey, half an hour from Manville. He and the group blazing down a rural road, past soybean crops, patches of maple, red barns worn from weather, a green John Deere windrower, farmland furrowed in the distance. They were headed to the back roads of Pennsylvania, Pop in the lead, as he always was. A steep dip ahead, a hundred feet away, eighty feet, maybe less. His buddy behind him cranked the gas, rushed up on the left, passed the pack of fifteen riders in the oncoming lane. But there was that dip there and you couldn't see into it. This guy thought he'd pass all his pals and then dash back into the right lane before he reached the dip, the leader now, the mighty one, the quick. But that dip wouldn't budge, and he was doing a hundred miles per hour on the wrong side of the road.

First the car's roof. Then the car's windshield. Then the

car's grille. The swordfish glint of this car, its chrome teeth. The car was right there, emerging up from the dip in the road. In less than a second it appeared there. Whatever color that car was, however the blue or green or red metal might have glinted in the day's light, that was the new color of death. Sixty-five miles per hour charging at one hundred–plus. And in that second – not *split* second, as the cliché has it, but *shattered* second – Pop had this thought: *He's dead and I'm clear.* Those were the five monosyllabic words that occurred to him when he spotted the swordfish glint of that car rise from the dip. *He's dead and I'm clear.* His buddy hit the car head-on with a velocity that exploded all his major organs. He launched through the air and was dead before he even touched the pavement. He was thirty-six years old.

Pop was right: he himself was clear. But when he glanced down, his bike wasn't under him anymore. The motorcycle had disappeared. He was moving through the air in the same seated position, at the same speed, but the bike was gone. It was then that he realized: his buddy's bike, when it collided with the car, went down and shot to the right, shot directly into Pop, taking his own bike out from under him. His thought just then: *I'm finished*.

The trees blurred by. He hit the road, then rose again. Hit the road, then rose, the blurring trees. He thought, *Keep tucked in.* So he tucked himself in, his limbs, his head, as he hit the road and rose. He could hear, could feel, the gritty rub, the coarse grind of his helmet against the asphalt each time he dropped. Then he thought, *I'm not breaking up.* And by some magic, he really wasn't. But now he was sliding, a bobsledder with no sled, and he thought, *If my leathers hold,*

I walk away. The leathers grated, scraped across the asphalt, but it was a good one-piece hide, a sturdy American-made product. And it held. He did not break up.

Three hundred feet from where he had just lost his bike and his buddy of many years, Pop collided into an oak, stopped there at the base of it, his face shield smashed but all his blood on the inside still. His bones, organs, memories all intact. And when he walked back three hundred feet to the body in the road – it looked like dropped laundry lying there – he walked on quivering legs, searching in the ditch and weeds for his bike.

I have the newspaper clipping here before me, stiff and stained flaxen from time and water damage. The bike is crumpled in the road, bleeding a lake of fuel from its tank. The car, a Datsun or VW, has its entire left side bashed in, the hood hideously buckled, the bumper hanging, windshield gone. A rope snakes in the shoulder to mark where the body landed, a full one hundred feet from the collision – shaped, it seems, like a man in fetal sleep. 'His helmet,' writes the reporter, 'was found in a field adjacent to the road,' and then the police chief is quoted: 'It just popped right off his head.'

The reporter begins his article with an odd choice of diction; the accident happened, he writes, 'as enthusiasts took advantage of the sunny day to again try the warm-weather sport.' That 'enthusiasts' makes them seem rather like stamp collectors, but what prompted these men could not be touched by the term *enthusiasm*. 'Warm weather sport' sounds as if it could be badminton, or miniature golf, or as if this reporter wants to write brochures for Carnival Cruise Lines. And why the formulation 'to again try'? The 'again' just floats there, challenging you to comprehend its place in that clause. Again *after what?* you can't help asking. And that awkward 'try,' as if every ride before had been a failure, as if these men were attempting to climb K2. *To again try:* it rings ominous in my ear. It means every Sunday was a fatality in the making.

The dead man's name was Robert Chittenden. He had recently borrowed four thousand dollars from Pop, probably to buy the very motorcycle that killed him, and Pop would never see that money again. He refused to ask the widow. Pop is mentioned only once in the newspaper clip: 'William Giraldi, 49, of Manville was riding in a group with Chittenden and lost control of his motorcycle at the time of the fatal accident, resulting in minor injuries when he hit the ground.'

The clipping ends with this tally: 'Surviving are his wife, JoAnn Fritz Chittenden; a son, Robert L. and a daughter, Cheryl, all at home; his parents, Mr. and Mrs. Lloyd Chittenden of Bound Brook; a brother, Richard, of Green Brook; and a sister, Susan Chittenden, of Bridgewater.'

The most stinging phrase in that tally? *All at home.* They were four and then they were three.

Four o'clock on a Sunday afternoon, May 7, 2000, the end of the semester for me, the weather an enticement to life. My girlfriend, Anna, and I sat reading in my basement dorm room at Drew University, and when the phone rang I went to the narrow window to look down a slope of grass at the cul-de-sac lying there in the perfect day, the cul-de-sac where I'd snapped photos of my father and his motorcycle just one month earlier.

My godfather was on the line now. He is my father's first cousin, born the same year; each resided in half the memories of the other. His calls were not unusual, and so the sound of his voice did not pull an alarm in me. But it was Sunday and I knew what Sundays meant. On Sundays they rode. That fact slammed into me within another second or two of hearing his voice on the line. Sometimes the phone call in the night is a phone call in the afternoon.

I've been struggling to recall precisely what was said in those opening seconds. He must have said, 'Your father crashed,' or perhaps the more evasive 'There's been a crash.' I can, however, recall precisely *how* he spoke: haltingly – all those *uhh*s and *umm*s – as if he was sifting through a litany of possible sentences, not a one adequate to the task. The task of telling me, but also the task of assimilating this news himself. I stood immobile there at the window, the day wrathful in its beauty.

The body begins to know before the mind; the body has its own knowledge, its own manner of knowing, a subterranean method, a wisdom from the chasm opening inside you. Too often it's described as a numbing, but that isn't right. It's true that for several seconds the head seems both to lighten and thicken, the sinuses seem to congest, there's the slightest toning in the ears. But what happens then is actually the inverse of numbing. As the stomach starts its plunge, as the heart begins its roll, all the senses are tuned, boosted. Your body is giving birth, but to what you cannot say. What you perceive as a numbing is really a cannonade of feeling, a waylaying of emotion. The dread of what the body knows does not deaden the body.

I must have asked, 'Is he hurt?' or else 'How bad is he?' because the reply was this, five words that thump in me still: 'I think your father's gone.' My godfather's fiancée was there in the room with him, and she must have lashed him for that line, because his next was 'Well, we don't know that for sure.' But he knew that for sure. And now so did I.

He told me that my grandparents and his own parents were just then on their way home from the Pennsylvania hospital, and then he told me that I should come home as soon as I could. All the family was being called about the crash, he said, all converging at my grandparents' house in Manville, thirty minutes away. Anna and I left campus; I remember hearing how the seatbelts clicked. She drove as I sat looking at the flora out of focus at the edge of the interstate, trucks and sedans dashing madly around us, all that metal propelled by human will, tearing along like two-ton bullets. Her hand on mine but not a word in that car, not one word I can recover in my memory.

We will circle back to May 7, 2000, to how and where my father crashed, to the suicidal cult of speed and his blood on the road, but first you should have the following facts about his life, facts that will show how he came to mount that motorcycle, how his death was a collision of chance and choice.

He was Pop's firstborn, the third William Giraldi in a patriarchal order of Italian immigrants, born into a severe family system of honor and masculine codes. Pop, a self-taught builder enraptured by motorcycles, bought my father dirt bikes when he was a kid. He rode them through the woods along the river, popped wheelies down backstreets. When my father turned seventeen in 1969, Pop bought him his inaugural street bike, a BSA 650cc with a chrome gas tank. For a time, he seemed poised and willing to inherit both the skills of carpentry and the mantle of biker eros.

But that's not what initially happened. Instead, he left Manville for college, the first Giraldi ever to attain escape velocity, to break from the persuasive pulling of the family and the town. A champion wrestler in high school, he went to Central Connecticut College in New Britain to pursue his goal of becoming a gym teacher and wrestling coach – Connecticut was far enough for him to shake loose from Pop, close enough for him to get home fast if he had to. His goal of teaching Phys. Ed. was sufficiently physical, masculine enough, to be deemed worthy of the patriarch while maintaining its autonomy – it was not carpentry, not Pop's path. Just as bodybuilding was for me sufficiently separate from my father's orbit, perhaps that's how he himself found the incentive to ditch the family mold, to ditch Manville for college, precisely because Pop could not identify with that incentive, could not have cared any less for classroom pursuits. Pop's dearth of respect for education was the only push my father needed to attain it.

Almost simultaneously, at nineteen, he married his beloved, a Manville girl. He was a residence assistant with an apartment in a dormitory, the walls an onslaught of cerulean, and he lived in this apartment with my mother, who had moved from Manville to be with him there. At twenty-one, just a junior in college, he was a father already, a family man already, his life now altered by the pressures he'd welcomed into it. Pop had advised him against this, against beginning a family at such an age. Just forty years old when I was born, Pop's ego had a galactic problem with becoming a grandfather so soon; he once told me that. He'd said to my father, 'If you have a child now, you're on your own, don't ask me for a nickel.' The opening months of my life unfurled on that campus in Connecticut; I was doted on by endearing hippies who passed me beer cans and then clicked bad Polaroids. When my father returned to Manville with a degree, a bride, and a boy, he saw that the annual pittance earned by high school gym teachers was many thousands short of what he needed. He saw, as so many new parents see, that his dreams would need downgrading.

With the solicitudes of a man much older, with an uncommon sobriety and urge to responsibility, and with no hand, *not a nickel,* from Pop, my father didn't stay young very long. The dirt bikes he'd been riding since he was a boy, the street bikes he'd owned at seventeen and eighteen? They were gone now. He had a tiny one wailing at home and another en route. The pressures, I imagine, were onerous, and I mean also the pressures of living up to Pop's example. And yet I'm told this by those who were there: all he wanted was this family-loyal life with my mother and his kids. Unlike Pop, he hadn't persisted in the multiple risks of motorcycles, in spending either his crimped time or money on them, because he was too devoted.

In addition to the new fiscal demands, it was this sense of devotion – and perhaps a half-conscious fealty to Pop – that lured him away from teaching and coaching and into the family trade of hammers and nails. He and my uncle

Tony formed a company they named Giraldi Brothers, and the work was daily brutality because they began as roofers. If you're a builder, you know there's nothing worse than roofing: a battering heat in summer, the unholy cold of winter, the lugging of shingles up ladders, the always-there hazard of falling and snapping your neck, your spine.

He was plighted, then, to remain Manvillian. Whatever liberation he'd achieved at college in Connecticut hadn't lasted. He was duly pulled back into the proletarian vortex, the Jupiter-scale gravity of Pop's presence, Pop's own pursuits. He gave everything to his family, in this sense. And that made it all the more disastrous, all the more humiliating – imagine the humiliation in a culture such as his – when his wife, after twelve years and three kids, abandoned him and, to boot, snatched half his money in the divorce. He was forced to borrow $150,000 against our house, half his net worth, in order to pay her. When she vanished from our lives, he had the look of someone who'd just lost his hearing in a blast, someone trying and failing to read your lips.

Again, he chose the hard path of duty; he raised my siblings and me himself, with help from Parma and Pop, when he could get it. Consider the nobility of that, and then consider the emasculation of it: first of not being man enough to hold on to his wife, and then of being burdened with distaff, with what many Manvillians considered the feminizing chores of parenthood, the dishes and the laundry – after pounding nails all day long. A single father who didn't flinch at sacrifice, at relinquishing his own pleasures in order to do what needed doing, he spent the next decade trying to labor out of the squelching suck of debt. All through my childhood, I'd heard this refrain from him: 'There was no way I was letting her take my kids.' But that hadn't been a problem – she didn't want us.

Yeats: *Too long a sacrifice / Can make a stone of the heart,* but not of my father's. When those debts were finally paid, and when his kids were finally grown, this man of duty, now in his early forties, returned to pleasure, to the patriarchal passion championed by Pop. It's perhaps a handy bit of irony that this cradle Catholic, who for a decade was weighed down by the slowness of duty, sought spiritual release in the cult of speed. He hurled himself into this eros with the abandon of one long denied. This was the letting loose, the exultation, he'd never had, an adolescent excess at last able to have its expression. He'd put in his time, and so he deserved this release. He'd *earned* it.

The transference of erotic energies into road racing, the focus and frisson given by that motorcycle, a red-and-white rocket called the Yamaha R1, the fiercest superbike on earth, a deific machine, racetrack-ready, light and tight, absurdly fast, a masterpiece of engineering. But the traits that make it dominant on the racetrack make it deadly on the road. A regular person can buy the thing but it's simply not meant for a regular person, not meant for America's erratic roads. It's the assault rifle of superbikes, much more than is sane, a dispenser of death.

He kept it under a quilt in the garage and shined it with new socks, and when he and his pals went on riding trips, he'd wheel the bike inside the motel room with them. The motorcycle as paramour that would not jilt him. I have a photo of my father, lying sideways on a motel bedspread, his head propped up with one arm, looking at the motorcycle beside him, the seductive gleam of new rubber and metal. He'd modified the bike with grade-A components: stainless-steel brake lines, titanium exhaust, Battlax high-performance tires. In his black-and-red racing suit – an Italian work of art he'd had custom made – and his red boots and black helmet, he looked like a rapid flash from Dante's feral mind, a demonic cosmonaut craving the speeds of some other realm. And why would a man crave such speeds? Because the world, our world, much too fast for many, is much too slow for some.

All his life force got poured into racing. He refused to sleep with his fiancée the night before his Sunday ride because his fluids had to be reserved for the red-and-white mistress. Racing brought him alive, yes, but it also brought him nearer the grave. There were crashes in that Sunday cult, lots of them, and there were injuries and funerals – lots of those too. But part of the prevailing attitude riders possessed was this: *It's never going to happen to me. He's dead and I'm clear.* Until you're not.

The young father of my youth, in his twenties, committed and abstaining, famous for his competence, his reliable level-headedness, most alive when providing for his kids, versus the early-forties father, heedless and harebrained, a high-stakes gambler. I want to say that his death was unavoidable, decreed by watchful gods. Nobody or nothing could have saved my father. His family history, his bloodline, was a Siren he was powerless to ignore. The Yamaha R1 was the howl, the homecoming he needed, his death the ultimate articulation of that need. But in my most rational, regretful moments, I consider that perhaps his fatality was not inevitable, that I or others might have saved him had we only tried. It's just that the trying would have seemed such a transgression against the familial code, and such a betrayal of his joy.

II

On May 7, 2000, an hour after I got the call, Anna and I were the first to arrive at my grandparents' house in Manville, and we waited on the red-brick steps of the front porch. This quadrant of town had long ago been dubbed Lost Valley, pinched between the railroad tracks and the Raritan River, accessible only by a tunnel at the west end and a bridge at the east. Lost Valley would soon become more literally lost as the river, that unmanageable artery of mud, kept breaching its banks and wrecking homes. The government, repeatedly galled by spending billions in disaster relief, would swoop in, purchase the homes, and then bulldoze them away. My father's boyhood home would be among those lost, just a patch of sick-looking grass where his memories once lived.

As we waited, there was nothing to do but look, and to feel the weather – eighty degrees, sun-filled, no humidity, incongruous with disaster. My aunt's house sat to the left of us, my uncle's to the right, those concrete sidewalks exploded in spots by stretching roots. In my grandparents' long concrete driveway, the basketball hoop still hung from the garage. On those front and back lawns we neighborhood kids had held riotous wrestling matches in summer and autumn, a band of ruffians who strove for much bruising and the minor blood of others. When I think of my childhood, that barely observable cosmos rushing farther away from me each second, I think of that house, that street, that driveway, those sidewalks and lawns.

Roil the mind with news of this death and it will attempt some form of focus, a stay against the new anarchy booming through it. The focus is diversion. I studied the shifting, devolving light of day as five o'clock came, as late spring slid into early summer. I studied the cracks in the pebbled concrete walkway beneath my sneakers, multiple cracks veining off into the grass. Pop had poured that walkway when he built the house, by himself, fifty years earlier, in 1950, not long before he left to fight in Korea.

My father was born two years later, while Pop was still there fighting, a forward observer directing mortar fire at an incomprehensible foe. There's a sepia photo of the day he returned from the war, dressed in a khaki uniform, unrecognizably good-looking and fit, a photo shot right there where I now sat. This photo was his first time meeting my father, already a year old. It was this photo I remembered now while waiting for the certainty of his death. And it was this very spot, on Easter Sunday, just two weeks earlier, where I'd last seen him alive. He'd handed me fifty bucks that afternoon and we'd given one another the clownish hug Parma loved to see.

Soon my grandparents' sedan turned the corner onto Huff Avenue. Anna and I stood, stepped away from the porch, reached for one another's hand. I tried to peer inside the car as they pulled into the driveway, tried to gauge their faces through the reflected foliage. They came slowly from the car, Parma's face a picture of hurt, a handkerchief pressed to her mouth.

Pop looked stoic still but walked somewhat unevenly, as if testing the earth before letting his full weight down, and when he reached me there on the walkway, he said four words: 'You lost your dad.' My father was forty-seven years old. I was twenty-five. Pop was sixty-seven, recovering from a double-knee replacement or else he'd have been on the ride that day. He embraced me in that tense, back-clapping mode familiar to men everywhere, and I brought my right hand to my eyes as if to shield them from a punishing sun, but the sun had begun its drop behind roofs an hour ago. And I noticed again the cracks in the concrete beneath my sneakers.

I cannot say if I'd thought of my brother or sister since getting my godfather's phone call two hours earlier, and I cannot say if I thought of them then, after learning for sure that our father was dead. It seems right that I should have thought of them: my brother, Mike, four years younger than me, eighteen hundred miles away in Boulder, Colorado, and my sister, Alisyn, two years younger, in Manville still. It seems right, but I cannot recall the thoughts, nor the probably lawless emotions to which they were attached, nor when I first saw my sister that day, or if I'd even seen her at all. We three have never been overly involved in each other's life; after childhood, our trajectories were too disparate, our interests too incompatible. But I must have thought of my siblings then in our grandparents' driveway. I want to believe that I thought of them.

There's much I can't recall. It's been sixteen years and the memory has its own wayward agency, its own mysterious volition, citadels in one spot, lacunas in another. When something momentous hits you, you are not always conscious of needing or wanting to seal certain details inside the vault of your mind. You are not predicting that sixteen years hence, you will wish to resurrect those details. You have faith – it *feels* like faith – that the memory will clasp onto what is vital, what is necessary to remember. But that faith, like all faith, is too often a letdown.

When I embraced Parma in the driveway that evening, she had four words of her own to say: 'This is so bad.' Her understated potency has stayed with me all these years. I could not tell her Tennyson's line, *Though much is taken, much abides,* because that line did not appear to me just then, and if it had, I would not have bought it. Nor would she have. This was the woman who, every afternoon for years, in every kind of weather, would carry a lawn chair to the cemetery and sit at her son's grave, in reverie and private requiem, as if she could make him remember her, as if he could know she was there.

Her faith, I could see from the outset, would only be strengthened by this blight. Pop, on the other hand: he'd never had any use for the divine and its dictates, and now he'd have even less. His indifference would turn to muffled scorn. That's how it works: a personal storm of this sort rends you one way or rends you the other but seldom leaves you right where you were.

* * *

Neighbors and family began appearing only moments after my grandparents returned from the Pennsylvania hospital. In a small town, news of death is fleet of foot, forever in a rush, much quicker than news of birth. Soon the driveway was alive with people in summer's colors, all those yellows and light blues, people I hadn't seen in months or years.

The phone would not stop; information trickled in with each call. The six other men with whom my father had been riding that day gave us what they thought were the basic facts. My father was thrown from his bike in a right turn on a remote country road, hitting a guardrail headfirst, though no one had seen the crash. He'd been at the rear of the pack, taking it easy that day; there was something wrong with his front brake, he'd said; it didn't feel right. He'd never been on that road before, didn't know the turn was there. The others found him beneath the guardrail, in a pond of blood leaking from his cracked helmet. I can't remember all of Pop's sentences from that day, but I remember this one: 'It's hard to crack a helmet.'

My father's younger brother, Nicky, himself an expert rider, walked me around the block and attempted to explain how the crash might have happened, how my father might have been calculating that turn as it ambushed him. Speed was the factor I'd return to again and again. What else but speed? Already I was accepting the rash of clichés as they came, the unexamined inklings as I maneuvered through the electricity of this new truth. Circling the block, I told Nicky that I anticipated being 'haunted' by my father's crash. I might have congratulated myself for not resorting to the most common formulation of all: *This feels like a nightmare.* In truth, it never did. What was so regrettable for me – what I was beginning to digest, even during those initial jolts, in those early hours of knowing – was that my father's death didn't feel nightmarish at all. It felt outright expected. Of course he'd kill himself on that machine. Of course he would.

Both of my father's brothers had inherited the motorcycle lust from Pop. Both had decades of riding experience, up-close knowledge of racing those machines on meandrous back roads, but both had been sensible enough to stop. They had young children and nervous wives. But my father's three children were already grown, and so perhaps he felt a less pointed responsibility to keep alive. Perhaps the risk of speed, perhaps all risk and recklessness, comes more easily to those who have finished the hard work of raising their kids. If that's what he might have thought, that my siblings and I needed him much less now that we were grown – my brother just twenty-one, my sister twenty-three – he was very wrong. His likeliest thought, though? No thought at all. Because it's always the other guy who dies. *He's dead and I'm clear.*

He'd been only a few months away from a marriage that promised a middle-aged fulfillment his youthful twelve years with my mother could not deliver. He and his fiancée had been about to move from their closed-in condominium to a sizable home backed against acres of woodland. I'd recently gone with him to tour the house, to hear his plans for mild renovation, where his workshop would go, where his bike would sleep, and I was gratified to see, to feel, his contentment – it felt forty-seven years in the making.

If I'd once thought of my body as a machine for living,

the motorcycle is a living machine. Parma detested the bikes. Pop had always taken several trips a year, week-long trips to motorcycle races and rallies, to Laconia, New Hampshire, and to Daytona, Florida. Each time he prepared to leave, Parma's rancor would rise, and we'd all sidestep her conniptions over being abandoned again, over the non-paranoid possibility that the next time she saw Pop he'd have coins on his eyes. Emergency-room personnel have a special argot for motorcycles; they call them *donor*cycles. If you need an organ, bet on that hearty young ignoramus winging down the highway at 105, twenty years old and strong, in flawless health except for his newly destroyed neck and skull.

The best pro racers in the world, the MotoGP maestros who top two hundred miles per hour on the straightaway – Valentino Rossi and Jorge Lorenzo and their intrepid brethren – those men won't ride on the road. Combining a maximum of sense with a prudent dose of dread, they know that to ride on the road is to shorten their lives. On a racetrack, there's nothing to hit. There are gravel-trap runoffs at the turns you're likely to miscalculate – they know where you're going to crash: it's always in a turn – and even if you lose it at two hundred, you slide for a while before tumbling into the grassy infield. The armored suit, with its padded humps along the back, saves you from a snapped neck and spine. But on the road? Trees, guardrails, telephone poles, streetlamps, mailboxes, trucks and cars intent upon grinding a rider into tinfoil. There's no escaping them.

Statistics tell a story. Death by motorcycle is nearly thirty times higher than death by car. Helmets are only 37 per cent effective in preventing death. In 2000, the year my father was killed, close to three thousand other American riders were also felled. Most motorcycle fatalities happen from May to August for the very reason you suspect: the weather is pleasant. My father crashed on the seventh of May. The time of day when most crashes occur? Between the hours of 3 p.m. and 6 p.m. For those who began riding in the morning, the late-afternoon crashes are due to fatigue but also to overconfidence. The longer you go without crashing, the more actively you believe you won't. A simple but deceptive equation. My father hit the guardrail at 3:06 p.m. More than 30 per cent of all motorcycle fatalities result from speeding – of course they do. The species of my father's bike (known technically as a 'super sports' bike or 'superbike' or 'sport bike,' rather less technically as a 'crotch rocket' or 'Jap bike') is four times likelier to kill a man than a soberer species of bike, a cruiser or touring cycle. You've no doubt seen those jolly, hirsute fellas in helmet headsets, grinning wives at their backs, a youthful Billy Joel crooning from a cranked-up radio about an uptown girl. Pop called those riders 'jackasses.'

I don't know what my father had elected to do with his organs, and I'm ashamed now that I was too stomped by sorrow to ask, or even to think of asking. My grandparents are not the breed of people to whom you can speak about such things. And certainly not when they'd just beheld their son lying dead on a steel table. A flesh-obsessed Catholic in her every cell, Parma no doubt believed that my father required his organs on those auspicious avenues of the afterlife, that his kidneys and liver would be welcome when a tarrying Christ finally came back to call up the dead. I've no notion how she squared this belief with what happens on an embalming table, the formaldehyde, the glutaraldehyde, the ethanol and humectants, the sewn-shut eyelids and lips.

In the kitchen, Pop was trying to land my brother on the phone in Colorado. Mike has never been easy to call or hear from. In 1996 he went out west to snowboard for a weekend and never came back. For weeks at a clip he's ungettable by phone or by email, hiking some hill, canoeing some ravine, camping in some off-the-map Edenic wild, backpacking through boonies, rock climbing, mountain biking, communing with bearded and tattooed others who puff enough weed to tranquilize a pachyderm. Our home state had never been a proper fit for him. He's long-haired with a hieroglyphic fresco inked onto his entire left arm, and he tends to favor women who are named after seasons. Jersey is short on those.

I haven't shaken loose this characteristically terse message Pop left on his voicemail that day, the last of the evening's light about to die: 'Mike, it's Pop. We've got a problem here. Call us back.' *We've got a problem here.* Fourteen years earlier, I'd spoken identical words to my father when I called him from the gas station, after I fed diesel fuel to a gasoline engine: 'I've got a problem here.' The problem upon me at the gas station was, by contrast, welcoming in its possibility of remedy, while the problem we all had on May 7, 2000 stood solid in its unfixability. A problem suggests the possibility of a solution, the chance of correction. What was the antidote to my father's fatal crash? How to fix *that* large thing? Death is not our problem, is not an algebraic equation to be overcome. It won't be solved. We make an adversary of a fate and then feel swindled when the adversary wins. Larkin: *Most things may never happen: this one will.*

My brother called back much sooner than we'd expected, and before Pop could speak, I jerked up from the kitchen table and told him to hand me the phone. 'Here,' he said to Mike, 'your brother wants to talk to you.' I hadn't planned on that, was not sure from what place that impulse had arisen, or what it meant that I wanted to be the one who delivered him this news. I was not aware of feeling a newfound parental obligation; he was an able adult who lived seven states away, and we'd never been very brotherly to begin with.

I said his name, I heard the opening notes of his panic, the quavering in his words: he knew. In his very marrow, he already knew. That's when my sobs began gradually to gyrate and then to spiral up from the well of me. For the last several hours I'd been somehow inoculated against tears, not prepped, unready for the fearsome work of real sobbing. As I stalled there on the phone with my brother, gauging the tremors as they moved along my fault lines, he wailed at me to tell him, to get on with this filthy chore. I spoke this wedding of words that would repeatedly spear me for the next several months, a linguistic pairing forty years premature, the most terrible sentence I've ever spoken: 'Daddy's dead.'

I suppose I'd had other options – 'Dad has crashed' or 'Dad's been killed' – but it was 'Daddy's dead' that came unthinkingly from my throat. The child's plea in *Daddy,* the decisive thud of *dead.* Even then, I see, in that stricken state, euphemizing was not possible, the placid dishonesty of *passed away,* the insulting gibberish of *a better place.* A loved one's place is with his loved ones; there is no better place than that. To miss a loved one without interruption is a special kind of torture, and talk of that supposedly better place does nothing to mitigate it.

In the coming days, many would mumble to me about that better place, about how sorry they were for the *passing*. It would be impossible to scorn them for such knee-jerk condolence, for relying on those euphemisms. Death makes people babble, makes them blunder. They don't know what to do with the thing, how to think and speak of it. Nor did I – I least of all – as I groped after answers that stood stalwart in their silence. And yet people do mean what they say at a funeral, are never surer in their intentions with language. It bothered them, I saw, when I refused to say *passed away,* when I insisted upon *killed* and *dead,* when I did not shrink from the unadorned truth of it. *Your father's gone.* Yes he was. Yes he is.

In the hours and days, weeks and months following his death, I developed a distracting fixation on word choice, as if the precision of language could summon understanding or deliver an atom of acceptance. It was a detour of obsessiveness over which I had no control. Whatever else it is, grief is a succession of byways. If words are instruments of revelation, my confusion and grief must have glommed onto them in an effort to be enlightened and ameliorated. Gather the right words, use them to fill in the many new frets of the spirit and heart, and maybe you'll give yourself a chance at healing. Our grief-eaten obsessions are never pointless trivia or pathologies; they are enactments of understanding, deep forms of meaning.

There on the phone with my brother, after I uttered

'Daddy's dead,' the emotional contractions of this labor that began several hours earlier at last ended in birth, a prolonged burst. Solar-plexus sobs that harnessed the body whole, vacuumed all the air from the room. It left me there panting on my knees. Then I was pacing between the living room and dining room with the cordless at my mouth; the telephone delivery of such news demands pacing, as if you can walk off the cramp of it. I tried to breathe through this eruption, this hefty tension in the head. I couldn't hear what my brother was asking or exclaiming, but I could tell that he was taking in the magnitude of *the problem,* this unmendable mistake.

Someone took the phone from me then, Pop or an uncle or cousin, and I reeled down the hallway into a vacant bedroom where I lay on the mattress and shook there, gnarled inward, convulsing with these sobs. My godfather hurried in after me, held me there on the bed, in the day's new dark. He'd always been the male member of my family least infected with machismo, and I've never forgotten his tenderness that night, his selfless lack of regard for the masculine protocol, so prevalent in our parts, that calls for a man never to spoon another man on a bed, no matter the sorrow.

After those sobs I felt unaccountably animated – I remember standing in the kitchen, trying to rally my family with motivating inquiries: 'Okay, everyone, what are we gonna do about this now? What's the next step here? What's the plan?' – but in a few hours I'd be back on a bed, in my dorm room at school, my quaking frame in Anna's hold, our faces pressed together. Sleep that night was the negation of rest, a wakeful, dreamless sleep in which I stayed conscious of my father's crash, and when we sat up at dawn, half the pillow was damp.

Because no one saw my father crash into that guardrail, no one knew what happened. But everyone knew this: the pack was a minute in front of him, pushing hard down that snaked Pennsylvania back road. They'd planned to wait for him at an intersection. And because he was unfamiliar with the road, another rider would then point him in the direction of the highway so he could return home. The place he hit was a ninety-degree right turn, 120 feet over a crest.

The morning after the crash, Anna and I drove to my uncle Tony's house, and we found him bent over the kitchen sink, his back to us, tears dripping into a cereal bowl. He couldn't turn around. My father's helmet sat looking at me from the counter, a crack in the lower left side – not a surface or hairline crack but a saw-toothed fissure, cracked clear through – and a dent just above it. Tony had taken it from the hospital and rinsed half a gallon of blood out of it. Soon he told me this, from his own experience on rides like that:

'Your father was on a road he didn't know, and he was trying to take it easy while the other guys were hauling ass ahead of him. He was afraid he'd get lost, wouldn't be able to find his way back to whatever highway he needed. It happens all the time. You get lost on those back roads, you're screwed. So he sped up to try to catch them. There was that crown in the road, and the sharp right turn just beyond it. He had what's called a high-side. As soon as he saw the turn, he locked up the back brake, which you never do unless you're going a hundred miles per hour and need to stop fast. Most of your brake work is done with the front brake.

'As the back brake locks, the bike doesn't want to stay up, it wants to go over, in whatever direction you're turning. When your dad felt the bike slipping under him to the right, he tried to save it. He didn't want to low-side – he was thinking about the bike. And when he straightened up to the left, the back tire stepped out, it caught on the road and flung him like a slingshot over the bike, into the guardrail. This all happened in two, two and a half seconds. If he had let the bike slide from under him, without trying to straighten up and save it, he would have gone feet-first into the side of the road and got up and walked away, I think, no problem. Maybe a broken foot or leg, but otherwise, no problem.'

Let the bike go and walk away, no problem. But he couldn't. He'd let *us* go, let all of life go, but not the bike.

III

If someone had asked me to help with my father's funeral, I would have said to bury him in his carpenter's clothes: the brown Carhartt hoodie, a torn T-shirt that still held his sweat, those beige and beaten work boots, the Lee dungarees scabbed with caulk and stained with paint. I would have said to place him in a plain pine box Pop and my uncles had built with their own hands, with my father's own tools, not the high-end mahogany casket, a capsule designed to keep out the moisture and the air, as if either now could do him any harm or good. I would have vetoed the mortician's art, the embalming, the sewing of his eyelids and lips, and that tiny smile, that vestige of a grin, they fashioned to his face for us.

They want to honor the dead, I know. They want to clean the tremendous mess. They do the noble work of giving the family what it needs most now: a last look that isn't violated by the vicious fact of the body's breakability, its fragile pumps and vessels. My family needed to see my father done up like a life-size doll, in just-bought clothes he did not buy, a hasty three-piece he'd have loathed. They needed, as so many need, not to confront the scowling fate of our flesh.

At the casket before the mourners arrived, my family formed a crescent wall of moans, a team's half huddle of grief, trying to prop each other up, literally hold ourselves together, gaping at my father and that clownish grin now stitched upon his face. This was the first most of us were seeing of him since he'd crashed into that Pennsylvania guardrail. My grandparents, my father's fiancée, and my uncle Tony had gone to the hospital three days earlier to identify his body. Sometime that week, I'd ask my father's fiancée how he'd looked when she saw him on the steel table. It was important to me to know how he'd looked. She'd seen the blood dried brown in his nostrils and ears, she said, and from her position slightly beneath him – she'd crashed to her knees beside the table – she'd seen his slitted eyes clouded and specked with blood, his pupils in permanent expanse, as if wanting to let in the light they no longer needed.

Now the rouge on his face looked perverse even though the mortician, in her overwrought voice – the voice she'd been taught to use, a sympathetic grating I felt along the notches of my spine – had told us before entering that 'he looks great.' For a corpse, she must have meant. Auden: *We are not prepared / For silence so sudden and so soon.* I leaned over the casket to touch his face and found that the texture of his skin was about what I'd expected: plastic or latex, an alabaster Halloween mask, not cold but cool. His fingers, too, had been sewn together. So much sewing, yet nothing mended. So much shutting, yet nothing closed. The foul breath of lilies, roses, mums kept pushing through the room's dormant air.

One of the many oppressive realities just then? In about twenty minutes I would be embraced by a score of friends from my past, a phalanx of well-wishers who'd come to offer their on-the-spot obsequies and homages, to show me kindness, yes, but in showing that kindness they'd no doubt have questions too:

Where've you been, Billy Boy?

What've you been up to since you left town?

Someone said you went to college. What's that all about? I don't remember you being too good at school. By which they would mean *When'd you become too good for us?*

Most of my boyhood friends were an odd fit for me. One pal was a muscle-car fanatic who'd somehow got hold of a half-complete 1969 Dodge Charger. The car sat for several years in his parents' one-bay garage, the hood always open, like a mouth with punched-out teeth, and I remember thinking what a terrific waste of a garage it was. At fifteen, another pal, with the aid of his mechanic dad, began revamping an ordinary VW bug into a turquoise show car. I was there the night its sheath was sprayed onto it, and the paint fumes nearly felled me. They and others were experts with wrenches; if it had gears or used gasoline, they knew how it worked, could break it down and reassemble it too, turn a lawnmower into a go-kart. I had trouble telling a flathead screwdriver from a chisel.

When it was time, a line formed from the casket, twisted through the panel-ceilinged room, filed through the double doors, down the glossy hall, out the front entrance, around the building, and into the parking lot, which wasn't wide enough to fit all the Chevys and Fords. I'd been hearing my whole life how beloved my father was in Manville, but this was the first time I'd ever truly seen it, truly felt it as a fact.

Mourners wanted to show my siblings and me what type of man our father was, strangers and once-a-year relatives who suddenly appeared, who knelt before us, trotting out vignettes in which our father had starring roles. He'd built one couple's lovable house twenty-five years ago, and it stands as unbendable now as it did then. When he'd been wrestling coach at Manville High School, he purchased the right kind of sneakers for one woman's penniless boy. He gave sandwiches and back pats to the town hobo, a toothless wobble, some smear of a man everyone else derided or shunned. A dozen other stories just like that.

After a while I could still see their lips moving but could not discern the words, only noises I knew were trying to become narratives. I nudged away a woman I'd never seen before, someone trying to assault my sister with memories she did not share, a tale about our father that involved, I think, a Dalmatian. That's what we do with the dead: we turn them into tales. How else can they help us now? How else to make them stay?

Earlier that day, my brother and I asked Pop if we could display a poster-size photo of my father and his bike, and that photo was the first thing you saw at the wake: my father grinning behind the machine that killed him. We wanted it there without fully comprehending why; we probably would have told you that he loved the thing, and we loved him, so there it was, an effort to honor his unstanchable passion.

But I suspect now that we were trying to remain faithful to our family's legacy of motorcycle eros, to those particular codes of esteem, to the cult of speed to which our father and uncles and Pop belonged, as if this cult were his singular source of definition. Why not photos of him as the devoted father and son, photos that vaunted his talent for friendship and carpentry? That lone photo must have been a dare, an act of macho provocation – *I dare you to say something about its tastelessness* – and perhaps I was waiting to see someone jump at the sight of it. This was the bike as crucifix, as True Cross, so fitting for a clan of Catholics. The instrument of death became the object of veneration.

The photo also must have been a form of self-protection, a way of burying the disruptive suspicion that our father died a fool's death, a pointless death, that he wasn't cut out for speed, and that he wasn't just chasing down an unhaveable dream but trying and failing to outfly a flock of demons. And so we needed that defiance, needed to boast of that machine, despite its being the reason we'd all been undone, all been collected in that room. To boast as if not to feel the shame of the waste, the wreckage wrought by such speed.

I sat slumped near the casket in a stupor that felt like the first work of sleep, near that nauseating smack of flowers, an obscene swelling of them. Flowers in a field let you breathe their beauty; flowers at a funeral punch at your lungs. Anna and my immediate family sat beside me, behind me, the oxygen in that room altering me in a way I could not then apprehend. It had something to do with physics, I was sure. But physics was a mystery to me. It shouldn't have been, I knew, because the physics was simple enough for any high-schooler to grasp: velocity, vector sum, acceleration, trajectory. *An object in motion stays in motion unless...* Unless it hits a guardrail, and then makes a void of your life.

Soon came the procession of carpenters and plumbers, roofers and masons, excavators and mechanics, electricians and general contractors with whom my father had worked for twenty-five years, men whose days were spent in begrimed boots and jeans, in T-shirts bearing their names and trades, all of whom looked awkward now, their faces tweaked by grief, hastily groomed and handicapped in decennial suits.

The most colorful in the procession went by, Woody, five feet tall with a mustard ponytail and chaotic goatee ('My lady likes a little tickle when I'm down for a visit'). A gearhead and backhoer whose business card read THE DITCHIN' MAGICIAN, he was a natural, enthralling storyteller – interstate car chases, dirt-bike crashes, sexual circus acts, wheelies in his pickup truck – who instantly improved the weather of whatever room he walked into. When Woody approached my father's casket, he performed as expected: hands somberly folded at his belt, head bowed in silent benediction. But when he turned to go, he put out both arms, as if they were gripping handlebars, and he cranked his right fist, his throttle hand, in a pantomime of acceleration, his mouth moving in what I knew was the sound a superbike makes. It was the energy we needed, that three-second respite from the funereal, an expression of *Hell yeah, live fast,* of *Gun it down the back roads of heaven* – of the Manvillian ethos to which I was trying to remain loyal with that lone photo of my father and his bike.

After the wake that night, my cousin said to me, 'You see Woody at the coffin?'

'Yeah,' I said.

'He's goddamn beautiful, ain't he?'

'He sure is,' I said, and we both grinned for the first time in four days.

I remembered that Parma had once told me as a teenager that she had never, in all her years of being married to him, seen Pop weep. A fabled tough guy who roostered through whatever room he was in, Pop had always seemed to us above the effects of common affliction. But now his giant frame quaked with sobs when we left him alone at the casket, and I could guess at the chief thought twisting in him: that this mess was his fault. He'd passed the motorcycle eros to my father. He'd taught him to ride. He'd been the only one with the influence to curb that passion, to convince him that the peril outdid the pleasure. But he never did. He never even tried. Because he didn't believe that any peril ever outdid its pleasure. And because he knew he didn't have that right.

Or maybe he preferred to cross his fingers and hope that my father might escape as he himself had escaped, hobbling away from a dozen motorcycle crashes, bruised, fractured, bleeding badly but conscious still, whole enough to heal, to ride again another Sunday. Never mind the yearly, sometimes monthly funerals of friends that Pop had attended, all those riding buddies who'd been flattened, broken beside him on the road. They were the unblessed. His mantra could have been *Some guys are lucky, some ain't*. Because funerals are for other people, never for you or your own.

If Pop could not, would not, do it, and if no one else could or would – not Parma, not my siblings, not his friends or fiancée – why didn't *I* try to convince my father that mounting that motorcycle each Sunday was probable suicide? Look at the statistics, see the chances of dying on a superbike; they aren't in your favor. I didn't try to convince him because I didn't know how they rode each week, the risks they took, how they pushed. No one had ever told me that each Sunday was a suicidal race against the road, against the others, against each rider himself. But how could I have been so willfully unaware? Those bikes are birthed for racing. They don't know how to do, how to be, anything else.

He'd stopped riding by the time I was born, and I'd been out of the house for two years already when he began riding again. In those five years before his death, I'd lived in three different states and was doing what some do in their late teens and early twenties: the fashioning of a selfhood far from the tug of family, from its corrosive influences on independence. And so I seldom had an accurate notion of the scenes and vicissitudes of my father's life. We exchanged letters and phone calls, and we emailed in the months before his death, when he at last stepped into cyberspace.

We saw one another several times a year, and I knew when he upgraded from the Honda CBR900 to the Yamaha R1, and I knew why. In the mid-1990s, the CBR had an aggressive, bent-over riding position, the foot pegs high and back, the handlebars low, lots of weight on the wrists, and it had a high-revving engine too, what my father's set called a 'busy motor.' The R1 had a larger engine and faster top speed, but it was also more comfortable to ride, and that's why my father switched bikes. I knew about his racing regalia too, the custom-made suit, the helmet and boots. I just couldn't have guessed at the intensity and seriousness he harbored, the degree to which he needed that velocity, needed to soar after decades of rectitude and responsibility. I just didn't think to guess. My own living seemed so paramount.

And if I *had* known about his road racing, the Sunday madness in which they all often came within a centimeter or second of oblivion? 'By the displacement of an atom,' said Wilde, 'a world may be shaken.' Just try to take away someone's fervor, try to dilute it. It can't be done. When what you crave is what you require, you *will* have it. And if by some hocus-pocus I had succeeded in taking that fervor from him, what then would that have made me? It would have made me a Promethean thief. Some fires can't be extinguished or exchanged.

I spoke at the funeral, spoke drivel beneath a slapping May sun, its light trying to sting my vision, light that did not illuminate but wanted to obscure the day and everything in it. 'Dismantle the sun,' Auden wrote – dismantle the son – and I thought, *Yes, dismantle this damn thing.* I can't recall ever being so bothered by a midday sun, the sizzling azure plate above. Here's how my heat-stroked mind was tacking in those moments:

We are sustained by explosions on the sun, its interior concussing of hydrogen and helium, such eruptive exhaling. The first sliver of a tick, when the pinhole universe became a grape, became a grapefruit, became a galaxy. In billions of decades, the scientists tell us, the sun will bloat in its dying, will ingest the earth. All the nothing out there that doesn't know our name. Space is curved and curving more, with no cure for us here, wide-eyed and inaudible. We never had a chance. Auden: *The day is too hot, too bright, too still, / Too ever, the dead remains too nothing.*

I don't know who nominated me to speak but I know I didn't nominate myself. Perhaps there was no nomination at all. I was the eldest son, so maybe it was assumed, all around, that this is what the eldest son must stand and do on a day such as this. I was, I *am*, the fourth William Giraldi, part of a familial structure whose grooves were worn long before my birth, and I was not exempt from certain expectations, certain rules of comportment. In my own conception of my placement in this family, I was a kind of low-level pariah, the only Giraldi male who hadn't gone into construction, who hadn't sworn a permanent oath to the primal ticking of the masculine. I'd made literature into my lodestar, and I always felt that in the eyes of my family there was something daintily suspect, something unmanning, about that choice, even though it was never in the strictest sense a choice. I didn't choose literature any more than I chose my lineage. Literature, rather, chose me. We don't always know what we're born into, and it can be either a blessing or a blow to find out. And what I've found out in the years since my father's death is this: haltingly manful though I may be, I am nevertheless the one my family goes to when something significant needs public saying.

For whatever reason, I can't remember the ceremony at the church, can't see in my mind the casket at the altar, can't hear the priest and his homily, the holy sentences he would have said. I have no reason to have wanted to bar this from my memory, but barred it is. The graveside scene I remember well, in part because this cemetery had been a daily sight in our lives. It lay between our house and my grandparents' house, and each day we'd driven past its gated green sprawl. People rarely visited this cemetery, but still it was tediously groomed, a placid last stop along the railroad tracks, beside the small regional airport. You could hear and see the red, the yellow, the blue prop planes descending just over the oaks and spruces at the rear.

As a depressed teen – after sunk friendships, after family quarrels, after breakups – I'd walk here with a pen and notebook and sit on some stranger's grave to vomit doggerel I wanted somebody to discover after my suicide. The child isn't certain of literature's personal utility; he understands storytelling but not storytelling's repeatable application to his own living. The adolescent, romantic though he is, begins to see, to intuit, how the right sentence or stanza, how the elevation of language, connects to his too-frequent upheavals, how it can offer the promise of rescue. My teenage melancholy buttressed my investment in literature; it was then, during those years of puzzling and private anguish, that I fully understood what my life would become, how my vista on the world would form itself.

And now – I was back at this cemetery much too soon. When Freud wrote that the death of the father is the most defining moment of any man's life, he must have meant that the son becomes the father if he wishes to keep the father's essence alive. He must annex the father's selfhood and spirit. I was agonizingly aware of that at my father's funeral: the immensity of it, a central largeness that made my mind buzz, made my senses dulled under such an insistent sun.

It's sweet to think you suffer as a unit, withstand the

barrage as a family, but each suffers, each tries to withstand that barrage, entirely on his own. Pain doesn't transfer; it insists on *you,* wants only you. What are those annealing properties of pain we hear so much about? We've turned Nietzsche's macho lie — *that which does not kill you makes you stronger* — into a T-shirt mantra for suburban moms and the many disciples of self-help. The truth is that there are plenty of forces in the world that diminish you in the process of not killing you. A human soul is not a bone; it will not necessarily become reinforced at the broken places. Pain does not put up with bright alterations to its meaning: it is not *a lesson,* not *a learning experience,* is never *useful.* Randall Jarrell: *Pain comes from the darkness / And we call it wisdom. It is pain.*

My family's silhouettes sat beneath a tent to my right, the sun throbbing behind them as I squinted, trying to make out their faces. Sweat-damp, I twisted in those miserable clothes, a cousin's navy three-piece, too baggy through the crotch, too cramped at the shoulders. Then I blathered graveside, telling a hundred mourners or more that this grief felt like arson, like acid crashing through my arteries. I said that no one had had the right to ask my father to stop riding that Yamaha, and that if he had stopped in order to mollify our concern, it would have been a death of another kind. To keep a man from his passion, to withhold from him the daring he needs, the ebullient, engrained desire that wakes with him each morning — *that* is death. We should all be so fearless, I said.

Then I told them that this day, May 11, was my twenty-sixth birthday, and to bury your father on the day of your birth is to become truly born. And I'm certain that when those last words left my mouth I didn't fully know what I meant by them. Only later did I understand how Freud's declaration lent them a sliver of meaning: I would have to become my father. In his absence, I would become him. Which meant, I thought, racing motorcycles – for several hours that seemed a very real possibility for me – and also impregnating Anna just as soon as I could manage it, having a child of my own in order to replicate my father, and in that way, keep him alive.

It was nonsense, of course, every inch of it. The next week, Nicky would tell me that a longtime friend of my father, a fellow carpenter, after hearing my spontaneous eulogy that day, said of me, 'He's a man. To stand there, to say those things. He's a man.' More nonsense, though, however pleased I was to hear it then. Later, I'd feel somewhat ashamed of this eulogy, the muttering of the expected bromides, just as I'd feel uncertain about our decision to display that lionizing photo at the wake. I'd acquiesced to my family's masculine code that day, done what the code demanded.

I'd internalized that code, after all, even though I'd been in violation of it my entire life, taking my father's own escape impulses much further, breaching the Manville version of manhood: with graduate school, with literature, with the eschewing of construction and motorcycles, with an awareness and deliberate expression of the code's frailty. Perhaps this made it all the more necessary for me to *man up* in these public ways, and at a time when the code was at its frailest. This meant muffling that internal scorn (*of course he'd be killed on that goddamn thing*) and conforming to the day's procedure, choosing allegiance over disruption. In my most self-disparaging moments, this felt to me like weakness and complicity. But I don't know that I had it in me to behave in any other way.

Still – someone else should have spoken that day, someone less conscious of the pathetic inadequacy of language when confronted with calamity, of how the mind and heart just hang there in a charcoal cloud. Someone less apt to exploit the romantic pitch and pull of cemeteries.

I was no less conflicted when, the day after the eulogy, my grandparents asked me, in a query that was also a mandate, to compose the epitaph for my father's headstone. I had thirty-six hours to come up with lines to last the ages. This was no assignment I wanted, the deadline about three decades too soon. My family, I knew, expected lines that sounded the way they imagined poetry to sound: 'Write something pretty,' Parma had told me. My preference for my father's headstone – a stanza by Herbert or Donne, by Father Hopkins or Auden – was so far out of the question as to make me seem ravingly garish for thinking it a preference at all.

How could I have been okay inscribing my father's headstone with lines that he himself would not have recognized or lauded or found remotely consoling? What is our duty to the dead when the dead don't care for duty? My answer is that the lines would not have been for him; they would have been for us. The dead don't need poems. In the end, it was that *us* which elbowed me into nixing the possibility of lines from Father Hopkins, because the *us* really meant my grandparents. They were the ones who'd be squinting at the lines each week, in whatever weather the season saw fit to give them. Their daily pilgrimage to the cemetery would last long after the rest of us had returned to our willed versions of normality.

I have a hard time understanding what I meant by the lines I wrote, and rather an easy time being embarrassed by them. I was conscious of having to maintain an obedience to the uncomplaining stoicism of my family, its strictures of manliness and daring. For the sake of my grandmother, I had to gesture toward the afterlife, at the inevitability of reunion with my father; what was illusory for me was essential for her. I also wanted to hit the right sentiment without swerving into bathos, to be able to live with whatever words I chose, not to sacrifice too much of my own selfhood in the completion of this task. This wasn't mere difficulty; it was futility. So the epitaph turned out to be my elegy in miniature, the propaganda everybody needed, declamations of his strength and his love, of riding hard and building well, and of our becoming him in his absence, which makes sense only so far. Truly becoming him would have meant a Yamaha R1, meant killing ourselves at a hundred miles per hour.

IV

While we're alive we live forever. Those aren't wheels; those are wings. High-performance machines raced to the brink of divinity. But cross that brink and you are not divine – you are dead. Even gods can be killed. Get killed in an instant and you're deprived of a final accounting. *He never knew what hit him.*

Imagine being too young and finding yourself about to die, conscious of dying by some ill fate, some wrong judgment – consider how downright mistaken it would seem. Your mind would speed before it slowed, would hop from yesterday to tomorrow before settling on the now, on the disappointment, the dread. And when it settled, you'd no doubt consider that negotiations were in order, a moment of diplomacy, some stab at deal-making to annul this error upon you. My father might have had that moment. Most likely he did not, not with his three injuries. That's what I learned after the funeral: he'd suffered three injuries, each of which was fatal – a broken neck, a crushed throat, and severe brain trauma. And maybe, in moments, I'm glad for that, for the quick obliteration, because negotiations with the Reaper never work.

Absence takes up space, has mass, moves from room to room. In its decisiveness, it seeks you. Someone ought to coin a term for that days-long stage between the buzzing of shock and the boredom of grief. Grief is much heavier, much stickier, than whatever precedes it.

Tiring and tiresome, grief will gain complete occupancy of you. On other days it felt as if a silent tearing had occurred at the hub of me, a ripping that sent vibrations out across my body, currents running just beneath the skin. After the initial jolt subsides, what you feel is closer to fear than grief. Lewis: *No one ever told me that grief felt so like fear.* You are a tangle of regret for what's left undone, and of remorse for what's now undoable. You quail four or five times before noon. The month, the season, feels all wrong.

Details began filtering in from the six riding partners my father had been with on the day he died. He had complained of brake problems at the gas station just prior to the crash. He planned to lag behind, let someone else lead the pack. Yamaha had recently done a recall on some element of the R1's braking system, but my father never followed up on the recall, so one guy was convinced that my father's brakes failed when he went into that turn, because an expert rider doesn't just collide with a guardrail on a day you could not have painted any better.

Two other guys claimed they'd heard my father say, 'I don't feel well,' a sentence he would not have spoken. A man who views the wordless enduring of pain as a sign of election does not gripe of feeling unwell, and certainly not to a clan of riders for whom machismo was a weekly contest. Someone else suggested my father might have had a heart attack as he went into that turn, but he was only forty-seven, and we don't have young heart attacks lurking in our family history. Another floated the idea that a deer might have bounded out in front of him, but just a minute before, a bevy of machines had screamed down the center of the road sounding like a war. No deer bounds out into that unless it's deaf.

There was also this: an irate old farmer in a pickup truck, not pleased by that scream of engines passing him at a hundred miles per hour. Someone offered the absurd speculation that, because my father was lagging at the rear of the pack, this farmer ran him into the guardrail. So, a homicidal old farmer, then. But even a five-year-old can tell you: it's not possible for a pickup truck, *any* pickup truck, to gain ground on a Yamaha R1.

And then there was this: my father had mounted a camera to the anterior of the bike so that he might study his riding style and make improvements for the following Sunday. But the camera was missing, and it took me two days to discover that another rider had taken it before the police appeared at the crash site. He knew the evidence would show a hollering catalog of traffic crimes. This information created a clog in my chest that would not wash down. A man I did not know was in possession of my father's camera, and on that camera was the crash that killed him. I made infuriated phone calls and finally got a hold of the wife of the guy who'd taken the camera.

'Let me talk to Frank,' I said.

'Frank is very upset about this. Frank was very close to your dad. Frank can't talk right now.'

'*Frank* is upset? Did you just say to me that goddamn *Frank* is upset?'

That week, Frank returned the camera to my brother but I didn't ask if he watched the footage, if our father's crash was on the tape. It was enough for me that the camera was back in our possession, whatever my brother chose to do with it. We had the equivalent of a black box, and I know it makes little sense – grief cares nothing for declarations of logic; it takes whatever egress it needs, whatever path conforms to the enigmas of its own internal working – but I never considered watching it, and I don't think anyone else did, either. I wasn't aware of being concerned about the acceleration of my sadness, about glimpsing scenes that would alter my conception of my father. But watching the crash would have no doubt confirmed his recklessness and blame, and I needed to soak in denial, to *imagine* my route into his death, and in this way perhaps imagine my way into the last moments of his life.

I could see the point of other investigations, other inquiries that yielded to the agency of the imagination – I'd soon be obsessing over documents and details and diction, the coroner's report and police report, the testimony of his riding partners about that day – but I must have been living in a low-level fear of that camera's proof. I could not have proof, one way or the other, because the omission of proof is the only way the sacred stays sacred.

When the pack realized my father was no longer behind them, they waited. When he didn't show, they doubled back and discovered him half beneath the guardrail, the bike on top of his lower half. The old farmer in the pickup truck was

217

there, and a couple who lived in the house nearby, and some others who had stopped. Another rider claimed he heard my father say 'Oh God,' claimed he saw him move his arm on top of his chest as he was being lifted into the ambulance. He'd said it all the time, 'Oh God': in jest, in sarcasm, in exasperation, in exhaustion. When Pop found out that my father had mumbled 'Oh God,' he said, 'He knew he was hurt.'

But how could my father say that, or anything else, with a crushed throat, with his windpipe ruined? With all three of those life-ending injuries? How could he lift his arm when I knew – *I knew* – he was already dead? That is one of our many unkillable wishes in the world: to keep the dead in conversation, in motion. Keep them talking, keep them moving, and you can keep them *here*.

Two days after the funeral, I phoned Christian, one of the men who'd been with my father that day, and asked him for everything he remembered, scratching these words onto a legal pad as he spoke:

'He was too good. He refused to lay it down, never doubted for a second he could take that turn. When we found him, he had one leg up over the bike, his head propped up against the bottom of the guardrail. The tires were pointed toward him. He hit the guardrail the same time as the bike. His legs lay in the direction he came from. I saw him lift his arm up and put it on his chest.'

But another rider would tell me that my father moved his arm onto his chest once he was laid on the stretcher, not when he was still on the road. Which is right? Is either right? Because only a conscious man moves his arm. Because if

218

there was consciousness in those last minutes, then he might have been aware of what he'd done and where it would lead. And if he had been aware? That somehow changed things for me – I'd have to reimagine, reconfigure his terminal seconds – even if it changed nothing for him.

'I didn't hear him speak,' Christian told me. 'Carlos did. I didn't hear him say "Oh God."'

'Tell me about the bike,' I said.

'Every Sunday that bike looked brand new. The brakes must have failed; there's no other reason. He never would've taken that bike out of the garage that day if the brake pads were worn down like everyone's saying. I think something failed as he went into that turn.'

I have these puzzling words from Christian looking at me now from a yellow page, words from sixteen years ago: *Possible pump malfunction, there was too much blood, it needed to be pumped out.* What can that mean? The heart, of course, is a pump, but that can't be what he meant. He must have meant the engine's fuel pump. But why, then, 'too much blood'? A bike doesn't run on blood, and a fuel pump would have had nothing to do with a crash. And 'pumped out' from where, with what, by whom? I've reordered those words in a number of ways, thinking I might have scratched them down wrong – bereavement is a garbled tongue, has no fixed syntax, is rife with tautology and non-sequitur – but no matter what I do, no matter their arrangement, I cannot make them click.

Christian said something else to me on the phone that day. He said that when they'd found my father under the guardrail, his head looked as if it had been wrenched around 180 degrees. And I did something terrible that night. In my grandparents' kitchen, just the three of us there, I told them of that detail, of my father's head wrenched around 180 degrees on his shoulders. The sound that came from Pop was part moan, part gasp, the name 'Jesus Christ' beneath it. And then I heard myself apologizing – twice, three times – in a voice lifted by a chest-swell becoming sobs. Why would I tell them such a thing? Why didn't I understand that what Christian must have seen was not my father's *head* wrenched 180 degrees, but his *helmet* that had turned on impact and given that grisly impression?

Through a wet tissue, Parma said, 'It's okay. I want to know. I want to know everything.'

New Jersey's population is the densest in the nation: it's a claustrophobic, comma-shaped state. Population density means more cars, and more cars mean clogged roads when they don't mean murder on motorcycles. And so, each Sunday, my father and his cohort retreated across the state line to the backroads of bucolic Pensy, roads that were curvier and better maintained than most of Jersey's. They weren't worried about Pensy's guardrails, lampposts, or ample oak trees because they maintained an intransigent belief in their own abilities. No – they worried about the distracted jackass in the convertible, the homicidal ditz dashing to the mall while applying eyeliner in her rearview, the silver-haired slaughterer driving east on the westbound side of the highway.

I'd grown up listening to my father carp about the average person, the average driver especially. Although he mellowed in his forties, as men are known to do – as sperm count dwindles, patience improves – he was ever sarcastic when he wasn't cynical, frequently complaining about humanity's lack of competence. 'It's amazing mankind has come this far with so many stupid people' was one of his favorite sentences. He had a proletarian's definition of intelligence, indistinguishable from efficiency and what used to be called common sense. You wouldn't have wanted to be in the car with him stuck behind some hapless sightseer doing half the speed limit. 'All it takes is one idiot,' he'd say – to make him late, he meant, but more generally, to *inconvenience* him. In my family's mindset, it's something of a capital crime for one man to inconvenience another. It's simply not done.

From start to finish, a typical Sunday's ride looked like this: Some guys would meet at Pop's house at eight thirty, look over their bikes, bullshit about throttles, tailpipes, handlebars. By nine o'clock they'd meet another band of riders in the next town, near the highway. They'd meet at the base of a water tower standing at the center of a honeycombed industrial complex owned by one of Pop's pals. A ramp led down to the tower, and as each new guy showed up, he'd pull a wheelie on the ramp to the cheers of those who were already there. More bullshitting and inspection of bikes until everyone arrived. By ten o'clock they'd have to meet the Pennsylvania batch of riders at a diner on Route 202, near the state border. They had a rule that turned into a joke because every man broke it: no racing before breakfast. Some guys never made it to breakfast.

They'd time the red lights on 202, deliberately slow to catch the red, so they could drag race, gun it to the next traffic signal, or they'd try to pass one another through the sweeping jug-handles on and off the highway. There was no plan for contingencies: if you crashed and were not killed, the best you could hope for was somebody dashing to a phone to dial a tow truck or an ambulance. Once, a helicopter was summoned when a rider ended up shattered in a ditch, bleeding everywhere on the inside.

Breakfast lasted half an hour, forty minutes at most. When my uncle Nicky first began riding with this group at thirty years old, none of the younger guys would sit with him at the diner – he sat beside Pop or his brothers, ignored by the rest – until he proved himself by passing one of the fastest guys in a jug-handle. After that, the rider he passed was full of reverence and affection for him. While eating: no family talk allowed, and no work talk either, nothing personal, domestic, nine-to-five. Motorcycle talk only: the MotoGP races, recent magazine articles in *Sport Rider,* new bikes, new parts for bikes, gossip about guys who'd recently crashed. Some couldn't eat much, toast maybe, their guts tied up in anticipation of the coming speed, of the concentration they'd need. But Pop's appetite was always unwavering; each week he'd speak the same line to the waitress: 'Pancakes golden brown, with sausage.'

After breakfast, the fifteen bikes lined up at a single pump at the adjacent gas station. Each topped off his tank and passed the nozzle to the next guy. Each began the ride on full. Those back roads had no gas stations, and if you found one, it was a mom-and-pop general store not open on Sunday. The price to top off fifteen tanks was normally twenty bucks, and Pop normally paid it. He and another alpha planned the route through the Pensy countryside. In the lead, Pop always knew the roads, every pothole, crack, and sudden curve, how to take a turn, where the dips were, the rises, where the elm root buckled the asphalt at the edge. And so the riders who crashed were usually those following him too fast into a turn: guys broke legs and backs trying to catch Pop.

The day had its clan lingo. *Don't go in the marbles* meant 'Don't run wide off the clean part of the road, into the stones, dust, and dirt on the shoulder.' *Stay off the paint* meant 'Keep your tires off the white and yellow lines,' because they were slick when wet. *I see your chicken strips* meant the tread on your tires wasn't worn on the outside, which meant you weren't riding aggressively enough. *The bike's on rails* meant the bike was stable, steady, smooth. *Keep the shiny side up* perhaps went without saying: it meant 'Don't crash.' And the day had its code for cops, too: *When the pigs light up their cherries and start to chase, split up: they can't chase us all.* And if you got caught, you never gave up the names of those who didn't. When troopers once snagged Nicky near a cornfield, they forced him facedown into the road, handcuffed him at the back, and hollered at him to name the others. He never did.

The day's racing in Pensy lasted a little more than three hours, an uninterrupted swath of time, unless a guy was lagging too far behind the pack – then you waited for him at an intersection. When the three hours were up, just before two o'clock, you needed to make it back to the highway or else you'd run out of fuel. By the time that refueling break came at two, the original clan of fifteen guys had been shaved down to twelve or thirteen: some crashed, some had mechanical issues, some couldn't hack it and went home. At the gas station, you hydrated, checked the bike, chattered about the ride's many glories and dangers. Pop always ate an ice cream cone. The Pensy guys then sped west, the Jersey guys east. And all week long, all they thought about was doing it again.

Several summers before his fatal accident, my father caused Pop to crash at the Flemington Circle, half an hour from Manville, only a handful of miles from where Robert Chittenden died in 1981.

Pop was behind him, pushing him hard into the turn, intense and tight on his back tire. My father must have felt him there, seen him there, because instead of keeping his speed and his line in the turn, he let off the throttle. Pop had nowhere to go; he had to lock up both the front and back wheels, and the bike went down right away, slid across the circle before colliding with the curb in a burst of fifty shards. Sitting there in the road, Pop saw his leg pointing north, the bottom of his foot facing east, his ankle cracked clean through, tibial and fibular fractures both.

The bike was unsalvageable, a purple Kawasaki Ninja ZX11, and the ankle would take six weeks, at least, at his age; he was in his early sixties then. He spent those weeks in a costly outdoor reclining chair my father had bought for him as a small recompense. When I visited Pop one morning as he recovered, I found him in that chair, in a strip of fluttering shade near the garage, his foot propped up on a spackle bucket, a Kawasaki logo beaming boldly from his T-shirt, beneath it this tip for living: LET THE GOOD TIMES ROLL.

'You know,' he said, 'Evel Knievel broke every bone in his body at one time or another.'

'Sounds like a lot of useless time in hospitals,' I said.

'Yeah,' he said. 'That's what happens.'

Pop wouldn't blame my father, and he certainly wouldn't blame himself, or even hint at the causality of the crash. That was a core element of the masculine charter I'd seen again and again since I was young: cowardice, hubris, culpability remained unspoken, as if it was shameful even to speak of such sins. Machismo demands a certain lack of reflection upon its own tenets, a lack of acknowledgment that such tenets swayed their behavior, their conduct on a construction site, on a motorcycle, in a family.

But I've been struggling to capture the nuance, the complication, of this crash between my father and Pop. There is no definitive version of what happened that day. My father never talked to me about it. What I have are the barest details from Pop. What I have is my speculation and my doubt, my imagined version, a ricocheting of loyalties. I have the aegis of the family's masculine code – my father went yellow in that turn; he had no business being on that ride if he wasn't going to gun it with the others – and then I have my heartpained inclination to defend him, to speak for him because he is not here to speak for himself.

Why did Pop feel he needed to push him through that turn? Was it his way of saying *I'll push you because I believe you can make it, because once you reach the speed you'll reach the sacred*? Because he believed, with the Great Santini, that the only effective method of inspiring greatness in his son was through the disgracing hostility that culminates in violence and injury? Some men love one another the same way they hate one another, through aggression and antagonism. By this red-blooded illogic, denigration somehow becomes celebration.

Or was it much simpler than all that, just another instance of an older general desperate to prove his value to the younger guard, to show them and himself that he still had it, that his stature wouldn't be abased by age? I have no trouble comprehending how some older men would crave that verification of their virility, just as some women want verification of their beauty. Pop was unreasonably competitive whether he was on a motorcycle or a racquetball court, in a boxing ring or at the bowling alley. (One of his most prized memories was of boxing in his garage as a teenager, pinning the other guy up against the bay door, and then slugging his head through a small square window.) We applaud the harsh competitive pulsing in our athletic heroes, so it should surprise no one when average American men, men who aspire to their own vocabulary of eminence, require the same competitiveness in whatever lives they've made for themselves.

Because the truth is that, by the standards of his own bearing, the humiliation belonged to Pop that day, not to my father. It was he sitting in the road with his foot hanging off.

I couldn't see it then but I should have known: the death of my father would also mean the death of my grandfather – a walking blank, a ceaseless, soundless abrading of the will. Never mind the will to power for a formerly powerful man. I mean the simple will to comprehension. He didn't look at you, he *blinked* at you, not because he was trying to place you, but because he was trying to place *himself,* to shake free of the grief, to remember how he'd ended up on the earth and how his firstborn had beaten him to the grave. You hear about this, about people *giving up on life,* but I'd never seen it before, and couldn't have guessed at its enormous languor.

Sixty-seven years old, he blinked for hours at the TV, blinked at the grass, immobile on the sofa, immobile on a kitchen stool, insomniac until the dawn, a hundred pounds too many, his only brief reprieve the hillocks of sausage and meatballs he wasn't supposed to be eating, the corrosive effects of which were combated by a daily fistful of pills. He'd sit in a lawn chair in the garage, both bay doors open, blinking down the driveway at the drowsy street, behind him an homage to masculinity from other eras. A portrait of a cowboy-hatted John Wayne, a still of Steve McQueen on a motorbike in *The Great Escape,* a yard of Louis L'Amour novels (his favorite, *Last of the Breed*), a shelf of motorcycle helmets. A shrine to his richly buddied past, a giant wall of blown-up photos in frames, he and his pals posing at some rally or race in '75, in '79, in '82, in '91, he and his three sons on their bikes in '95 and '97, a kinship of leather, brawn, blood, Pop always the chieftain at the center of the shot.

To see that wall-sized shrine was to see what brotherhood meant to him, what certain men mean by 'a full life.' And to see him slumped before it after my father's death, oblivious and blinking, was to feel the cold contrast of what's gone and what remains: his atrophy of spirit, his persistent bracing against a stridor only he could hear.

Flipping through albums of my boyhood, the mood of

the late '70s and early '80s upon me like a stain, it's hard to find a photo in which one or more motorcycles does not appear in the frame with me. On Pop's lap on a Harley Davidson Sportser V-twin in 1975, again on a four-cylinder Kawasaki 1100 in '79, a Yamaha VMAX in the background in '81, a Suzuki 1000 in '83, a Yamaha FJ1100 in '85. Sifting through the thousands of loose family photos Parma keeps in plastic bins, eighty years' worth of shots, I find that fully half of them contain a motorcycle of one kind or another. The history of my family in photographs is a photographic history of motorcycles. Considering this, it's something of a wonder that I escaped the two-wheeled contagion.

V

After my father's death, I found this among his many papers: a letter he'd written to the daughter of his fiancée. I've preserved his spelling and grammar:

Dear Tracy:

Your mother said I should write you a letter on your graduation. So this is it.

1st you should thank me for talking your mother into not reading the letter she wrote at dinner!

2nd your mother kept me up all nite with Childhood stories of you. And so today I am tired!

3rd Why do they have to have a graduation on Sunday, when everybody knows that is motorcycle riding day!

4th Thank You God for not making me ride two hours with Millie in the car. [Millie would have been his future mother-in-law.]

5th Do not buy beer with your graduation money.

6th and finally let me give you some advice on your graduation day.

LIFE IS SHORT RIDE HARD
Love Bill

When he strapped on that helmet, when he woke that engine and gripped one hand to the throttle and the other to the clutch, when he eased from the driveway of his home for a Sunday of road racing – a race against his own skill, his own hunger for risk – then he shut out the regular world and its quotidian concerns, the daily grating of domesticity, that work-week attrition, and he welcomed his new isolation, the monastic focus on the asphalt, on the yellow lines at the center and the white line at his flank. He welcomed that focus because it was wanted but also because it was required for the spiritual thrill of being able to maneuver such an unforgiving machine, to keep such power from slipping into disaster. Milan Kundera, at the beginning of his novel *Slowness:*

> *The man hunched over his motorcycle can focus only on the present instant of his flight; he is caught in a fragment of time cut off from both the past and the future; he is wrenched from the continuity of time; he is outside time; in other words, he is in a state of ecstasy; in that state he is unaware of his age, his wife, his children, his worries, and so he has no fear, because the source of fear is in the future, and a person freed of the future has nothing to fear.*

All of our lives are set by a certain terrible inevitability, causality ruled by the forces of speed and momentum, energy and force. Those superbikes, and the way my father's clan rode them, took that fact and boiled it down to its most brutal and thrilling essence. They demonstrated the perhaps uniquely male quality of submitting to the insane, the great, and the deadly almost exclusively within the dynamic of a group, a setting in which, on Sunday afternoons, time collapsed into itself at excessive speeds, in which social rules melted away and were replaced by Homeric codes.

The brotherhood, exaltation, and worship my father found on Sunday rides was no different from the brotherhood, exaltation, and worship I found training at the Physical Edge. 'After a certain age,' wrote Proust, 'the more one becomes oneself, the more obvious one's family traits become.' My father and I were not as far apart as I sometimes pretend. We both had the unignorable impulse to extremity, an impulse passed down from Pop.

A day after the burial, the men of my family made the hour-and-fifteen-minute drive to the crash site, to the town of Springfield in Delaware County, Pennsylvania, ten miles west of Philly, five miles north of the Delaware River, which divides the state from our own. Pop, unwilling or unable to see the site, remained behind. My two uncles, my cousin, my brother, and I left Jersey before nine in the morning on a day when the weather matched perfectly the day that saw my father's death. Before we left, Parma had given me a white wooden cross to hammer into the soil near the spot where he died. I didn't ask where she'd got it – though it occurs to me now that she'd made it herself in the garage – and I took it without protest. What good would have come from my telling her that the heavens have absconded, that God was unworthy of His rule?

On Route 202 in western Jersey, we drove past the diner

where the pack of riders had met before crossing the state line, the place that served my father's last meal. My uncle slowed the car as we passed, but not a one of us had the appetite to suggest we stop.

The name of the road he died on: Slifer Valley Road. I'd spent abundant hours thinking about that name; it put me in mind of Robert Lowell's alliteration 'a savage servility slides by on grease.' The word *Slifer* gives off a serpent's hiss, suggests sinews and dips. Eliminate the first and last letter and you are left with *life*, with the inverse of what that road now meant to us. Eliminate only the *S* and you have *lifer*: one who gives a lifelong commitment – to motorcycles and manliness, yes, but there's no commitment as lifelong as death, no commitment like the commitment to the grave. For all of everybody else's life, you are dead. Eliminate the first two and last two letters of *Slifer* and you have the silent emphasis of *if* – if only he'd craved slowness instead of speed, if only we hadn't tolerated that craving, if only I hadn't been too preoccupied to ask about his Sundays.

As we approached the spot, we saw the road sign before the crest, that black arrow inside a yellow diamond shape that warns of the ninety-degree right turn ahead, and that yellow square beneath the diamond shape, the number 20 inside the square – not the suggestion but the insistence of only twenty miles per hour. And as we came to the other side of the crest, when I first saw the sharp right, my thought was this: *That warning sign is way, way too close to the turn.* You'd better not be speeding, not even a little, because by the time you see that sign you won't have space enough to make the right without crashing.

It's a secluded spot, near a rock-cluttered rill, an umbrella of trees repelling the sun, farmland etched onto the earth and stretching into the distance. A calming road, only the occasional Buick, the intermittent Ford. We parked off to the side and began looking. A crimson smear from his helmet on the guardrail. Beneath it, spread on the asphalt, a large oval of his blood, laminate in a rhombus of sun punching through the trees, a brigade of black ants feeding in it.

I found pieces of the bike in the road: white and red paint chips, metal shards, small plastic shapes from the fairings, a steel foot peg. I collected them all, the relics, and slipped them into my pockets, and in the coming days I would spend untold hours touching them, turning them over in my hands, inspecting them with a magnifying glass.

Up the road thirty yards, in the direction from which we'd come, on the near side of the crest, the two skid marks began. They were each over fifty feet long, punctuated by a space of nearly forty feet, evidence that the bike was moving at a lunatic speed as it emerged over the crest. He must have seen that ninety-degree turn waiting like the grave. Those skid marks – a skid means panic. If only I could have lifted them from the pavement. It all began with those skid marks, and ended where the skidding stopped, where the panic was no more.

My grandparents had an itch to blame anything or anyone but my father: the brakes, his riding partners, a homicidal old farmer in a pickup truck. Pop was convinced that my father hadn't miscalculated, hadn't made the tyro's error of speeding at a crest when he didn't know what lay beyond it. My father wasn't speeding at all, Pop reasoned, because there was relatively little damage to the bike, only a gouge in the gas tank. If my father had been doing a hundred miles per hour, as some of us suspected, then the bike would have been demolished when it hit that guardrail.

A middle-aged couple from the nearby house came out to greet us. They hadn't seen the crash but they went to my father's side soon after. The husband wore aviator glasses and looked to be recovering from extensive plastic surgery – the peculiar tautness and sheen of his face, the stiff-jawed talking, the sentences of a ventriloquist. The wife was gnomish, recently popped free from the pages of a storybook. We all shook hands and introduced ourselves there in the road, at the mouth of their driveway.

'I unbuckled the helmet strap and told him to hang on,' the husband said, 'told him that help was on the way.'

'That means a lot to us,' I said.

I did not ask: *Was he alive then? Was he breathing then?* And I did not ask about the blood that must have been on the fingers of both hands after he unbuckled the strap. I don't know why I didn't ask: I'd arrived at this spot in hope of discovering such information, and yet when the time came to know it, to hold the facts, I could not.

'Anybody would have done it,' he said. 'It's what a person does in a situation like that. What was his name?'

'William Giraldi,' I said. 'The third.'

He looked at his wife, then back at us.

'Our son was the third William, as well,' he said. 'He was killed, five years ago, on April 7, just one month earlier than your father. Same day, though, the seventh. Someone shot him in the head. Only thirty years old. We never did find the killer, though we tried. God knows we tried.'

My uncles, brother, and cousin were uneasy now, I could see. They didn't want this reconnaissance to turn maudlin, were highly suspicious of the mushy, and I hoped that, whatever else he did, this husband would not start sobbing on our necks right there in the road.

'It's a funny thing,' he said. 'Both of them William, both of them dying on the same day.'

My brother glanced at my cousin, then my cousin glanced at me, and both of my uncles weren't sure where to glance. They only nodded, maybe in agreement of some kind, their own ilk of understanding, and they nudged around some stones with their sneakers. I couldn't see the husband's eyes behind his mirrored glasses, and for some reason I thought that he might not have eyes at all, just two black holes, a hellish vision out of Lovecraft.

'There was an old man here at the crash,' I said. 'An old fella in a pickup truck?'

'Yes,' he said. 'He wasn't happy. When the other guys arrived, he kept screaming at them, saying, "See what happens? See what you did?" At one point he wanted to drag your father out from underneath the guardrail, get the bike off him, but I said not to do that. Said it was best to wait for the paramedics.'

Get the bike off him. Then the bike was *on* him. How did the bike end up on top of him if he'd been flung over it?

'This old guy was very concerned, though,' he said. 'His hand was crippled, very strange.'

'A crippled hand?'

'Yes, a crippled hand. He unloosened your father's jacket

235

to give him some more air. There were some others here too. Some motorists who'd stopped. Everybody was very concerned.'

'That warning sign is too close to the turn,' I said, gesturing behind us to the crest.

'It's way too close,' he said. 'There's an accident here at this guardrail once a month, at least. We've petitioned the county, a couple of times, to have it moved farther down so people have time enough to slow, but they won't move it. I don't know why.'

I wanted to interview this couple, ask them the specifics they remembered, what they saw and felt, how it all seemed: colors, scents, tastes, the sound the wind made through the boles. But I couldn't do it just then, not with my family there. The husband gave me his telephone number and said I could call him whenever I wished. We had this weighted thing between us now, this affiliation of hurt: his son, my father, both named William, both dead before their due, killed on unlucky number seven, their deaths tinged with unknowables, without completion, without condolence. I never did call him, and I'm not sure why – because although I wanted facts, I didn't want too many of them? – and I can't call him now, sixteen years later.

Mike hammered the wooden cross into the soil, and as I squatted near him at the guardrail, I thought this: *What did you expect at the other end of that crest, at a speed I cannot guess, the trees a blur on both sides of you? My hours will be ravished by wonder, seeing these Pennsylvania paths of asphalt and your color gashing through the countryside. Your death is black and red, bright white and chrome. Now my own life shrinks and swells on this road, at this spot,*

this right-angle right turn you didn't see until much too late. Where are
we now? How can our planet expend the energy to spin? I want to sink
into this spot that claimed you, to see for myself in hope of knowing. I
can see you now, lying here broken, life leaking from you. Perhaps a lone
thought survives long enough to let you know: this Sunday will never
end, and the race is under way. The ruin in the wake belongs to me, not
you. Who will reverse the heart and allow our blood to run backward?
How can I choose to live in the hypothesis of reverse? Dad – what did
you do?

Before we departed that afternoon, I made a point of
locking within my memory everything about that road and
its surroundings: the shallow rock-filled brook, the broad-
leaf trees, the furrowed farmland, the nearby pond, the
costly homes set back on acres of coifed grass and shrubs.
That day was the only time I've ever been there, though the
place appears periodically in my dreams. That's one of the
pastimes of the dead: bored invigilators, spying sprites, they
breathe on us while we sleep.

Two years later, Mike returned to Slifer Valley Road,
and when he did, the middle-aged couple once again came
to the road to greet him. It must have been a necessary
hobby for them, to sit watch over that right turn, no doubt
remembering their murdered son, praying – they seemed like
the beseeching sort – that another motorist wouldn't mangle
himself in sight of their home. The cross Mike had pounded
into the spot of our father's crash was still there, although
altered in an unexpected way: a swan had built her nest and
laid her eggs against it, so that only the top, the T-section of
the cross, was now visible. Mike's initial thought was that
sacrilegious landscapers had been heaping their sticks and

cut grass onto the modest monument to our dad's death, but then the wife told him about the swan.

In their thirty years of residing in that house, she said, they'd never seen a swan cross Slifer Valley Road to nest away from the pond. But during the first nesting season after our father died there, a rogue swan built her large bed and laid her eggs directly against the cross, on top of our father's blood stained into the asphalt. Each day when she crossed the road from the pond to reach her nest, she'd linger there in the center, on the yellow line, just before the right turn. As if, the wife said, in caution – a swan warning speeders to slow down.

Slifer Valley Road as my father's swan song, the sound of the bike a music he loved, a rapturous tune for those with ears to hear it. Swans don't actually sing before they die – one species is known to whistle – although you see that superstition at certain spots in literature: in Plato and Euripides, in Cicero and Seneca. Some Greek myths speak of Apollo, the god of music, as a swan. Homer was the Swan of Meander, Shakespeare the Swan of Avon. In *Othello,* Emilia says, *I will play the swan, / And die in music.* In Andersen's famous fairy tale 'The Wild Swans,' the swans are heroes, brothers who have been turned into the birds by a malefic witch and who rescue their sister from the executioner.

The wife gave Mike a photograph she'd snapped of the swan in the nest, its question-mark head and neck beside the white cross. When Mike returned that day and showed me the photo, I said, 'Please don't tell me you think our father is that swan.' He didn't tell me that, no, although his face said otherwise. The swan, our father, as hero-crooner. That photo is still framed above his bed in Colorado, and every so often his dreams are filled with floating, singing, waddling swans.

In the months after his death, my father did not appear in the wilderness of my sleep as an apparition or omen. He did not arrive to say 'Remember me.' He had no advice, no wisdom or warnings to impart, no events to foretell. No ghoulish haunting to undertake. He was simply *there*, the image of him projected into my sleep. I maintained the awareness that he was dead, and so his appearance in my sleep seemed a resurrection, and that's what I felt while asleep and dreaming: the awe of this Lazarus act. There he'd be, just standing in whatever room I dreamed I was in, his typically wry countenance, unaltered by burial, comfortingly at ease, with nothing to say or do, no will remaining, and I'd look open-mouthed at him and weep, wonder how he'd climbed from the grave.

And when I'd wake I'd be weeping still on a wet pillowcase, feeling drugged, fatigued by the dream, trying to crawl fully awake, away from its lingering, but also wanting it to last, because I could feel him still, the way scent from a candle stays in the room after you've stanched the flame. The tears were actual, both in and out of sleep, and this merging of one realm with the other – the dead with the living, the unconscious with the conscious – is how our dreams manage to feel so pertinent to whatever quest we're on. In one dream I approached him, in Parma's kitchen as he leaned against the counter, and I held him but he did not hold me back, would not or could not, and I soon woke myself with the shock of that, with the shuddering of sobs.

* * *

My brother and I had the tearful task of going through my father's van, sorting through the many tools, papers, envelopes, sitting in the sawdust and dried dirt. A hopeless junk-food fiend, my father had littered the van with chocolate wrappers and cookie boxes – Snickers, Reese's, Lorna Doone, Fig Newtons – and we grinned at that, though grinning seemed impossible. The letters I'd written him over the years from the various places I was living – from Myrtle Beach, from Boston – and some of the photos I'd enclosed: they were all folded into an overhead compartment.

On one envelope, the back side of a bill, he had written, in caps, SPEED VISION, and above that was a telephone number: 1-888-SPEED. He was a nostalgic keeper of tiny things, and now I needed to keep everything too, every receipt that held his signature, every square of paper that showed his scrawl. Since my brother lived in Colorado, we agreed that the van would go to me, and I would drive it for the next two years. My brother wanted all the tools, our father's utensils of creation. There was still the mission of going through his clothes, smelling, touching the fabric that had touched him. And then the task of the items he'd stored in blue bins in the basement of the townhouse he shared with his fiancée. Cards and letters, photos and notebooks and pamphlets, medical records and our report cards, sales papers for the motorcycle, keepsakes from wherever he'd been over the years, on vacations, on weekend motorcycle jaunts.

And I remembered this: when I was a sophomore in high school, after my first girlfriend dumped me for a football star, just prior to my discovery of bodybuilding, my father asked what in God's name was the matter with me, when was I going to shake myself out of this doomsday funk? I was miserable to look at, and as a single father with enough misery to brook, he didn't want to be living with a depressed romantic. My mother had been out of our lives for five years at this time.

'Move on,' he said. 'You're a teenager. This is called normal life. It happens every day to everyone.'

I clomped upstairs into my bedroom, retrieved the perfumed, rubber-banded brick of love notes the girlfriend had scribbled to me, and then clomped back down to present them as evidence to my inexperienced father.

'Here,' I said, and clapped them into his gut. 'Read these notes and maybe you'll get it.'

There at the counter in our kitchen, he unfolded the notes and read a high-school girl's words of eternity. He didn't smirk; he barely blinked. Very carefully he refolded those fragrant pages – their familiar scent slapping me as I stood there watching him – and he said, 'Come on, I want to show you something.'

In our garage, in a cedar chest that had always been with us, my father had stockpiled every note, letter, and card my mother had ever written to him – fifteen years' worth of regal blue loops and dots, beginning when they were themselves in high school.

He plunged a hand into the chest, yanked out a clot of paper, and said, 'It's all bullshit. It doesn't mean a thing. Words, that's all. Lots of goddamn words. Nothing but your actions count in this life. Words are easy. A person's words aren't worth shit.'

Words are easy. This in-the-garage pep talk mollified my grief not one bit, and yet the significance of that gesture trails me still. Auden: *The words of a dead man / Are modified in the guts of the living.* My father wasn't wrong. In his nook of the world, from his manly vantage, actions mattered, actions elevated and saved. But I wish he were here for me to tell him how hard the right words really are. I wish, too, that I could say this for the sake of drama: my father and I took that cedar chest into the backyard that afternoon, doused it with gasoline, and set it ablaze, the two of us shoulder to shoulder, staring at the fire, at all of my mother's untrue sentences disappearing in black smoke.

VI

Gravity, velocity, trajectory, horsepower and torque, Newton with a notebook and quill. The aggressive greed of it, gravity's single-mindedness, the self-serving mandates of momentum, how velocity or traction won't be talked into changing its mind. The motorcycle as finely tuned organism. The front and rear suspensions are correlated to the tires: the tires won't work right, won't have optimal stick or spin, if the suspension isn't tweaked to the rider's weight and height, nor will the brakes, the always singeing brakes, work properly. The best acceleration and deceleration rates, winning and losing, dying and living, are often a product of centimeters, of quarter pounds.

The motorcycle as a kinetic presentation of physics, of those numinous equations that altered how we see and build. In a turn – at a lean angle of seventy, sixty degrees – a rider shifts his weight, lowers the bike's center of gravity so it can take the curve, keep its speed of forty, fifty miles per hour, and keep a contact patch with the pavement so the bike doesn't slip away from underneath him. Heading into a turn quickly, very quickly, as the rider is leaning and cranking the throttle, centrifugal force is determined to pull the bike to the outside edge of the road or track – he's got to hit that turn just right, at the right angle and the right speed, and exert the right amount of force to keep the bike going where he needs it to go.

You want a 60/40 weight distribution from the back tire to the front, and you get that ratio when you're on the gas – the bike is happiest when you're on the gas. That's when it handles. It gets glum when you're on the brake and in a turn, and a glum bike is a deadly bike. The bike *wants* to go straight, and it *wants* speed, was designed for it.

Newton's First Law of Motion, the law of inertia (if only my father had been tempted by inertia and not its opposite) – an object in motion (the motorcycle) wants to remain in motion unless acted upon by an outside force (brakes or guardrails) – is not good news for a speeding bike. It means that the quicker it's traveling, the less apt it is to turn. Not a problem if you're on an airport runway; a giant problem if you're on a Pennsylvania back road.

To take the turn and come out the other side of it with all your bones intact, you've actually got to nudge the bike slightly away from the direction in which you're turning. The wheels are basically gyroscopic at this point, and so the counter-lean has the inverse effect: it sends the bike in the other direction, into the turn. While that's happening, the rider takes himself off the seat, leaning into the turn – you can see it in MotoGP races, the riders dragging their knees and elbows on the track. The bike, though angled, retains that crucial contact patch so it doesn't go down, but the rider is hanging off the thing like a monkey to redistribute the weight.

And when it all goes wrong – when the forward, downward, outward forces don't get along – then what you have is this: the laughable fragility of the human skull, no better than an egg. How unprotected we are on the earth, nothing sufficient to shield us, tissue all-too-easily torn, bones cracked, veins and arteries tearing under pressure. How did *Homo erectus* endure the peril? How did Cro-Magnon relax? Rubber and steel, asphalt, chrome, and gasoline: just begging to kill you. The human form will not fit in the world now. A yurt is sturdier, an armadillo better equipped.

In the night I fell prey to magical thinking. I had a child's notion that I could undo what had happened, buy back my father from the Olympian forces that took him. The money he left my siblings and me must have caused an uptick in my guilt – that reliable Catholic guilt, never tardy – because I wanted to trade the money, blood money, for his life. Half-asleep, I thought that if I could just find the right administrator, invoke the proper deity, I could hand over the cash and walk out with my father.

Anna and I spent that summer at my godfather's house in Maplewood, New Jersey, just south of a bombed-out Newark, thirty minutes from my grandparents' place in Manville. The house sat behind a scrubby lawn on a wide suburban street lined with oaks that reached their arms over rooftops. It was a capacious two-story Colonial built in 1926, brick front with cedar-shake siding, detached garage, a back deck with a space-age grill for barbecuing. The original owner of that house had grown up in it, had become a wealthy banker, never married, and then in his eighties committed suicide in the downstairs office, I don't know how. Lots of money, no love.

But we made lots of love that summer, in that house, and in that downstairs office where, unknown to us, someone had once ended his own life by rope or razor or gunshot. We had the house entirely to ourselves because my godfather passed the days at his business and the nights at his fiancée's condo. We moved into the pink bedroom upstairs – it was like living inside a watermelon – the bedroom that was supposed to be reserved for his daughter. Both of my godfather's children resided in Pittsburgh with their mother, eight hours away, and barely ever visited Maplewood. Lovemaking inside the shell of grief is an uncommon salve: the emphasis on *love*, the emphasis on *making*. It eased that grief by millimeters on some days, by inches on others. A ravenous bonding as if in hormonal defiance of death, half-aware of that timeless sex/death duet and dance, their almost rhyme. Sex brings life, life brings death, therefore sex brings death. But it didn't – it doesn't. The death of a beloved can be an unwelcome reminder of the restorative potency of lovemaking, and then lovemaking in turn becomes a stay against the always-shuffling, always-approaching umbra of your own death.

The trance of grief, its squashing calm, how it reduces you daily. Even TV commercials make you lachrymose, those ads selling pills for the many ineptitudes of your life, or a father and son test-driving a Ford pickup. The future seems cruciform. On those ninety-degree, sweating summer midnights, I lay looking into the pink bedroom's dark, feeling the multiple vibrations of grief, quickened by an inability to sleep, to forget, to pinch shut my eyes and not see Slifer Valley Road, not see the physics of my new grief. Sleep always eventually came, but I woke with the sun and I woke with the sunder and it was as if I'd never slept at all.

During the days, we'd lie reading in the backyard sun and then walk into town to fetch the night's dinner at the fish market and grocer. We'd make use of the grill on the deck, sirloin and corn and skewers of shrimp. Food, like sex, is better than prayer. After dark we'd watch films in bed – Kurosawa, Bergman, Fellini – and read again until we were tired enough to attempt sleep. The daylight world was all atilt for me. Only at night did things seem flush, steady in darkness, the black as ballast. I preferred those days of crippling rain, unexposed by sunlight, hidden indoors but near enough the window to savor the storm.

My brother had returned to Boulder, Colorado, just days after we'd gone through our father's van. One night before sleep, the heat of the day still held in the dark like a memory, he phoned me, his voice altered by tears because he'd just remembered something that happened when he was a child: In 1988, when Mike was ten years old, our father and uncles began renovating a four-story warehouse into apartment units. The building had once been Redfern Laceworks, where Pop toiled as a machine operator after Korea. It was a Saturday morning (our father worked Saturdays too), and Mike went with him to the job site that day, perhaps because there was no family member available to watch him. Since the divorce two years earlier, our father had been ceaselessly arranging for the three of us to be looked after, tended to, checked on, picked up, dropped off: with my grandparents, with aunts and cousins and kindly neighbors. There was always in the air a pestering smog of dread, an anxious sense that without them all we'd perish.

Our father must have had no other option but to take Mike with him that morning, because in the initial stages of renovation, the building was a filthy, jagged trap of hazards, an invitation to injury for any ten-year-old. Floors two, three, and four each had a rectangular gape where the elevator would go, a gape that someone had neglected to cordon off. Despite the warnings, Mike wandered and then fell through it, from the second floor to the first, fifteen feet onto the cracked concrete foundation.

Our father watched him drop, and then from the bottom floor Mike watched him rush, jump, panic down the open staircase. He'd landed on a mound of scrap lumber and broken cinder blocks, plywood and two-by-fours, and because our father was unlucky but not *that* unlucky, Mike wasn't impaled, his liver or kidney not perforated by a ten-penny nail, nor did he drop crown-first or else fracture his spine or neck on the concrete. He was not, in fact, injured at all.

So that was how he was able to see our father dashing down the steps after him, his grimace and panting impossible to mistake for anything other than uncut terror. And that's what Mike was remembering now on the phone with me, not two weeks after our father's death: the panicked look on his face as he bolted down crumbling steps after his youngest boy, the wayward one whom he expected to find unfixable.

It was, Mike said, exactly what love looked like, and we wept there together on the phone.

That summer of death was also the summer of something wrong with my plumbing, an involuntary pause in urination, a caesura in my stream, and also an unclear rectal annoyance that often had me sitting sideways. This, I knew, was the body looted by emotion: intestines, rectums, urethras sacked by feeling, bowels squeezed by grief. The soul will show itself, will manifest its damage, and the most intimate precincts of your body will take the hit.

I saw a urologist who, without any type of test, was rapid in pronouncing 'prostatitis': an inflammation or infection of the prostate (and not, as one friend thought, 'the disease of seeing too many prostitutes'). It would require a blitzkrieg of elect antibiotics because, said my urologist, the prostate is notoriously stubborn, a foul-tempered gland — it doesn't want interference from us. And because I didn't have health coverage of any kind, my canary-maned and boylike doctor gave me a week's starter dose of pills, and then charged me only $35 for the visit, not his standard fee many stories north of $35. Perhaps this was pure and unprompted kindness on his part, but I think it's likelier that I told him about my father's death, that I hunted his sympathies — that I was being exploitative, in other words, manipulative with my mourning.

All that summer, I'd noticed, I had a loose relationship with the sentence *My father's dead,* in part because my grief needed to let you know, needed not to pretend, but also because I had a new intolerance of empty exchanges, the void-filling chitchat everywhere, the false automation of *How are you?* and then *Good, thanks, how are you?* My reply to the opening nicety of *What's up?* or *How's it going?* was always *My father's dead,* as if an insistence on this ruthless candor would make the world clear again, and that clarity would then allay my despair. Obnoxious and unjust, that's obvious to me now, and my only excuse – I won't call it a reason – is that grief can be both a puppeteer and a ventriloquist. It attaches to your limbs, puts you in contorted poses, walks you in unnatural gaits, speaks for you in words and lilts that are not wholly yours.

In certain moods, grief can also taunt, chide, lash, as if in rageful challenge to what it perceives as the good luck, the non-grief, of others. It can choose convenient targets for our ire when the true target is not present. The day after my father's crash, the long drape of dark about to uncoil, Anna and I lay on a spare bed in the condo he'd shared with his fiancée. We lay looking at a ceiling fan, registering the upticks and falloffs of our shock. Then my sister and a band of her friends gathered at the picnic table beneath the window to smoke and talk, to be with one another, to do what people have always done in times of trauma.

And soon there was laughter, and this laughter, neither too raucous nor shrill, nevertheless lanced my efforts to register the shock on me, unsettled the already slow-coming cognizance of what my father had just done to himself and to us. I went to the window and raised the screen, and down into the dark I yelled for an end to that laughter, that sudden affront to my own suffering.

Several times that summer I behaved in ways I later wished

I could reverse, and I'd start with that night: my sister, and the friends who loved her, who had arrived to support her, *needed* the lightening of laughter. How else to endure the many waterloos of living except through laughter? It was also the innocuous, nervous laughter of people who didn't know how else to process their friend's affliction, how to express their own discomfort with death.

Why could I not see that? Why was I not on guard against this displacement of rage? Why didn't I just shut the window and embrace the woman I loved?

Perhaps because that's one of the other characteristics grief picks up: near-total self-consumption. The griever is by definition a solipsist; he can grieve in groups, with other grievers, and there's some balm in that, but the exhaustive work of grief can't be lessened by giving some of that work away. It is his, entirely his, and so he labors as he knows how, his gaze narcissistically inward. The griever can thus become very precious to himself, and protective of himself, which doesn't mean that he can't be helpful to others in pain – I hope I was, in whatever way I was able – only that later he had best feel some remorse for that solipsism and have an apology at hand.

My urologist's blitzkrieg of antibiotics didn't work, not even a little, and two weeks later I was back in his office, this time to be given that medieval procedure called a cystoscopy. Into the urethra slides a tubal scope so that we might spy upon my bladder's liquid privacy. We could see the bladder on the screen, that blank pouch, undefiled by tumors or whatever badness my doctor sought. My bladder wasn't as blank as its computerized image of blacks and grays, because when he retracted that seeing tube, there came an unpreventable cataract: onto my shins, onto the linoleum, onto the doctor's Italian wingtips.

He mentioned then a possible colonoscopy, if things didn't improve – that bit of barbarism that would no doubt turn my colon into a semicolon. But for now, more antibiotics, a mightier genus this time. I was on them all summer, for naught. When school started up again in the fall, I saw a different doctor, who let me know that I didn't have prostatitis – 'You're much too young for that' – but rather IBS, or irritable bowel syndrome.

'Any stress in your life?' he asked.

'My father was killed in May,' I said.

'That'll do it. It's IBS. It's not a serious case, from what you're explaining. It's a nuisance, I know. Exercise, meditate. It'll go away when the stress goes away, I'm certain.'

The IBS abated as he said it would, but slowly. I'd been on a regimen of antibiotics for four consecutive months, a combative regimen with nothing to combat, and so my immune system was defanged, worthless now. In December of that year, I'd be abused by a lionhearted flu: two weeks of weeping murder, twelve straight days in bed, one overnight stay in the hospital, fevered hallucinations, phantasmal visits from my father, cared for by friends in medical masks and latex gloves, the ugliest illness of my adult life. People toss about that tiny three-lettered word 'flu' like it's made of nickels, but when the flu comes for you, *really* comes for you, it comes with the full force of nine quarters: *influenza*.

False cures, whether antibiotics or displaced rage, are not only false, they are injurious. They offer not relief but remorse, compounded problems to heap upon the pile you already have. I'm hesitant to speak of literature as a cure or corrective for anything; it can deliver pleasure, and beauty, and wisdom, but it can't eradicate personal or social sickness, can't undo a damaged soul. When Matthew Arnold suggested replacing religion with poetry, he understood that religion *is* poetry. And yet, in the weeks and months after my father's death, literature was, as it had always been, my only hint of solace, the only medium equal to my woe, the only effective accomplice in the arduous work of return, of returning to some version of myself before my father's crash, a self irrevocably altered but one I might still recognize in my midnight. From Book VI of *The Aeneid,* as rendered by Dryden:

The gates of hell are open night and day;
Smooth the descent, and easy is the way:
But to return, and view the cheerful skies,
In this the task and mighty labor lies.

That is literature's unkillable value, what Kenneth Burke called 'equipment for living.' Literature turns us all into Adams naming animals: that assortment of animals inside us, all that hisses and coos. I sought the right words to wed to despair, entered into consultation with eminent voices of anguish. All summer it was Eugene O'Neill, all fall John Donne – the palliative pathos of *Long Day's Journey into Night,* the ecstatic desolation of the Holy Sonnets – and they ministered to me in a tongue no priest, no therapist, no doctor owned.

VII

The death certificate appeared one afternoon in the mail and my grief had fresh details to focus on, new items with which I could try to reconstruct my father's final moments, and perhaps solve the agonizing unknowables. That was the illusion, anyway, that a fixation on documents and language, on what could be established and known, would soften some of my disquiet. I would obsess now over the details of my father's dead body just as I had obsessed over the details of my own body during my muscled teenage years, the minutiae of diet and training that were the largest part of my every day.

I was too cowardly to view the footage of the crash on my father's camera, or even to ask my brother about it. I needed facts, but not too many of them, and not the wrong kind, not images. Images would be dispossessing, a glut at the tree of knowledge. I did not feel able to trust or manage images – they are not my medium – but I'd requested the death certificate because writers, if they have any hope at all, have hope in language.

The coroner's name was Scott M. Grim. How could I have made up such a name? The registrar who signed the certificate was Sandra P. Vulcano. So: Sandra the Vulcan and Grim the Reaper. To name a coroner 'Grim' in a novel would be a witless move, and yet our lives deliver us these witless facts and then leave us to be confounded by them.

In the part titled 'IMMEDIATE CAUSE (Final disease or condition resulting in death),' Grim had typed MULTIPLE TRAUMATIC INJURIES in clangorous caps. Underneath that, on a line labeled 'DUE TO (OR AS A CONSEQUENCE OF),' is MOTORCYCLE ACCIDENT. Under MANNER OF DEATH, the 'Accident' box is X-marked. Under PLACE OF INJURY is ROADWAY.

And then there's this:

DESCRIBE HOW INJURY OCCURRED: OPERATOR OF
    MOTORCYCLE
THAT STRUCK GUARDRAIL.
LOCATION: SLIFER VALLEY RD., .18 MI. E. OF WALNUT LN.,
    SPRINGFIELD TWP.
PLACE OF DEATH: DOA.
TIME OF DEATH: 3:26.
TIME OF INJURY: APPROX. 3:06 PM.
DATE OF DISPOSITION: 5-11-2000.
PLACE OF DISPOSITION: Sacred Heart Cemetery.
PLACE OF BIRTH: Manville, NJ.

A curious document – dull mint-green paper, heavy stock, watermarked – because it bears my father's name, yes, but also because of its seemingly arbitrary capitalizations and peculiar diction. Not 'road,' but 'roadway' – is there a difference, I wonder, to the eye of a coroner? The tautology of 'due to' and 'as a consequence of.' The use of 'that' instead of 'who' in the description of the injury, which makes it sound as if only the bike struck the guardrail (if that were so, I'd be penning a different book). There's 'disposition,' with its multiple meanings: we dispose of trash and the unwanted; your disposition is your temperament. The discrepancy between the time of injury and the time of death: twenty minutes, which means he might have had those minutes to know, to suspect, what had befallen him, and where he was falling.

There's the capped triad of 'MULTIPLE TRAUMATIC INJURIES,' its nonnegotiable decision, such stubborn finality. And then the stamp of 'DOA': no bothering with periods between letters, and no mistaking it for its twin, 'Dead or Alive,' since the second half of that formulation was not possible for my father. On the certificate, DOA describes 'place of death,' but DOA is, of course, not a place. It's a manner of arrival, the condition in which you are gurneyed into a hospital. Slifer Valley Road is, will always be, the actual place of his death. His dying happened there on that asphalt, beneath that guardrail.

Manville was not the place of my father's birth. No one's born in Manville except by accident; it doesn't have a hospital. His nativity happened one town over, at Somerset Medical Center. Why did the coroner make this error? The 'INFORMANT'S NAME' on the death certificate is William Giraldi, Jr. – Pop. Not 'informer,' but 'informant,' with its connotative stirrings of cloak and dagger, intrigue, whistle-blowing. Pop must have given all the personal data that appears on the death certificate, and he must have given it on the afternoon of the crash, when he and Parma went to the hospital to identify my father's body.

He gave Manville as the place of my father's birth because he wasn't present for it; he was directing mortar fire on a mount in Korea. Also because he was walloped by shock. Also because my father was *conceived* in Manville. But mostly because in every dilating chamber of his heart, Pop felt that my father should have been born in Manville. It's not equal to the early Christian framers changing the birthplace of Christ from Nazareth to Bethlehem in order to fulfill the necessities of a Jewish prophecy, but it suggests some of the visceral importance of being, really *being,* from Manville.

Pop would not have noticed that the hospital in which he stood giving this data on his dead son, St. Luke's Hospital, was located in the town of Bethlehem, Pennsylvania. Nor would he have cared to notice the coincidence that Saint Luke the Evangelist is the patron saint of lace makers. Pop himself worked in a laceworks factory for extra income just after my father was born. These coincidences meant something to *me,* though, as if they could coalesce into something significant, some coherence I could wield in order to see my way through this.

I know too that it was Pop who gave the personal data because under DECEDENT'S USUAL OCCUPATION — another unexpected choice of diction, 'usual,' as if assuming the dead was a job-hopper; and consider too the link from 'descendent' to 'decedent,' a decedent's descendants, deceased too soon and he doesn't leave any — Grim had typed 'Self-employed.'

Under KIND OF BUSINESS/INDUSTRY, he typed 'Builder.' For Pop, *self-employed* was a tag to be proud of. It suggested Emersonian agency, a man not shackled to an overseer. And 'builder' was how he insisted on referring to himself and his sons, never 'carpenter.' He heard a dignified toll in *builder* that was missing from the more pedestrian *carpenter.* Pop didn't care that Christ is said to have been a carpenter too, and not because he knew that *handyman* comes closer to the Greek term *tekton,* but because he had no patience for the Nazarene's unmanly meekness, his turn-the-other-cheek masochism.

I called Grim's office one morning, and his assistant, who had worked on my father, notched out some time to speak with me. I quickly jotted down these notes as he spoke: *fractured neck; inter-cranium damage; massive head injury; helmet pulled up on neck upon impact with guardrail; fractured larynx; fractured lower part of cranial vault; possible chest injury; knocked-over lung; air in chest outside lung.*

I said, 'Would it have been possible for him to talk? One of his buddies said he heard him talk.'

'Not possible,' he said.

'What about move his arm? Two of his buddies said they saw him move his arm.'

'Not possible.'

The notorious unreliability of eyewitness reports. Two of his fellow riders had said they saw my father move his arm onto his chest, and both of them were mistaken. How, why does the mind bamboozle the eyes into seeing what cannot be there, what the body cannot do?

'Do you think he suffered?' I asked.

'No,' he said. 'That wasn't possible, not with those massive head injuries. There was no suffering.'

And then, unprompted, he told me this: 'Once, when I was an EMT, years ago, we responded to a suicide on the train tracks. A guy got cut clean in half. It was a real mess. I took his bottom half, my partner took his upper half, and we loaded him in the ambulance. On the way to the hospital the guy woke up and started walking on his hands, trying to get to his bottom half. Imagine that, the guy walking on his hands, dragging his bloody waist across the floor, trying to put himself back together. That lasted about six seconds, I'd say.'

And then this: 'I once had a mother punch me in the jaw and then pull her dead eight-year-old daughter off the table. She dragged her all the way down the hospital hallway by her ankle, trying to get her home. She punched nurses who tried to stop her – she was a big woman. Security had to restrain her. Meanwhile the dead girl is just naked there on the floor in the middle of the hallway.'

Grim's assistant, that soldier of truth who had literally peered inside my father, left me with those stories: the dying who won't die even when they want to, the bereaved who refuse to accept, to bury, their dead. And he left me with those nouns, *larynx* and *cranial vault*. They split like thin, sunbaked shale. Human evolution had no way of anticipating steel and speed and asphalt, and so we are like graham crackers in the grip of some furious, defective child. Our bodies, adapted to the African savanna of one million years ago, are now just waiting to be minced on the macadam of civilization.

What must it feel like in the blood, that lust for speed? How do some men come to crave it? Milan Kundera: 'Speed is the form of ecstasy the technical revolution has bestowed on man.' He called it 'pure speed, speed itself, ecstasy speed,' and when I first read those words, I knew Kundera was speaking about my father.

Before we finished our call that day, Grim's assistant solved for me the niggling riddle of why the motorcycle wasn't demolished, as it should have been. My father's chest and lung injuries were caused by the bike itself. It didn't splinter into fifty pieces because his body came between it and the guardrail. Right till the last, even when the physics was wildly, irrecoverably beyond his grasp, he was trying to save the bike.

The next morning I called the hospital and spoke to one of the EMTs who'd worked on my father, and, unaccountably, I asked about my father's racing suit, about the possibility of my recovering it. The noble soul on the line had some trouble barring the disbelief from his voice. That's when he told me he'd sheared the suit from my father in the ambulance before he was fully dead. It was so 'soiled,' he told me, it had to be incinerated with other medical waste.

'Soiled' did the trick; he saved himself from saying, and me from hearing, the indignity of all that word meant, of what can happen to the bowels of the fatally injured. I remember feeling touched by that, by the linguistic gesture of this stranger whose job it is to save other strangers, to attempt to save those who have raced themselves beyond saving.

My unbelief had not inoculated me against this morbidity, this Catholic fixation on flesh. Once Catholicism gets its talons in you, it clasps you for life, regardless of whether or not you remain a believer. Our hometowns, our families, the myths and modes we were given, those first ten years of life gusting through our present: we try to block their persistent power but they seem to form a net from which we cannot wiggle free. The narrative drama of the Mass – the music, the ritual, the pageantry, the architecture, the imposing gore-specked crucifix at the fore – helped to form the lineaments of my psyche, nor was my father subtle when it came to the sanctity of blood. As children, whenever I unloaded cruelty onto my brother, our father would grab my forearm, grab Mike's, slam our flesh together, and say, 'What runs through your veins is the same,' and for fifteen minutes afterward his finger marks would be ochered onto our skin.

The primal focus on my father's body, on how and where it was ruined, on the helmet and suit in which it died – each dusk and dawn his helmet watched me from my dresser where I'd placed it in memoriam – was another way my bereavement sought vent. That obsessiveness was one with which Catholics have long been familiar: a re-creation, a playing out, of the Passion, the view that the body's suffering is its ultimate expression, that agony is above all redemptive, that only through the dumping of holy blood can salvation be had, the books balanced, harmony restored. The helmet and suit, the paint chips and metal shards I'd collected at the crash site, the bike itself? The hurt in me must have processed them as Golgothan relics, hints of the crucifixion, items that would escort me into belief.

But belief in what? In my father's death, in his life before and after that death? Father Hopkins writes:

Christ plays in ten thousand places,
Lovely in limbs, and lovely in eyes not his
To the Father through the features of men's faces.

Wounded at my core, I must have been trying to spot one of those ten thousand places, reaching for some welcome back from the wreckage, back into the palm of the Father. And yet I'm certain I didn't truly think that reprieve was possible for me through obsessive investigations, or by waking my faith from its long dormancy. My grief simply didn't know what else to do with me, and so it reverted to those ancient methods of reverence. It tried to switch me into the child I once was, the parochial school student who clutched the gospels and crucifix and believed without strain. That is grief's encore: transforming you into a child without defenses, without devices.

A letter to the editor of *Sport Rider* magazine. I discovered it among my father's papers. He wrote it four years before his death, in unruly black scrawl, on lined notebook paper, with copious crossouts. I've preserved his spelling, grammar, and punctuation:

Dear Sir:

I would like to thank you for the many things I have learned from reading Sport Rider Magazine. I would also like to tell you a story you might find interesting.

I am 43 and the oldest of three brothers, we have been riding motorcycles since the age of 12. In the past three years we have become very interested in sport bike riding, and have joined a group of sport riders who is led by a 63 year old man.

My brothers and I ride a CBR900, ZX9, and a GSXR 1100, the leader of this group presently rides a ZX11. He has been riding for over 40 years, and he knows every bump rise and curve on all the roads that we ride. He is an exceptional rider and i'm sure if he had ever gotten involved in racing he would have done very well.

Over the course of the past 30 years many riders have come out to follow him and many have tried to pass. Some of the riders were able to pass him, but very very few, and many of them crashed. Through out the years he rode consistently and fast, but always faster than one should ride on the streets.

In the past three years I have seen a change come over this man. It seems he is not riding as fast as he once was, and I know what has slowed him down. It is the three brothers who are following him in the turns and he's wondering if they will make it out the other side. In the past few years I have gain a great confidence and trust in this man, and I know he would never lead me into trouble. He is my father and I thank God for the lessons he has taught me.

There is a simple lesson for everyone in this story. The next time your headed into a turn and your confident that you will make it, think about the rider behind you. Does he have the same skill to make it out the other side? There is nothing more tragick than leading a rider into a situation that he can not handle and have him crash. Ride safely and always think of the other guy.

The letter is unsigned; he never mailed it. I can't pretend not to notice the tremendous chasm between Pop's *He's dead and I'm clear* and my father's own *Think of the other guy.* But I see from this that Pop did eventually slow down when all three of his sons started riding with him. The man described here is not the same man who'd crashed pushing my father through the Flemington Circle the year before. So mercy did come to him, albeit more slowly than it comes to others.

The possibility that his brakes had failed, had either locked or disengaged when he went into that turn on Slifer Valley Road, would not stop stalking me. When I learned that the insurance company had sent the bike to a repair shop to have the brakes inspected – *both* of the women I'd spoken to at the insurance company were named Regina – I phoned the guy at the shop who had done the inspection, a motorcycle expert named Myron.

'There was a recall on some element of those brakes,' I said, 'but for some reason my father never did it.'

'Right, he never did the recall,' he said. 'I can't say why that is. But the brakes didn't fail on him, so it didn't matter. One is worn down to the metal, but they wouldn't have locked up or failed to stop. In my opinion he was trying to save his rotor by applying the back brakes because it's three hundred dollars to replace the rotor. The one pad is about twenty miles from worn down to metal, but the recall Yamaha did was for a bad adhesion connection pad, and that wasn't the problem here. They're original R1 brakes, never changed, but they have a life of nine to twenty thousand miles.'

'So the brakes didn't fail?'

'No,' he said, 'the brakes didn't fail.'

I thanked him then, thinking we were finished, not wanting to inconvenience him with grief-born queries.

'Listen,' he said, 'if it means anything to you, I could tell that your father was an expert rider, a serious racer, not one of those typical Sunday dudes who don't know what they're doing.'

'How could you tell that?'

'From the tires,' he said. 'The tread is worn in such a way that shows me how he rode this bike, and he rode it hard, seriously hard, I mean. They're worn in the same way as the tires on MotoGP bikes. You've probably seen them on TV, going two hundred miles per hour. They lay those bikes down practically horizontal in the turns, knees scraping the track. Your father had tires like that. You should be proud, is what I'm saying.'

I should be proud of two hundred miles per hour, a ludicrous speed no man was ever meant to reach. It sounded incorrect to me, that application of pride, and yet, against such a weakened will, I *was* proud of that number, that racer's tread on the tires. And I remembered, too, what a friend had said to me shortly after the funeral: 'To die like that, to go out doing what you love. That's the only way to die, man. It's honorable.'

W. S. Merwin once put it this way: *We were not born to survive / Only to live.* But I did not believe that then and I do not believe that now. Wanting to be helpful, friends dished me the curative rhetoric they thought I needed to hear, the formulations that might have helped them had it been their father dead on the road. There's not one thing honorable about dying a violent death at forty-seven years old, leaving behind a score of family members whose worlds are all wrecked in ways both major and minor. We don't live in Homer's warrior society where a man's vicious death on the sand of Ilium is a guarantee of panegyric, of immortality in song.

I said to Myron, 'Can I ask you something?'

'Anything,' he said.

'What's it *feel* like?'

'What's what feel like?' he said.

'That speed. The bike beneath you at such speed.'

'You never rode before?' he said.

'Never,' I said.

'Well, I can't really explain it,' he said. 'It just feels like... like you're alive for the first time, like you're gonna live forever.'

Myron told me then that he was keeping my father's bike, buying it from the insurance company for a mere $1,500. Not bothered by a curse on that machine, undeterred by the blood he had to wipe from the gas tank and engine, he planned to modify it into a drag racer and run it at the track at Raceway Park in Englishtown, New Jersey.

I wasn't sure what to say to that, although I know I didn't like it – not the way it sounded, not the way it made my intestines clench. I wished this young man good luck. What else could I do? In the weeks after this phone call, I kept checking Englishtown newspapers for information on fatalities at Raceway Park. And to this day I wonder if he died on the machine that killed my father.

VIII

After my father's crash, I sifted through his stacks of motorcycle books and magazines. One book was titled *The Soft Science of Road Racing Motorcycles,* and you can ask yourself if you'd ever choose to trust your life to *soft* science, because when you hit the guardrail, it will most assuredly be the opposite of soft. I also found a trove of DVDs about the aptly named Isle of Man and the annual race that happens there, called the TT, or Tourist Trophy. This was motorcycle porn for the velocity-addicted. My father watched these DVDs on Saturday nights to charge himself for the next day's ride, to fall asleep with the Doppler-effected scream of a 1,000 cc engine still in his ears, to let that speed infiltrate his dreams.

The Isle of Man is a green, cliff-rich arcadia in the Irish Sea, midway between Ireland and Britain, and the TT is the deadliest motor race ever devised. A thirty-eight-mile, time-trial motorcycle race on narrow island roads, roads of cambers and dips, bends, bumps, kinks, wet in some places, dry in others, uneven textures everywhere, gravel when you don't want it, ridges to the left of you, ditches to the right, average speeds of 130 miles per hour, the smudge of 200-plus on straightaways, mere inches from stone walls and hedgerows, street signs and spectators, cottages, lampposts, objects made of concrete. Road racers call it 'the furniture.' A rock in the road and you're dead.

Since its inception in 1907, a staggering 246 racers have been killed at the TT. In 1970 alone, six racers died. This risk is inbuilt, and the coterie of riders not only accepts it, but thrills at it. Crash on a racetrack and you slide into a patch of grass. Crash at the TT and you hit a house. One you walk away from; the other makes sure you never walk again. Try to envision the stupendous violence a house inflicts upon a human body at 160 miles per hour. In little more than a gesture of safety, hay bales are strategically placed in some of the deadliest spots, but hay bales haven't kept men from killing themselves. The chances of calamitous injury or death at the TT are so high that a casual observer is left with a dislocated jaw, incredulously agape, speculating about the mental hygiene of these racers. Edgar Poe called it 'the Imp of the Perverse,' that mischievous force within that prompts us toward our own demise.

Here's further testament to the lunacy or purity of the TT, depending on your view: the prize money for winning is a pittance. There's no large purse because sponsors are slim, and sponsors are slim because those roads are ruby-hued with blood. It's a mite bad for business when your product adorns a 'death race,' which is what one disillusioned racer recently dubbed the TT – although 'disillusioned' isn't literally right, since these men are not gripped by a single illusion. They know better than anyone what can happen, what *will* happen, on those island roads each summer.

No man is an island proves demonstrably untrue on the Isle of Man. On those bikes, each man races and wins or dies alone, and each dead man is enisled in his grave. The *pas de deux* is between either the bike and the rider, the rider and the road, or the rider and his death. There's the incontrovertible skill and fearlessness of these riders, yes, but another reason my father admired the TT was this: they are overwhelmingly working-class family men who have to keep their day jobs. Coarse-palmed carpenters and plumbers, mechanics and truck drivers with perpetually blackened fingernails and worried wives. You'd have trouble finding the pampered and the privileged among their number.

At the urging of my brother, I recently spent an hour and forty minutes with the film *TT: Closer to the Edge,* a docudrama about the 2010 TT. 'If you want to understand Dad's mentality,' Mike told me, 'then watch this film.' During the dramatic opening images you hear a mélange of riders in voiceover, their unmistakably British lilts, measured, contemplative, soothing in the slowness of their gravitas, a slowness that belies the speed within:

'There is nothing to compare it with.'
'It's the most exhilarating place in the world.'
'It's like being able to fly. Just like growing wings.'
'If it's in your blood you can't get it out. You just want more.'
'My mind goes completely blank. My mind just turns into madness.'

Just like growing wings. It's a felicitous simile. The TT racers, like the MotoGP pros, are easily thought of as kin to fighter pilots: cool heads, quick vision, superior eye-hand coordination, and blood that welcomes the rush of it. Guy Martin, the charismatic, uncontainable star of the film, his hair styled by a storm, has this to say: 'I can imagine, from the outside looking in, anyone who's racing the TT looks like the lights are on but no one's home.'

That's one way to put it, I suppose. Throughout the film Martin cranks up the wattage on those lights, an illumination of what it's like to be a conquering pale rider, to live in triumph bestride the white horse of death. And if he seems mad to you, if he and the others seem to have vacated their braincases, well, that's the cost of the glory they want. Here's Martin on the many perils of the TT: 'You do end up in that position where it looks like it's gonna be game over at any moment. But those positions – money cannot buy the buzz you get, that *thing* you get when you think, *That's it, game over.*'

The sober and sensible adult person strives, I think, never to be in that position. The 'buzz' to which Martin refers is, for most of us, a gut-clapping fear. Whenever I've come close to being killed, in a car or on a bicycle, it didn't feel to me like the buzz of being alive. It felt like being *almost dead*. That's one of the danger-seeker's bromides, the first clause in the credo of every skydiver, cliff diver, bungee jumper, road racer: in order to be fully alive, you must come to the very lip of death. You see the logic. Only Martin and his brethren of extremity are really living. The rest of us are effectively dead, zombies in bondage to the mediocre. Yeats: *The years to come seemed waste of breath, / A waste of breath the years behind / In balance with this life, this death.*

Near the end of the 2010 TT, Guy Martin must have had

more buzz than he knew how to feel. He came within an inch of dying in a filmic fireball when he went down in a lethal corner called Ballagarey. In the prologue of his memoir, *Guy Martin: My Autobiography,* he writes this of Ballagarey:

This is the kind of corner that keeps me racing on the roads. It's a proper man's corner. You go through the right-hander at 170 mph or more, leant right over, eyes fixed as far down the road as it's possible to see, which isn't very far. Like so many corners at the Isle of Man… it's blind. I can't see the exit of the corner when I commit fully to the entry.

And then Martin describes the crash that resulted in his bike tumbling across the asphalt in an inferno, igniting the hay and hedgerows along the road. The model of Honda he was riding is aptly called a Fireblade, a 210-horsepower missile on wheels. The front end tucked, the tires lost grip, the bike began to slide. He thinks, *I've got it, I've got it, I've got it, I've got it…* But he doesn't have it. And the bike is 'steadily skating, increasingly out of control toward the Manx stone wall that lines the outside of this corner.' And then what happens?

Then the thought 'Game over' entered my head. At those speeds, on a corner like that, you're not jumping off the bike, just letting it go. I was leant over as far as a Honda CBR1000RR will lean, and a little bit more. I released my grip on the bars and slid down the road. I didn't think, 'This is going to hurt,' – just, 'Whatever will be, will be.'

Or, perhaps a bit more accurately: whatever will be will be

271

what I made happen. You can't choose to enter a famously fatal turn at 170 miles per hour and then throw up your hands to providence, appeal to predestination, blame the caprice of fate. Providence has a hard time caring about you when you're standing still, never mind when you're a nearly airborne blur in the Ballagarey turn. Barring blindsides, the lightning strikes of God and man, our living or dying is the outcome of the decisions we make.

In *TT: Closer to the Edge,* the wife of a rider remarks that if you love the men who do this, you support their wishes, apparently even if those wishes are death wishes. Two riders died in the 2010 TT: the New Zealander Paul Dobbs and the Austrian Martin Loicht (the film spotlights only Dobbs's death; he was forty years old). 'Climbing without a safety net' is how another rider describes the road race. No margin for error. One minute miscalculation toward glory and you are no more. A white-haired reveler and speed fan, referring to 'the bravest men in the world,' imparts this wisdom about the TT: 'If it doesn't excite you, you're not alive, and that's a fact.' But, sir, here's Larkin: *Being brave / Lets no one off the grave. / Death is no different whined at than withstood.*

The film gives you the unassailable integrity and strength of Dobbs's widow, Brigid, even as the torment is stamped onto her face and her voice begins to break from the grief of it. If you're looking for genuine bravery, you can look no further. Her dignified resilience, the umbilical to joy she maintains for her two fatherless girls (she speaks of their nightly dancing in the kitchen), and her steadfastness at the hardest task there is, the successful rearing of children. Her class of courage is more capacious, and more important, than the suicidal brand of bravery of men doing 180 miles per hour through antique villages lined with stone walls, a bravery indistinguishable from imprudence. You can't watch Brigid Dobbs in the lush scape of her New Zealand home, and those tiny beauties riding tiny motorbikes in homage to their dead father, and not feel whole segments inside you collapse.

Another rider remarks, with ample sadness, that Dobbs died in his pursuit of love. That might be true enough, but the syntactical inverse is also true: he loved the pursuit of dying. Here's what Brigid Dobbs herself says: 'You can't love the death, you can't love the loss, but you can't love the excitement and the thrill without knowing that that's part of it. It wouldn't be so exciting if it didn't have the risk. That's why they want to do it.'

And that's what I'll never understand: how his lust for the thrill conquered his love for the two blond beauties he and Brigid invented together. Because they needed him more than he needed that blast, that bang in his blood, and now their kids will grow up without the ballast of a father. They were four and now they are three, and that minus-one, that gap, never heals. What is our responsibility to our passion when measured against the responsibility to our children? Watching Dobbs's kids – and feeling a stab of that late-night mawkishness when the house is still and the ale bottles empty, that supernatural deal-making with imaginary magistrates – I knew I'd swap my own father for theirs. The Reaper could keep mine if only he'd bring theirs back.

There's a shot near the center of the film that lives in me still. The camera, fixed to one side of the road, aims intently across at the bucolic calm, at the silence and stillness on the other side, only the slightest sighing of the hornbeams, a flutter from a kingfisher, the whistle of a skylark, a gray-stone church, its steeple arrowed at clouds, a megalithic crucifix watching the day. And then you begin to hear them in the distance, coming from the right, coming to kill this pastoral pause. You've heard the sound of the approaching high-pitch gasoline scream, how it ripples on air, an exhaling to a needled crescendo. And when the crescendo comes, directly in front of the stationary lens, you can *hear* it, yes, it's right there in front of you, but you can't *see* it. There's only a green, then a blue, then a red blear: blink and they're gone.

On the Isle of Man or on Slifer Valley Road, that's what two hundred miles per hour looks like. Chromatic ghosts caught on film. But barely.

I had to see, to touch, my father's bike. There was no getting around that. I had to see and touch it the same way family members of the deceased aren't satisfied, aren't on the footpath to acceptance – not *closure,* ludicrous untrue term: doors and windows get closure – unless they have a body to behold. Doubting Thomases all of us, we must finger the wounds and then lick the blood. Look at Caravaggio's searing work called *The Incredulity of Saint Thomas.* That is us. *Blessed are those who have not seen and yet have believed.* But it's not easy being blessed.

A week after the funeral, my uncle Nicky went with me to the cycle shop in Pennsylvania where Myron had inspected my father's bike. I had to unsuction myself from bed at dawn and meet Nicky at a rest stop somewhere on I-78 in western

Jersey. For the hour it took us to reach the cycle shop, he told me stories – they tumbled from him in such nostalgic glee – about the Sundays he'd spent riding with his brothers and Pop, how commonly close they'd all come to getting crushed, shredded on the asphalt, and the day he'd spent in jail after surrendering to state troopers, after hours of outrunning them, cat-and-mousing them, through the vales of eastern Pennsylvania.

'It was fun,' he said. 'It was so much fun. I miss it.'

One of the riders who often joined their pack was a Pennsylvania outlaw they called Crazy Chris: mid-thirties, Norwegian complexion and mane, outfitted in all-white racing leathers and white helmet as if to mock the virtue of angels. Crazy Chris had racetrack experience and was, Nicky said, one of the most naturally gifted riders he'd ever seen, a guy born with his hand in the throttle position, gasoline in his blood. His bike was a hodgepodge he'd built himself, a Suzuki GSXR 750 cc frame with a 1,000 cc motor: a faster engine in a lighter, tighter scaffold. He knew all about the proper geometry, the desired rake of the forks to the frame. If you're road racing, you want the front wheel at the proper distance from the rear wheel. If that distance is too far, the bike won't tip into turns at high speeds. You want the front wheel tucked under the bike and not too far out on elongated forks like a Harley chopper. Choppers have to slow to a near stop in order to make a turn. On the Suzuki 750's frame, the wheels were closer, so it handled much better in sweeps, but Crazy Chris wanted the extra torque of a 1,000 cc motor, and so he Frankensteined his bike into a frightful anomaly.

The bike wasn't legal, not even a little, neither registered nor insured, and his homemade license plate was a greeting card for cops: it said FUCK YOU. A loner who never stayed long with the pack, he went off to taunt police into chasing him. He'd flip them the bird, peel out, rip doughnuts in front of them. There wasn't a police cruiser in all of Pennsylvania that could catch his bike, and so he'd deliberately slow, wait for them to gain some ground on him, flip them off again and then scream away, sirens wailing uselessly in his wake. Once, after disappearing for an hour to play with cops, he rejoined the pack, was suddenly there again among the others, doing an effortless, mile-long wheelie at seventy miles per hour, looking at Nicky as he passed. His helmet seemed to be smiling.

We arrived at the cycle shop by nine that morning. Inside, each bike gleamed, the scent of fresh rubber and polished chrome, of new plastic and oiled metal. It took no effort at all to see how some men felt an aphrodisiacal tug toward these machines, their amped-up sex appeal screaming for release in speed, a release never fully achieved and so ever renewable. Every Sunday the needle moves farther to the right, farther toward the red, because all week long you've felt it building in you, accumulating through your loins. And when this ravening hunger for release becomes not *la petite mort* but *la grande mort*? Then the fluids that are lost can't be replaced, and the desire remains one of eternal unfulfillment.

Watch some MotoGP guys whisper to their bikes before a race, watch them caress the gas tank and handlebars, listen to them speak about those bikes, about feeling *through* the bike to the tires, to the track, and you'll hear tones of *amore*. They're speaking about a love affair, a zestful devotion, a thrilling bliss only sex comes close to matching. In Italian – the top two racers in history are both Italian: Giacomo Agostini and Valentino Rossi – the term for a motorcyclist is *centauro:* centaur, the fusion of life forms, animal and man, machine and man, the fluidity, a symphony of movement.

At the cycle shop we met Myron, the one who'd told me on the phone that I should feel proud of my father. He and the other men at the shop looked at my uncle and me and nodded, most solemnly, in what seemed reverence or honor. A comrade had fallen, and we were that comrade's kin. I thought they were about to salute us. Don't underestimate that: these men on motorcycles revel in the camaraderie, the familial bond they make, a flashy caste of primitives, hunters out for the sustaining kill. It was, my uncle told me, half the reason he'd ridden each week, because it calcified this link with other intrepid men, this elite and clandestine club breaking laws on back roads, engaged in *deep play,* that irrational frolic in which the risks far outshoot the rewards. You see it with rock climbers, with base jumpers, with loons in wing suits.

Many a middle-class domestic male has a blood-need for the daring, the dangers of this tribalism, the dynamite of speed that for half a day elevates them above the routine of their lives. (Larkin: *Those living ghosts who cannot leave their dreams.*) It was soul-enhancing to be one of the worthies tuned into this thrill; every Sunday the ride replaced a disappointing God, the ride as rapture, the speed a substitute deity that saves or smites you. I almost understand it.

We went out back and saw it there, leaning on a boulevard of sunlight: the red and the white, the steel and the chrome that laid my father on a gurney, not the chariot he'd hoped for. Its wounds were oddly minimal, telling little of such irreversible work. The slash in the gas tank looked like a claw's quick swipe at doughy flesh. The left handlebar was bent inward from impact with the road, the left mirror and blinker gone, the foot peg ground off.

My uncle squatted to inspect the front brakes and tire tread. Astraddle the bike, clasping the clutch, the brake, the throttle, balancing its heft beneath me, seeing the speedometer, I tried to imagine what my father saw at a hundred miles per hour, the odd and unfocused world, how it must have seemed to him as he dashed through it. What else could I do but put my hands on this machine and try to imagine? We'd driven all this way so I could touch the bike for six minutes and be enlightened about nothing, no closer to whatever knowing I sought. An addled mourning has that effect; it spins you through cycles of pointlessness as you try to adjust your compass to death's terrain.

IX

Twelve tedious pages, stapled in the upper left-hand side, typewritten, and next to the insignia at the top, these words, in caps and italics: *COMMONWEALTH OF PENNSYLVANIA ACCIDENT REPORT*. But the first word you see when you slide the report from its manila envelope, the lonesome word perched there in caps, centered at the top of the page, is FATAL, the de facto title of the report. I'd mailed fifteen bucks to the Springfield Township Police Department and they in turn sent me this photocopied document of my father's death, more pages to feed the mandatory obsessiveness of grieving.

On the first page the data lie in blocks under headings – police information, accident information, accident location – and there are a total of seventy-seven numbered boxes. My father's bike (and sometimes my father himself) is referred to as UNIT #1, which has its own block. Some of the data are exceedingly clear: box 13, labeled # KILLED, is marked with the Roman numeral I. (What insouciant shorthand, that particular use of the #.) Other data are deliberately cryptic:

box 47, BODY TYPE, is marked with the number 20. Box 50, INITIAL IMPACT POINT – meaning, I think, the guardrail – is marked with the number 9. They didn't think to include a key for me to decode these digits, and so I'm left wondering what '20' means for my father's body type, and why the guardrail has been designated a '9.' You can make yourself batty with this.

More mystifying is box 55, DRIVER CONDITION, which is marked with the number 1, and most mystifying is box 52, TRAVEL SPEED, which is marked with a 0. So my father's condition as a driver was number one and his speed was zero. If either of those numbers had been accurate – if my father indeed had been the number-one driver and if his speed really had been zero – then he would still exist and this accident report would not. Of course those digits signify other things, things to which only officials are privy, and those things naturally have no metaphorical reach. For instance: box 14, # INJURED, is marked 0 but should contain 12 at least, one for each member of our immediate family, beginning with Parma, whose injuries were evident each time she spoke, evident in her eyes, her gait, her gaze. It's an unbelievable sight, how emotional ruin bleeds into physical ruin, how an inner agony forms to the face, heart-scourge camped in the bones.

There are more cryptic digits at the top of the second page: ILLUMINATION is given a 2 (meaning, perhaps, that I could have rather dismal expectations for being illuminated), ROAD SURFACE is a 1, and WEATHER is a 0 (is it possible to have zero weather?). But at the center of the page, the report commences with a narrative. In fact, box 87, which takes up most of the page, is labeled just that, NARRATIVE, and the rest of the ten pages consists of this unusual mode of storytelling.

It's not storytelling as most prefer it – beginning, middle, end; development, denouement, resolution; narrative arc and readily workshopped themes, the A-B-C of O. Henry – so consider the Latin source of 'narrate,' *gnarus,* which means 'knowing.' These policemen narrators want you 'to know' right from the start of their story, because at the base of the second page, in box 89, VIOLATIONS INDICATED, next to the line marked unit UNIT #1, they dish you this bit of info: DRIVING VEHICLE AT SAFE SPEED, by which they mean, of course, the opposite of safe. It begins this way, from the middle of page two to the middle of page three, in the prose of investigator Daniel J. Branch:

Weather: Hot & humid
Temperature: 90 degrees
Road Surface: Black top
Upon arrival at the scene, I observed Driver of Unit #1 being attended by emergency personnel. The operator of Unit #1 was transported to St. Luke[']s Bethlehem Trauma Center by ambulance where he was pronounced dead.

Evidence: I observed two single skid marks from Unit #1. The first skid mark started in the east-bound lane of Slifer Valley [Road], and was 56 feet in length. There was a gap of 40 feet, then the second skid mark was 54 feet in length. There were scrape & gouge marks in the west-bound lane. Unit #1 was moved approximately 30 feet [from] the point of final uncontrolled rest by bystanders. The damage on Unit #1 indicated it landed on its

*left side. A puddle of fuel from Unit #1 located on the roadway
indicated the point of final uncontrolled rest. There was a yellow
warning sign that warns drivers of the right curve ahead. The
recommend[ed] speed posted on that sign is 20 MPH.*

Notice how Officer Branch begins the rapid drama of my
father's death: with stage directions, and no periods, as if
those three conditions — of the weather, the temperature,
and the road surface — exist in perpetuity. For my father,
they do.

The temperature is not insignificant. At three in the
afternoon, after five hours of racing in ninety-degree heat,
you can maybe imagine the rider's burnout, how hot both
he and the bike are. The heat isn't a problem for the bike;
the hotter the day, the happier the parts. Everything works
better in the heat. (Pros run a warm-up lap before the race:
the fluids don't flow and the tires don't stick if the bike isn't
hot enough.) But an overheating human body is a drained,
sluggish body, and a drained, sluggish body errs against the
sovereignty of physics.

For sixteen years I've been looking at that common phrase
at the end of Branch's first full paragraph, 'pronounced
dead,' and I've never got used to it. The passive voice of it
agitates me, and also that 'pronounced,' as if the state of his
cessation, the reality of his being dead, was contingent upon
somebody saying so. *I now pronounce you man and wife. I now
pronounce you dead.* The verb I want there is *confirm*. A doctor
confirmed he was dead, had died, had killed himself with
speed on Slifer Valley Road.

I wondered too why Officer Branch starts his second full

paragraph with 'Evidence' and a colon, because, following the pronouncement in the previous line, it seems as if what he's going to present after his colon is evidence of my father's death. And what would that evidence look like rendered in narrative? Is a story ever really proof of anything? Of gigantic grief or being gone? Of a fractured neck and larynx, of intracranial devastation? No – the stories we tell are suggestions of what's possible, intimations of verity, stray vestiges of knowing. You see after a few lines that what Officer Branch wishes to put forth is evidence for the conclusion he'd stated on the previous page: the failure to drive at a safe speed.

Add up those three numbers: the first skid mark is fifty-six feet long, then there's a space of forty feet, then another skid mark fifty-four feet long. Total: 150 feet, a tidy round figure – fifty yards, or half a football field, or the average length of a block in Manville. Those three numbers tell an unambiguous tale:

He emerged over the crest in the road, saw the curve, locked up the back brake – it's what you do when you need to stop immediately – and skidded for fifty-six feet. Then he let off the back brake for forty feet. Whether or not he was trying to slow with his front brake, the one with too-slim padding, I can't say. Then he locked up the back brake again for fifty-four more feet. By that time, the bike was beginning to tilt at the start of the curve. It won't stay upright when the back brake is locked, not when it's still moving at eighty miles per hour. And he wasn't going to have any of that. He wasn't going to let the bike go over. He wasn't going to lose it. So he released the back brake then. He righted the tilt as he went into the turn. And that's when the rubber caught the road. That's when the catapult happened. That's when all of this happened.

For sixteen years I've been trying to imagine my father's thought – singular, because there wasn't time enough for more than a lone thought, one that is nine-tenths emotion – as he emerged over the rise in the road and saw that ninety-degree turn there waiting, with patient and deadly resolve, with infinite terminus, on the other side of it. I've tried to imagine his feeling – singular too – as he went into that skid. He had to know it was bad. You lock up the back brake only when it's bad and you're trying to keep it from getting worse. But he couldn't have known much more than *This is bad*.

There were perhaps two seconds, three at the most, from the time he saw the turn until the time he was too damaged ever to see anything else again. Count it: *one, two, three, done*. And two or three seconds don't produce enough oxygen, aren't expansive enough, for an intelligible thought or completed feeling. Conception or death, the beginning and the end, can happen in that abbreviated span, but little else. A sneeze, perhaps.

Near the start of *TT: Closer to the Edge,* from a head-on camera angle, there's a high-side accident that approximates what happened to my father. I've watched it fourteen times over, pausing it every half second so that it plays in slow motion, and still I cannot fathom precisely how the physics of the crash unfolds. Even in slow motion it happens too quickly, too minutely, to understand with the eyes.

When you let off the brake and come out of a slide, the

back tire gains grip, and if the bike doesn't have the right position, if it's not exactly vertical on the road, it goes from no traction to instant traction, from sideways to straight. When the tire grabs asphalt it has no choice but to force the bike straight. And then the bike's momentum gets pretzeled, wants to twist itself over, and so it does – the bike always does what it wants – and then the bike and the rider both get flung. It's a matter of weight transfer, from the front tire to the rear. The bike is heavy in front and light in back when the front brake is applied, but light in front and heavy in back when the back brake is applied. This weight transfer affects everything that happens on the bike.

YouTube has plenty of high-sides for the crash-curious, and most are just like that, from upright to upended so rapidly you can't make out what's happened. Which tells me this: even if I had perfect video footage of my father's crash, or if I'd been present that day, observing from some clear vista on Slifer Valley Road, I would not have been able to process the microseconds in which it all went irredeemably wrong.

In a different context, Kipling made the phrase 'thinking with the blood,' and maybe that fits here. My father reacted with his blood, not his brain, and his blood told him to save the bike, not to lay it down. We can't calculate correctly in only three seconds, and so the viscera makes its own decisions. Often there's not time enough even for that. If you've ever crashed your bicycle you know that you can be horizontal on the sidewalk with a leaking gash in an elbow or knee before you even understand how you went down. Before you have the chance to prepare to fall, you're already fallen. Car crashes are similar: one second you're in the sane and reasonable direction on the road, and the next second you're askance in a ditch.

There are certain troublous situations where, in that second when you understand with your blood, with your saliva, that you will not make the turn, you can glance for a spot to crash, 'to jump ship,' as Guy Martin puts it. You glance for anywhere that's flat, unmarked with immovable objects made of metal or wood, a patch to lay it down and slide or roll, or preferably a very soft place. A wheat field would be nice. A child's bouncy house in a large front yard would be ideal; you'd aim your crash for that, if your crash were in any way aim-able, which it usually isn't. It happens much too quickly for anything other than the controlled chaos of physics.

That wheat field or bouncy house, frequently there when you don't need it, is never there when you do, and that's what makes the street such a perilous place for a motorcycle. Everything, everywhere is a solid object against which the organs and skeleton have no chance. My father didn't get that one crucial second for that one crucial glance, and anyway, there was no good place to crash on Slifer Valley Road, unless he could lay it down and low-side, let the bike slide out from under him. The broken vertebrae would have hurt but he would have lived. As it was: I believe he had no time to understand that crashing was guaranteed, no time for rationality to declare *I don't have this one,* and so no time to let it go. No crash options. He didn't *decide* not to lay it down. He didn't decide anything. A decision takes time he didn't have.

At that speed, in that turn, with that guardrail curved there before him and elms standing ancient and obstinate on either side, his only option was dying. You can add better brakes to the equation, subtract ten degrees from that miserable heat, change the time of day to eliminate his fatigue, but at that speed in that turn, the outcome is still a trinity of fatal wounds.

Crashes are usually relayed in seconds. The famed *split second*. Or the finger-snapping *just like that*. The always popular *in the blink of an eye*. The much-hyped *out of the blue* and its globetrotting twin, *out of nowhere*. Avert a roadway fiasco and it's usually done *in the nick of time* – *nick*: 'a small broken area that appears on something after something else hits or cuts it.' The escape is always *narrow*, the call always *close*. Any closer and it'd have flung you far away. The miss is always *near*, and yet it's the *hit* that was near. Mourning happens when the bike *hits* the guardrail, not when the bike *misses* the guardrail. Don't avert that roadway fiasco and you're *at the wrong place at the wrong time*, although the truth is that you'd be at the wrong place at the *right* time, or the *right* place at the *wrong* time. We'd do well to get our *wrong*s and *right*s right. It was the wrong speed on the right road, the wrong speed in that right turn.

We're pawns of causation, of *because X then Y*. Bodybuilding was no different: training hard equals getting strong. To live uncrazed in the world, we require a comprehension of the nexus from A to B, a knowledge of the strings making objects dance. We prefer to calculate the effect from the cause, of course, but when we're already battered in the ditch, or dying beneath a guardrail, then we're forced to calculate the cause from the effect. The speed, the rain, the ice, the multitasking derelict with only one hand on the wheel… the Yamaha R1 tearing down Slifer Valley Road. *He never knew what hit him.*

But *I* know what hit him, and I live now with knowing that he didn't. No final tally of forty-seven years, no concluding thought of his children, parents, all the good work he'd done. What does that matter, a final thought? Final thought of us or no final thought of us, the result was the same. But it matters to me. To believe that those last seconds don't count because the result was the same is to believe that *all* seconds don't count because the result is the same. If his thoughts were important that morning, if they were important the day, the week, the year, the decade before, then they would have been equally important as he was skidding, screeching, beneath the guardrail bleeding.

Perhaps he had the famous flash you've heard about – *My life flashed before my eyes* – but flashes aren't thoughts. Nothing gets tallied, no daughter, mother, son fully conjured, in a flash. *To go peacefully in my sleep:* that's the understandable wish of many, and I don't dispute the peaceful part. But to die and not be aware of it, not digest what's happening to you, not *experience* it, not glimpse the narrowed glare of the Reaper? That seems to me a stupendous deprivation and injustice. Next to being born, dying is the most important thing that ever happens to you.

Officer Branch's formulation 'point of final uncontrolled rest' – not once but twice – is an idiomatic marvel to ponder. He means where the bike stopped when the crashing was done, I know, but 'uncontrolled rest' is a new concept to me, a deliberate contradiction, as if a chaotic calm were possible. *Final rest,* on the other hand – that makes sense if you insist on the euphemism *R.I.P.*

('He's at rest now' was one of the more irritating declarations I had spoken at me during the funeral, always delivered in that pastel tone, mostly neutral but with a trace suggestion that it was *better* to be at rest, to be dead. It took rappelling down into auxiliary wells of politeness not to respond with 'But he didn't *want* to be at rest now.' Still, that wasn't as loathsome as the popular nonsense that says *Everything happens for a reason.* To those who uttered that to me, I wanted to reply, *Yes, and the reason is pointlessness and pain.*)

My father was in control of the bike until he was not. Under the guardrail, he and the bike were not both resting; they were both bleeding. I'm struck by that image mobilized by Branch, 'a puddle of fuel,' the bike's gasoline mingling with my father's blood, the propellant of one meeting the propellant of the other, both of them propelled no further, no farther.

I was struck, too, to learn in Officer Branch's version that bystanders had wheeled the bike thirty feet away from where they'd found it, because I'd been told by the other riders that my father was with the bike against the guardrail, his leg or legs partially on top of it. Which means that these bystanders weren't standing by, but rather had repositioned my father to get him off the bike, or to get the bike off of him. More conflicting reports from Calvary.

It's the impulse, I suppose, in a situation such as that, to attempt some form of rescue, however meager, however futile (to watch a man die and do nothing must cause a permanent ruction to the self). But I'm pretty sure that the repositioning of someone with those injuries isn't in the protocol. Not that moving him or not moving him made any difference at all. At that point, nothing for him made any difference anymore.

On page three, Officer Branch concludes his narration with 'Scene was photographed by police.' For several hours after first reading the report, I'd thought that what the police had photographed was my father under the guardrail, on the stretcher, his body and his blood, and I went about preparing myself, preparing my own blood, to behold those shots, because of course I'd have to see them eventually, the photographic work of an anonymous police artist for whom my father was the model. Until I realized that the photographs Branch refers to are the standard shots of any accident scene: the skid marks, the bike, lipstick-like smears on the guardrail, gouges in the asphalt. By the time the police began taking photos, my father would already have been in the ambulance, en route to the ER, having his racer's suit sheared from him, being tended to by hands incapable of reversing the hurt.

From the middle of page three to the end on page twelve, another narrator takes up the thread: Robert L. Bell, the police chief himself. (Daniel Branch and Robert Bell: wholesome American names. You can picture them: sandy-haired and sideburned, slightly freckled, a pinch overweight, highly Protestant in that Pennsylvania vein.) Chief Bell's narrative of my father's crash is taken up mostly with 'witness testimony': to say what you saw, and in saying it, to make it true. Remember the irate old farmer in the pickup truck, the one with the crippled hand? He was 'startled to discover one of the motorcycles was traveling 5 feet behind him' – tailgating, he means, and he got the word right. If ever you've turned to find on your bumper what looks like a Crayola cosmonaut astride a two-wheeled rocket, startled is exactly what you feel. The farmer was then startled some more when the bikes began roaring past him, that distinct silver roar, the sexed-up scream that sounds like nothing else on earth.

The farmer is sure to mention 'an oncoming white van that came very close to colliding with one of the cycles, head on.' A white van: he remembered the color. Then he pulled to the shoulder and waved on the other bikes, watching them 'across a valley as they accelerated quickly away from him.' For some reason he doesn't mention what the married couple told me when I visited the crash site weeks earlier: that he unzipped my father's suit in an effort to give him more air. He doesn't mention the blood that must have been on his fingers after he did so. How could he have forgotten? This farmer who remembered the detail of the white van doesn't remember my father's blood on his own crippled hand. Or else he considered it too indecent and upsetting to say so.

Another witness was at a stop sign on Hickory Lane – what a pleasant-sounding American street: nothing awful ever happens on Hickory Lane – waiting to turn onto Slifer Valley Road, and that's when he saw the bikes go by 'well above the speed limit.' He himself was about to pull onto Slifer behind the pack, but that's when he saw my father coming, 'traveling faster than the previous group of motorcycles, apparently trying to catch up with the group... He believes Unit #1 was traveling approximately 80 MPH.' (That's a good guess, eighty – I wish it were true. At eighty, an R1 is just getting warmed up. The faster it goes, the better it works. Unless there's that turn you don't know is there, in which case both it and you cease working altogether.) When this witness found my father on the road, 'he felt for a pulse, but did not feel one.' It's uncertain just what he would have done if he *had* felt a pulse – in my father's neck or wrist, which did he touch? What does a bystander do then except ogle and be relieved, by turns fear-lashed and inwardly glad, grateful to his god that today is the day of another man's death and not his own? *He's dead and I'm clear.*

After that, Chief Bell has what looks like an irritating time in conversation with the riders who were with my father that Sunday, every one of whom retches up the same lie: their average speed was forty-five miles per hour. One guy says he 'believes Unit # 1 was doing around 35 MPH,' a comedy any way you cut it. Another guy says that 'they traveled no more than 50 MPH,' as if he could appear consummately truthful with an admission that they were indeed speeding, but only by five miles per hour above the limit on those roads. What's the harm of a measly five miles per hour over the limit? Everybody does it.

And after hearing the same bullshit line from the last rider he interviewed, Bell had had enough: 'I confronted him on that statement and explained to him that numerous witnesses and the total of over 100 feet of braking skids by Unit #1 contradict that stated speed. Nevertheless, he maintained they were not going over 50 MPH at any time.'

Each rider tells Chief Bell the same sequence of events: the pack stopped at a Mobil gas station for a breather. My father was complaining of his front brakes; they didn't sound or look right. He said he had a headache, 'didn't feel well... was going to take it easy and head home.' When they saw that my father wasn't with them anymore, they waited at a stop sign (some say the pack waited three minutes, some say it waited thirty seconds; that's a two-minute-and thirty-second discrepancy in the conception of time). After waiting, two riders went back to look for him. About two minutes later, one of the riders returned to the pack to inform them that 'Unit #1 had been involved in an accident.'

Involved in an accident: the word choice of the rider who returned to tell the others what had happened. Not *crashed into a guardrail*. Not *killed himself in that right turn*. The linguistic sleight of hand is telling for how it strives to absolve my father of blame, how it strives to absolve them all of blame. *Involved in an accident* sounds rather like *involved in a lightning strike*.

This same rider confesses that he 'did not know if Unit #1 was familiar with the road.' To him, for his willingness to indulge the obvious, I'd like to put two questions. After what happened, how can you still not know if he was or was not familiar with the road? And if *you* were familiar with that turn, and if you doubted that he was, then why didn't you warn him of it? *Think of the other guy.* Why wasn't anybody thinking of him?

My father's riding pals are all ashine with admiration for him – 'was an excellent rider... the best rider in the group...

293

more than 20 years of riding experience... a highly skilled rider' – which is the reason they have to lie to Bell about his speed, about how fast every one of them rode every weekend of every summer. To tell the truth would be not to risk a summons for themselves, but to betray my father, to snitch on a fellow Sunday soldier, to transgress against the code and camaraderie. They are, in that way, identical to the cops they badmouthed, outmaneuvered, outran each week: the brotherhood and the bond, clan-thinking, tribal solidarity – it always and everywhere trumps the truth. A tribe of warriors protects its own, even when, especially when, he has fallen in battle.

I can guess Bell's sensible query as he listened to the laudations for my father: *How does such 'a highly skilled rider,' an 'excellent rider,' end up dead beneath a guardrail?* Because it would seem to him, as it no doubt seems to you, that the inverse of skill and excellence are required to find yourself smashed and bleeding to death on a Pennsylvania roadway.

A detail I can't explain: halfway into Chief Bell's narrative, he begins referring to my father by name: 'GIRALDI stated he was going to take it easy... GIRALDI was lagging behind... Two riders went back looking for GIRALDI.' But on the final page of the report, under 'OPINION and CONCLUSION,' Bell reverts to form, as if invoking my father's name here, in this most pertinent section, the section of his ruling, would be a debasement of the dead:

While a recall exists for the front brakes of the involved motorcycle, there is no indication the defect in the front brakes contributed to this accident. The existence of lining on three of the four brake pads, although very thin, was sufficient to stop Unit #1 when driven at legal and prudent speeds.

The statements of uninvolved witnesses and the length of the one-wheel skid mark both indicate excessive speed, well above the posted suggested speed for the curve of 20 mph.

Operator of Unit #1 was solely in violation for failing to drive at a safe speed.

There's no revising the word choice, no erasing those terms: *legal, prudent, excessive, safe.* But it's the word *solely* I feel trembling in me now, because it means *solely responsible.*

X

Calamity usually results from the confluence of bad things. On May 7, 2000, on Slifer Valley Road, that confluence was present for my father. The day's cruel heat, the condition of the front brake pads, the fatigue at the end of the ride, his ignorance of the road, the warning sign much too close to the turn, his not wanting to keep the other riders waiting for him. Eliminate just one of those factors and perhaps there's no crash that day. But you can eliminate all of those factors and it will make no difference if he's kissing a hundred miles per hour at the near lip of that crest. And those men, I know, were always kissing a hundred miles per hour.

May 7 was always my father's self-made fate; the month and day don't matter. The big crash, the last crash, was chiseled into his tomorrow from the moment he bought that bike. *If it's in your blood you can't get it out.* Not unless you get *all* your blood out, unless it spills from you onto the asphalt. Those are your choices. The men who are frightened into stopping, close-called into quitting, persuaded by the good sense of spouses and children? It was never really in their blood, never encoded in them. The blood won't be persuaded.

Recently, for the first time in sixteen years, I asked my brother what he saw on the footage from our father's camera. All along I'd been thinking that my father had filmed his own fatality. But the crash was not on the camera. He'd stopped filming that morning, several hours before they reached Slifer Valley Road. We don't know why he turned off the camera so soon into the ride, except that this was the first day he'd tried filming. The camera was shakily mounted to the fore of the gas tank; he'd rigged it there himself, aimed it through the windscreen at the road, the speedometer visible at the base.

You can see him passing cars, see the needle hit 110 miles per hour on a snaked, wooded road called Dukes Parkway, just outside of Manville. The speed limit through the dips and rises of Dukes Parkway is forty, and some cars do much less than that. Deer bound out everywhere from behind boles. But for my father on an R1 passing cars, it's glance and go – the glance makes the call. No car in the opposite lane? You go. The bike is so irrationally fast, you need no more than that glance. You can be around a car in under three seconds.

At one point near the end of the tape, my father and another rider pull to the side and park in a depressed shoulder to wait for the others who weren't as fast. You can see his unclear reflection in the windscreen, see him remove his helmet, and you can hear him say, 'It's too hot for this shit today.' But the reflection is faded and you can't make out his face, an image refracted in sun, marked with bubbles of light. And then the camera shuts off and the image is gone. His blurring out of the world had already begun then. In just a few hours from this final glimpse of him, he will hit the guardrail, and his blurring will be complete.

When I was old enough to suspect that it mattered, I must have told Pop that I doubted if I'd ever be able to ride a motorcycle. I remember being stumped by how something so engine-heavy didn't topple, how so much metal stayed in motion atop two wheels. He responded with a sentence that's never left me: 'If you can ride a bicycle,' he told me, 'you can ride a motorcycle.' And that's why so many men ruin themselves each year on American roads: because they think that riding a Yamaha R1 is no different from riding a bicycle, which is a bit like thinking that there's some connection between being able to bird-watch and being able to fly.

Three years ago, more than a decade after my father's death, my uncle Nicky, fed up with tamping the weekly temptations, bought a Yamaha R6. He'd quit riding not long before my father was killed – the danger was too much with him then – and in all that intervening time, he'd had persistent fantasies about new screams of speed, those inner gales of adrenaline. But he didn't buy the R6 for the road; he bought it for the racetrack in a south Jersey town called Millville.

In the warmer months, from April to October, he's part of a coterie which pays to be instructed in the physics and art of racing motorcycles. And what he's learned during these track days, both in the classroom and on the asphalt, is that he and his brothers and Pop, and the bevy with whom they rode each Sunday, did not have the tiniest clue what they were doing, either how a superbike works or how their bodies need to function on top of it. Not the tiniest clue.

'We had the basics all wrong,' he told me recently. 'Everything was totally wrong. Your father and me, Uncle Tony and Pop – we didn't have the first idea. No technique at all, no understanding of how the bike moves or how we should handle it, how we should approach a corner. What I'm doing now, it's a science class, and when you consider how stupid we were, it's a goddamn miracle we didn't all die. When you do these track days, you really, really get why so many guys are killed on the road every day. They just have no idea.'

I've been living with that sentence: *They just have no idea.* Those bikes, in other words, have no place on the road. They are far too sophisticated and fast, far too supreme for the common thrill seeker unschooled in physics. The man on the throttle is tricked by such willing horsepower, by his own will to power, his desperate will to release. You might not be surprised to know that the organizations that host the track days cater to ex-military men, offering discounts and benefits. I recall a news headline from 2008 that blared: MARINE MOTORCYCLE DEATHS TOP THEIR IRAQ COMBAT FATALITIES. Those stats aren't different for the other branches of the military, either. After you've flown a helicopter gunship or fighter jet, after you've unloaded with a .50-caliber from a Humvee, or sent a fusillade from an Abrams tank, what are you supposed to do once you return to society? What then is your intoxicant? Where to let out the clamor in you?

'The blind force of the sub-cortex,' Pavlov called it. You see why these soldiers mount superbikes, why they turn to

Yamaha and Kawasaki, to Honda, Suzuki, Ducati. It tells you something about the matchless exhilaration of those machines. Here in our humdrum world, they are the only thing that approaches what the blood feels in war.

A few summers before his fatal accident, my father crashed on a different Pennsylvania back road, farmland running to hills in the distance, plots of elm and spruce, wide expanses of grass. He was riding a black and red Honda CBR900 then, the first bike he'd bought after years of not being able to afford one, of literal dreaming about those sinuous roads, the quick of those machines. He could see the sweeping right up ahead, but it swept more sharply than he'd anticipated. His approach was much too fast, his angle in the road all wrong. Centrifugal force will not be fooled with, and he crossed the yellow line at the start of the sweep, then crossed into the opposite lane. Had there been an oncoming car, a family on its way to a Sunday service or the farmer's market, we'd have attended his funeral a lot earlier.

Instead, he veered into a ditch and flipped over the handlebars, shoulder-first, into an unsuspecting somebody's front yard. The impact broke his right collarbone in two spots. The bike was dented, bruised, but otherwise undamaged, and he rode back to Jersey that way, 150 miles on highways and back roads, with a broken right collarbone. Because the throttle and brake are on the right handlebar grip, all the weight and pressure from the suspension, from gassing and braking in turns, spike up into the right arm and directly into the right shoulder. So he rode those 150 miles home in agony. For two weeks after, the entire right side of his torso, front and back, was a mottle of indigo and amethyst.

He was with one other rider during that crash, a father figure to him and Pop's closest friend of forty years, Kurt, a man of incorruptible dignity and style – his silver crew cut, his leather jacket with the Yamaha patches, his voice calloused from the cigarettes of his past. The other riders had for him the same reverence they had for Pop. Kurt helped my father back onto his bike that day and then guided him home. When they finally made it, the two men stood in the kitchen, trying to fool my father's fiancée into thinking that everything was all right, that no one had crashed.

Why did his body not hold on to the memory of that pain and what birthed it? Why was he not deterred by the pain and its promise of more? I want to ask Kurt about the crash that afternoon, what went wrong in that turn, but Kurt is dead. He killed himself on his motorcycle, later that same year, when he collided with a tree. It was the only time I ever saw my father weep.

One morning, while Anna was still asleep, not long after I received the police report, I saw half a dozen cars parked in front of the house directly across the street from my godfather's. The men wore black suits, the women black dresses. The wife, a young mother of two small children, had just been killed in her car on a slick interstate, her body twisted with the steel. I saw the husband, the now-single father, standing on the walkway, greeting some, saying farewell to others. On the lawn lay plastic toys, in the driveway a red tricycle, all abandoned by the disloyalty of toddlers. A car drove away; the new arrivals walked inside. And then, for a moment, he was alone. It was just the two of us now on that shaded street, across from one another, our hands searching our pockets in the same way, both looking at the space between us. Neither of us waved, neither nodded. Just that empty space there.

CODA

The author's father, in the final photo he took of him, Drew University, Madison, New Jersey, 1999

I began this book on the day of my father's death, but I didn't know it then. That night, after returning to my dormitory, before Anna absorbed my quaking till dawn, I opened a notepad and penned a single line: 'Absence takes up space.' In the days and months, in the years, that followed, the lines accumulated, one by one, sometimes in twos, rarely in threes. They were often the words of others, lines that crooned to me out of the depths of memory, as I was eating or driving, mostly in the mornings after waking, or else in that liminal murk between the dark of sleep and the light of day: Wordsworth or Coleridge, Kafka or Auden. Over the years the notepads multiplied, stacked on my desk as if a bulwark against further dismay. But I could do nothing with them, could find no arrangement, could not complete the story of my father, or my own story among men. From where would that apprehension come? How to find the language, the armature, for such telling?

Benvenuto Cellini's magisterial *Autobiography* begins with this: 'All men of whatsoever quality they be, who have done anything of excellence, or which may properly resemble excellence, ought, if they are persons of truth and honesty, to describe their life with their own hand; but they ought not to attempt so fine an enterprise till they have passed the age of forty.' For me, those words crouched like a dragon at the gate of autobiography. When Cellini advises us to wait until after forty to embark on 'so fine an enterprise,' he means that most of us need that long to acquire the psycho-emotional skills in order to execute our life stories properly, to envisage the proper angles of comprehension – to begin to see ourselves as we really are. I've never approached what Cellini means by *excellence,* but by the age of forty, I'd been born as a father, and with that comes its own brand of staggered excellence.

In his memoir *Experience,* Martin Amis remarks that the childless never fully understand their parents. My sons, Ethan and Aiden, were the spur I'd needed to decode the deceptive phonics of memory, to transcribe the notebooks, knead them into a shape loyal to the vicissitudes of truth – to tell the story of my family's masculine order so that my sons might know the grandfather who was killed many years before their births. And so that they might know what made me, as well, and by extension, what helped make them. It's simple for them to comprehend that I am their father, but shuffling through photographs together, I can see their faces straining to comprehend that *I* once had a father too, and that he now lies in the earth. Small children must conceive of their parents as outside of time, not tripped by the many lurchings of the past. A child is all present; he has no firm conception of his past, and his future seems an incredibility that never will come. Just try to tell a child he has to wait a week for something – for him that week might as well be an eon.

Schopenhauer: 'The first forty years of life give us the text: the next thirty supply the commentary.' If that's accurate, my father had only seven years of commentary. After the birth of my sons, I began to feel the onset of a duty – the duty to continue that commentary because he could not continue for himself. We all of us want our stories told, and the tellers should perceive the debt they owe to the heroes of those stories, and to the stories themselves. The firstborn son, duty-bound by definition, will take on some debts but not others. I would not name my own firstborn William, would not make him the fifth in that lineage, shackle him with a name to a particular fate he must then labor to overcome, as I had. I'm not one to traffic in curses, or that sins-of-the-father fatalism, but I was certain that four generations of William Giraldis were quite enough. Born in Boston, reared in Boston, half-Asian, my kids are fully Boston boys, not the provincial Manville boys I and my father were. They speak Mandarin and live in a home besieged by books. If Parma and Pop had expected Ethan to be named William, they never said anything to me about it.

My grandparents are eighty-five years old now; I imagine the elderly care less and less about issues that once shrilled with such urgency. Maybe family legacy doesn't mean very much in the hoary grip of exhaustion and grief. How annihilating that must be, at day's end, slouched there at the rim of such blackness. I was spared from having to see my father wither – he will never be old – but I am not spared from having to see the withering of grandparents who were never merely grandparents to me. No shawl-knitting frump, Parma almost singlehandedly rescued us from destitution after my mother vanished from our family. She's never been sick, she's never been slouched, never been an ounce over ninety-eight pounds. Give her a habit and she could pass for Mother Teresa. A gallon of Breyers ice cream for dinner and an economy-size bag of Lay's potato chips afterward – they cannot kill her. Once, I watched her frost twelve cobs of corn with toxic quantities of salt and then gnaw each one with the flitting thoroughness of a squirrel. Currently, five days a week, she ministers to several cyclones of great-grandkids, including my sister's two sons. 'They're my heart,' she says, and that's true in more ways than one.

Wordsworth did much of Freud's work in one terse line: *The Child is father of the Man.* Six years from now, when I reach my father's age at his death, that line will assume a freshly skewed meaning for me. We are meant to outlive our parents; the cosmic order balks only when parents are forced to outlive their children. The grief of Pop and Parma has not slackened in sixteen years. But to outlive our parents by such a margin, to become my father's elder so soon, and for so long, will no doubt be a disorienting perversity. Though perhaps not only that. I suspect there will be a boost in the obligations I feel toward my father, chiefly the obligation to adopt his verve for living. Not to live for us both, as it were – I can't accept the speed that brought his blood alive, that emptied his body onto asphalt, the risk that meant valor – but somehow to let my senses be amplified by the quickness he beheld in the world. Living well might indeed be the best revenge against those who harmed you, but it is also the best homage to those who made you.

The son as father, the father as son. It took no great powers of prediction to see that once my own sons arrived, I'd experience a further onloading of my father's absence. He adored small children with a silliness that was wonderful to see, a toy-giving clown and tickler. (If you're looking for the most accurate measure of a person's character, watch him with children; how he treats them will be the best or worst you can say about him.) Even during the many twitchings of my teenage years, when I wrongly thought he was being tyrannical, I never doubted that he'd make a perfectly loving grandfather.

Having children diminishes your need for your own parents. You become the thing you need. Adults don't make children; children make adults. Six and three years old, my kids are boisterous as only boys that age can be. The daredevils scale the twelve-foot built-in bookshelves in our home and then drop, in skydiving form, to the bed below. Destructively physical in their trampling and grappling, their nonstop superheroing, my sons don't notice that someone essential has gone missing. They don't see that they need my father. But I see it for them; he is a daily lacuna in their lives. I feel a reluctant pride in their athletic talents – they'd *really* rather swing a bat and speed on bikes than read Lewis Carroll with me? – but there would have been nothing reluctant in the pride my father felt. He would have been heroic for them in a manner I can never be. Their loss of him is enormous, and yet minor compared to his loss of them, his loss of the world.

That term, *hero*, thrives within its sundry meanings. From the Greek *hērōs*, it literally means 'protector.' Like *love*, it's a term in constant flux: a term with wings. Messiah and messenger, saver of the day. *Christ* derives from the Greek *christos*, 'anointed one.' Oedipus and Romulus and Robin Hood, Shakespeare and Joan of Arc and John Brown, Oskar

Schindler and Michael Jordan, Batman and Obama. The distressed damsel's squeal of 'My hero!' A story's protagonist, in battle with an *anti-hero*. Quester, explorer, guru. The rebel as hero – James Dean, or else Milton's Satan – an up-ender of order. The hero as witness: Trotsky, Emma Goldman, Anne Frank, Primo Levi. The hero as leader, statesman, murderer-in-chief: Augustus, Napoleon, Lenin, Castro. The hero as Everyman, your unruffled parent or selfless sibling, the grandmother who sacrifices years for you, or the donator of a kidney, the neighbor who unsticks your snowed-in automobile. But I keep coming back to its origin: *protector*.

In *On Heroes, Hero-Worship, and the Heroic in History,* Thomas Carlyle separates his study into six units: the hero as divinity, as prophet, as poet, as priest, as man of letters, as king. Joseph Campbell understood heroes as embarking upon cyclical journeys: the departure from their comfort and unknowing, the initiation into wisdom and their true selves, the return to assume roles of leadership or deliverance. It looks like tough work being a hero; no woman or man should sign up for it. The pedestal all too easily becomes a pillory. But here's Ortega y Gasset: 'A hero is one who wants to be himself.' Or rather, one who has no choice but to be himself, which means the unheroic are those who hide, or who never really comprehend who they are, what they were meant to do. When I say that my father would have been heroic to my sons, I don't mean only that he would have seemed superhuman in his red-and-black helmet and racing suit, in his mastery of tools and the masculine arts, supremely cool, supremely *fast,* in all the ways I am not. I mean also that he would have appeared to them as he was, a man wholly and convincingly himself, a seeker of speed who would not be denied release.

My boys want to know if my father's death is a *tragedy*. They've heard the term employed to describe everything from a school shooting to a rained-on picnic. I tell them that the term has become tired through overuse, but still, they want to know: Is my father's death a tragedy? For me, and for our family, yes, I tell them, it is a personal tragedy, although *private disaster* is how I've thought of it all along. Sophocles would not understand our bandying about of the term *tragedy* whenever something unhappy occurs, and he'd no doubt wince at the widespread redundancy *terrible tragedy*. The Athenian innovators of tragedy had very different, much loftier, notions of what constituted the tragic: a great figure's about-face of circumstance brought on by a concussion of the accidental and the ordained. Oedipus's fate is a maddening paradox, both predetermined *and* his own hubristic fault. Perhaps my father's fate shared some of those classically tragic strands: his hubris on the machine he was ordained to ride.

'Why didn't he just stop riding?' Ethan asks me, his six-year-old simplicity sobering, shaming of all rationalization. But that's the rub, I tell him; he could not stop without forfeiting who he was. 'Well then, why didn't he just slow down?' Because the Yamaha R1 wasn't engineered for lethargy; it doesn't work without racing. His own sneakers, I point out, were engineered for running. What is he compelled to do, helpless *not* to do, in those lustrous new sneakers – what's the first thing he does in them? He runs, he sprints. But the analogy is defective, and he knows it. There's that slight strain in his forehead, the slight pursing of his lips, evidence of the thought he suspects is an upsetting accusation and so he pauses before he says it: 'So then he did it to himself. He asked for it.'

Those are my own words he's returning to me, precisely what I say to him when he's heedless on his bicycle, when his headlong riding puts him on the pavement with bleeding elbows and knees. Both he and his brother have been fearless on bikes since they were two years old; they skipped training wheels entirely. When Ethan turned two, the smallest pedal bike I could find was still too big, and so I had to modify it, hacksaw the seat post, swap the handlebars. The other parents in our neighborhood often pointed, gasped when one of our tiny two-year-olds sped by without training wheels, and then looked to my wife and me with a weave of accusation and awe. The skill of balance and lust for speed seem to have been encoded in their very cells. Unable to live in me in that way, my father lives in them. I never attempted to curb those abilities, was in fact mutedly proud of them – I couldn't ride a bike until I was five – though they frightened me then and frighten me still.

When Ethan is there on the pavement with bloodied elbows, I tell him: 'Show some caution. You're responsible for your own safety. You did that to yourself. You asked for it.' I say that to him – with a sternness born of fear and love – because it is true, but also because I never got the chance to say it to my father. Caution was anathema to his Sunday clan, and one of my missions as a father – a mission persistently hounded by my own father – is to make sure that caution is never anathema to my sons. When we talk about my father and Ethan accuses him of causing his own death, I honor his perception while honoring the complexity of the truth. I tell him that he is right – yes, my father did it to himself; yes, my father asked for it – but also that he will have to wait several years to read this book, to see that my father's death was much more complicated than mere recklessness, that he lived in the grip of a powerful legacy, of enormous pressures from the patriarch, pressures that many of us are not fast enough to outrun.

New memories, I've found, shout away old ones. Looking at early photos of my kids, I can't recall them at those ages. I can see them there in the photos, and I can see myself with them, and I know those moments, those events, occurred, but I simply cannot locate them inside myself. And never mind the photos of ten, fifteen, twenty years past, photos of my father and me. I yearn to recall the details of those days but cannot. I cannot sift through the addling fugues of memory in order to hear the individual notes I want. Our memories, I'm sorry to say, aren't up to us. And if the neuroscientists are to be believed, the mechanisms of memory are so organically unsound, so prone to disruption and deprivation, to revision and error, it seems paranormal that we can remember anything at all.

One of the things I'm sure I remember is this: for a brief while after my father's crash, I comforted myself with the thought that the gods were surely finished using me for target practice. The thought, steeling in one way, was a near masterpiece of self-pity in another. After the childhood abandonment by my mother and the violent early death of my father, I was clear. No more ill tidings for this orphan.

Self-pity is by its very nature a cloistered, incestuous view, a fundamentally privileged conception of self, and mine smugly assumed that losing my parents as I had was the worst that could happen to me. Not until you have children of your own do you understand what breed of anguish can be visited upon you.

I'm never not nervous about my kids being maimed or killed, abducted or abused. The fear is always there, at one register or another, an almost distracting hum of anxiety. When they leave the house in the morning for first grade and preschool, there's not even a flake of certitude that they will return in the afternoon. The way they won't return is one of the ways children have always not returned: traffic disaster or collapsed roof, drowning or inferno, fall or flood, or else another American warp with an assault rifle. We do what we can, take caution, take care, but for many of us, all of life is a crossing of the fingers, a letting go and hoping we'll be spared by calamity. When you have my history, my sense of certain chaos and injury, you're always waiting for another phone call. My phone doesn't ring without my muttering of Dorothy Parker's immortal line: 'What fresh hell can this be?' My life is a passive struggle against forces I cannot harness. 'Things,' Larkin says, 'are tougher than we are,' and that fact impelled me into weightlifting at sixteen years old. It was my attempt to balance the scale. At forty-one, with two small children I try gravely, daily, to protect, I know there's no balancing of that scale. Things will always be tougher than we are.

The child-rearing differences from generation to generation are usually distinct, and each day now I feel those differences with the particular force of my own history. As children we all rode in vehicles without car seats, toddlers on the unbelted laps of Camel-smoking mothers. My own boys, by contrast, don't get on a scooter or skateboard without looking like scaled-down Michelin Men. They've never been inside a moving car without being strapped to seats fit for spacecraft. Come near them with a cigarette and expect a tirade. The notion of handing them a BB gun or hunting bow strikes me as criminally incompetent. The men of my family didn't raise me with much praise or affection, and so for the past six years I've unleashed so much verbal and physical love upon my sons, so much you're-number-one rhetoric, that I fear I'm building coddled autocrats with no notion of necessary struggle. They're only six and three, I know, but nothing ever completely undoes what we do to them at these ages: not religion, not education or medication, not nonstop sorties of psychotherapy. We damage them one way or we damage them the other.

We also mislead them without meaning to, with ambitious diction, *always* or *forever*. In the saddest scene in John Updike's story 'Separating,' Richard Maple, after telling his teenage son that he's leaving the family home, says, 'No matter how this works out, I'll always be with you.' When I first read that story at eighteen, it had what felt like a teleporting effect on me. I instantly remembered what I'd long forgotten, that scene with my father slumped on a stool in our darkened kitchen when I was nine years old, when after an hour-long quarrel with my mother, he said to me, 'No matter what happens, I'll always be your father.' That sentence had a particular meaning when I was nine: disruptions were coming to our home, my mother would be leaving us, but I could count on him to remain. And he did; he was overwhelmingly there. Now, since his fatal crash sixteen years ago, the sentence means something else altogether. He is still overwhelmingly here. What he told me was much truer than he could have realized: *I will stick around now, yes, and I will stick around long after I'm gone.*

In Updike's story, in the buildup to telling his son about the impending divorce from his mother, Richard Maple must have rehearsed his line, 'I'll always be with you.' It's exactly the right sentence at exactly the right spot in the story, the assurance the boy needs from the parent about to leave home. But my father's nearly verbatim sentence to me was unplanned and maybe ill-fit to the circumstances. He was not the one leaving our family, and of course he'd always be my father. In what possible way could he not be? On that evening of schism, the assurance I needed was being issued from the wrong parent. But he knew then, didn't he? That night in our kitchen, at what was for me the very start of our family's unstringing, he knew that I wouldn't have any assurances from my mother. He knew she'd soon be disappearing. And so he offered me his own assurance as consolation. He didn't dish me the false pop-song banality *I'll always be here for you,* but he also meant something other than the self-evident fact of 'I'll always be your father.' He meant, I think, precisely what Richard Maple tells his son: 'I'll always be with you.' My father's *always* wasn't a lie, not then and not now that he's gone, because for me it means *I will always* have been *your father.*

I tell my sons what I tell myself: my father lived and

died attempting to be worthy of an ancient code. His story remains the story of most men, writ large, writ fast, writ in blood. His story is my story too, because he breathes in me, in whatever hopes I have for a larger life. One of my family's narrative threads speaks of us as an unlucky bunch: diseases and deaths, divorces and depressions, the manifold injuries and injustices. But we are no unluckier than average, and I'd say a good deal luckier than most. Luck, anyway, is a knave's game. Our luck is the work and the love that await us.

Acknowledgments

With enormous thanks and much love to:

Bob Weil, maestro and shepherd, without whom this book would not exist.

Steve Almond, who gave these pages more dedication than I had a right to ask for.

Nick Giraldi, uncle, pal, pursuer of speed.

Will Menaker, tireless mind of many insights.

Bill Pierce, who listened without complaint.

Katie, Parma, Ethan, Aiden and Caleb: my heroes.

David Patterson, steadfast 007.

Steve Attardo, graphic artist extraordinaire.

The committed staff at Norton/Liveright, paragon of publishing. The editors of *Kenyon Review, Antioch Review, The Pushcart Prize 2010,* and *Best American Magazine Writing 2011,* where sections of this memoir first appeared.

HOLD THE DARK

A terrifying literary thriller set on the Alaskan tundra, about the mystery of evil and mankind's losing battle with nature.

At the start of another pitiless winter, the wolves have come for the children of Keelut. Three children have been taken from this isolated Alaskan village, including the six-year-old boy of Medora and Vernon Slone.

Stunned by grief and seeking consolation, Medora contacts nature writer and wolf expert Russell Core. Sixty years old, ailing in both body and spirit, and estranged from his daughter and wife, Core arrives in Keelut to investigate the killings. Immersing himself in this settlement at the end of the world, he discovers the horrifying darkness at the heart of Medora Slone and learns of an unholy truth harboured by this village.

When Vernon Slone returns from a desert war to discover his son dead and his wife missing, he begins a methodical pursuit across this frozen landscape. Aided by his boyhood companion, the taciturn and deadly Cheeon, and pursued by the stalwart detective Donald Marium, Slone is without mercy, cutting a bloody swathe through the wilderness of his homeland. As Russell Core attempts to rescue Medora from her husband's vengeance, he comes face to face with an unspeakable secret at the furthermost reaches of American soil – a secret about the unkillable bonds of family, and the untamed animal in the soul of every human being.

An Alaskan Oresteia, an epic woven of both blood and myth, *Hold the Dark* recalls the hyperborean climate and tribalism of Daniel Woodrell's *Winter's Bone* and the primeval violence of James Dickey's *Deliverance*.

NOW IN PRODUCTION WITH NETFLIX, STARRING
ALEXANDER SKARSGÅRD

ISBN: 978-1-84344-575-3   £8.99